A flamboyant polymath, General Augustus Henry Lane F[ ] was influential in four fields during his lifetime: military[ ] archaeology and public education. Yet very little is known a[ ] or motivation.

Mark Bowden has written an entertaining and thoroughly[ ] the General which describes his stormy relationships with l[ ] leagues, tenants and dependants; his military career; his activit[ ] _._ education; and his contributions to anthropology and archaeology. In particular he assesses his impact as excavator, field archaeologist, theoretician and first Inspector of Ancient Monuments on the development of British archaeology.

This is the most complete biography of a controversial man whose methods and ideals have been much quoted but frequently misunderstood and misrepresented.

Pitt Rivers

Pitt Rivers

The life and archaeological work of Lieutenant-General Augustus Henry Lane Fox Pitt Rivers, DCL, FRS, FSA

Mark Bowden

Field Officer, Royal Commission on the Historical Monuments of England

The right of the
University of Cambridge
to print and sell
all manner of books
was granted by
Henry VIII in 1534.
The University has printed
and published continuously
since 1584.

CAMBRIDGE UNIVERSITY PRESS

Cambridge
New York   Port Chester
Melbourne   Sydney

CAMBRIDGE UNIVERSITY PRESS
Cambridge, New York, Melbourne, Madrid, Cape Town, Singapore, São Paulo, Delhi

Cambridge University Press
The Edinburgh Building, Cambridge CB2 8RU, UK

Published in the United States of America by Cambridge University Press, New York

www.cambridge.org
Information on this title: www.cambridge.org/9780521106221

First published 1991
This digitally printed version 2009

A catalogue record for this publication is available from the British Library

Library of Congress Cataloguing in Publication data

Bowden, Mark
    The life and archaeological work of Lieutenant–General Augustus
Henry Lane Fox Pitt Rivers, DCL, FRS, FSA / Mark Bowden.
      p.   cm.
    Includes bibliographical references.
    ISBN 0 – 521 – 40077 – 5
    1. Pitt-Rivers, Augustus Henry Lane-Fox, 1827 – 1900.
    2. Archaeology – Great Britain – History – 19th century.
    3. Archaeologists – Great Britain – Biography.   4. Generals – Great
Britain – Biography.   5. Great Britain – Antiquities.   I. Title.
DA3.P53B69   1991
941.081′092 – dc20   90 – 45313   CIP
[B]

ISBN 978-0-521-40077-0 hardback
ISBN 978-0-521-10622-1 paperback

For my parents

Contents

Illustrations

Maps

Genealogical tables

Preface

The subject of this biography changed his surname in mid-career from Lane Fox to Pitt Rivers. Before 1880 I refer to him by his Christian names or as 'Fox', and after 1880 as 'Pitt Rivers'. In the Bibliography all his works are brought together under the name Pitt Rivers. It is perhaps appropriate to explain at the outset why he changed his name. When Horace Pitt, sixth Baron Rivers, died childless in 1880, his property would normally have descended to his senior surviving cousin, George Lane Fox. However, the will of George Pitt, second Baron Rivers, had specified that his estates and the estates of the late Lord Bingley should never be the property of a single person as long as there were two descendants of his sister, Marcia Lucy Fox, between whom they could be divided. As George Lane Fox was already the owner of the Bingley estates at Bramham near Wetherby, West Riding, the Rivers property devolved upon the next surviving cousin, Augustus Henry Lane Fox. According to Horace, the sixth Baron's will, Augustus Lane Fox could inherit the property only on condition that he took the surname Pitt Rivers and the arms of the Pitt family within one year of taking possession of the estate. Change of surname at the moment of inheritance was a common occurrence amongst the English aristocracy of the eighteenth and nineteenth centuries (Stone and Stone 1986, 88–9).

The wide range of the General's activities, especially his parallel careers in anthropology, archaeology and public education, make a straightforward narrative difficult to achieve. I have followed a similar pattern to that adopted by Thompson (1977), a thematic rather than a strictly chronological approach, despite the problems in this scheme, notably the tendency to make artificial divisions between the General's interests, identified by Bradley (1983, 2–3).

The primary sources for a life of Augustus Pitt Rivers are not extensive. He never kept a diary or journal and rarely retained copies of his own letters. The Papers now kept at the Salisbury and South Wiltshire Museum consist of a fortuitous selection of letters received, notes for papers, lectures and addresses, documents relating to the Ancient Monuments Act, newspaper cuttings and other miscellaneous items. Other letters, notebooks and papers are scattered amongst various other institutions. The General claimed that his mother was addicted to destroying documents (Constanduros 1953 unpublished) and this seems to have been a family trait. Much that was left at Rushmore and Farnham at his death was subsequently destroyed or lost. Other unpublished sources consist of the reminiscences of his archaeological assistants, members of his family and local inhabitants of Cranborne Chase. Aside from these sources we have to rely on the General's own published works and those of his contemporaries. There is, however, a rich harvest of secondary material beginning with the paper by Hawkes *et al.* (1947). All the sources I have used are listed in the Bibliography which is divided into separate sections for unpublished and published material. I have not included a complete bibliography of the General's published works; this is available in Gray (1905, xxxvii–xliii).

Acknowledgements

It is a pleasure to acknowledge the generous help I have received from many individuals and institutions, notably John Barrett; Dr David Brown, Ashmolean Museum; Dr Tim Champion; Jo Chaplin; Dr Clive Gamble; Pamela Grace; Martin Green; George A. Holleyman; Dr Jessica Kuper; Donnie Mackay; David McOmish; Ralph Merrifield; Henry S. Middleton, Maidstone Museums and Art Gallery; the staff of the National Army Museum, Chelsea; the staff of the National Portrait Gallery; Roger Peers, Dorset County Museum; the staff of the Public Records Office, Kew; Peter Richards; Dr E. Clive Rouse; Dr Chris Smith; the library of the Society of Antiquaries of Newcastle upon Tyne; Christopher Taylor; Dr Robin Taylor; Emma Theakston; Professor Charles Thomas; Dr Julian Thomas; Adam Welfare.

Very special thanks go to Peter Saunders, Clare Conybeare and all the staff at the Salisbury and South Wiltshire Museum for their help and hospitality over several years; to Dr John Chandler (formerly of Wiltshire County Council Library and Museum Service) for assistance beyond the call of duty; to Mark Corney for supplying much information and for preparing the maps; to Lorraine Mepham, not only for word processing in the early stages but, more importantly, for her sound editorial skills; last, but by no means least, to Professor Richard Bradley who first introduced me to the General and who has been a source of inspiration ever since.

Illustrations acknowledgements
I am very grateful to Mr Anthony Pitt-Rivers for permission to reproduce Plates 1, 4, 5, 6, 7, 9, 10, 11, 13, 25, 28, 29, 30, 31, 43, 44, 45, 56 and 57. Plates 1, 3, 4, 5, 6, 7, 8, 9, 10, 11, 13, 14, 15, 16, 20, 21, 25, 26, 27, 28, 29, 30, 31, 33, 39, 41, 42, 43, 44, 45, 46, 47, 52, 54, 56, 57, 58, 59 and 60 are reproduced here by courtesy of the Salisbury and South Wiltshire Museum. Photographic copying and printing was undertaken by David Cousins.

The contemporary photographs are largely the work of H. St George Gray. Plates 8, 20, 26, 33, 41 and 47 are by David Cousins and Plate 58 is by Lynn Rivers.

I

Introduction

The name Pitt Rivers is now associated with a magnificently eccentric museum in Oxford and, for many people, with the memory of an equally strange museum in the depths of rural Dorset. This is the story of Augustus Pitt Rivers, the founder of both museums. He was a soldier, landowner, archaeologist, anthropologist and government inspector; a splendid Victorian autocrat who determined to carry out scientific research and to that end caused all kinds of excavations and other activities to be undertaken. His burning desire to educate 'the masses' was the driving force behind his endeavour, for Pitt Rivers was a political animal; but it was as an archaeologist that he made his greatest impact.

Lt-General Augustus Henry Lane Fox Pitt Rivers has been recognised as a central figure in the development of archaeology ever since Sir Mortimer Wheeler declared himself a disciple. Hawkes (Hawkes *et al.* 1947), Crawford (1953, 31, 33) and Wheeler (1954, 13, 25–9) were clear about the General's role in the growth of the discipline, and they were followed by Piggott (1959, 44–50), Fagan (1972, 141), Daniel (1975, 169–74), and Barker (1977, 13); Thompson (1977) gave the General more extensive treatment and Bradley (1983) argued for a different interpretation of his significance. The General has been called 'the father of scientific archaeology' (for example Bowden 1984) and yet some ambivalence exists concerning his treatment by modern authors. Rahtz names the General among the top five archaeologists of all time (1985, 52) while Carver (1989, 669) gives an opposing viewpoint, but neither of these writers document their arguments. Meanwhile others see him as little more than an amusing eccentric with a private band and menagerie of exotic animals. However, if for no other reason, the General has had a significant influence on British archaeology as the excavator of over forty sites including such classics as Wor Barrow, South Lodge Camp and Woodcutts, all of which have been sources of reference and reinterpretation for later researchers. An appreciation of the historical context of the General's work is fundamental to our understanding of these sites (Barrett 1987).

Pitt Rivers cannot be judged by archaeological criteria alone. He was, like most prehistorians of his day, also an anthropologist and an early follower of Darwin. In Stocking's words he occupies 'an important secondary place in the evolutionary pantheon' (1987, 180).

1 Lt.-General Augustus Henry Lane Fox Pitt-Rivers

The intellectual circles in which Pitt Rivers moved were remarkable. They included Darwin himself and his earliest and ablest champion, Thomas Henry Huxley, as well as Herbert Spencer, who interpreted Darwinism for the humanities and created sociocultural evolutionism, the dominant sociological mode of thought of the later nineteenth century. They also included geologists such as Sir Joseph Prestwich and Professor Boyd Dawkins, the leading anatomist Professor George Rolleston, the philologist Friedrich Max Müller and the anthropologist Edward Burnett Tylor. Archaeology was central to the concerns of the disciplines represented by these men in the later nineteenth century because it was able to address questions, such as the antiquity of the human race, which were seen as fundamental to science. Pitt Rivers worked alongside some of the greatest British archaeologists of his generation: Sir John Evans, Sir John Lubbock, Augustus Franks and Canon William Greenwell.

The outstanding qualities of this group were the intense intellectual excitement generated at the meetings of learned societies which they all attended, not surprising in view of the momentous discoveries so frequently communicated throughout this period, and the wry humour which is apparent in much of the personal correspondence between them. Enthusiasm was strong. The archaeologists, all of whom with the exception of Augustus Franks must be considered amateurs, thought little of dropping their everyday business to visit gravel pits in the Somme valley with Boucher de Perthes, or to travel to the Swiss lake villages, or to Hallstatt, or to Neanderthal, or to any of the major continental museums.

General Pitt Rivers was to take a leading role within this group from the late 1860s until the end of the century. In the first place his organisational skills were much in demand and he served as an officer on the councils and committees of several learned societies. His colleagues' perceptions of his success in this field are surely reflected in his appointment as the first Inspector of Ancient Monuments in 1882. The General's success as a fieldworker and theorist was of much greater significance but was, ironically, less appreciated by his contemporaries.

This lack of appreciation may in part be due to the novel aspects of much of his work. The General's greatest innovations in archaeological technique fall under three heads. Firstly, he excavated a wider range of sites than did his predecessors and contemporaries. He escaped from the prevailing obsession with burial mounds and studied hillforts and settlement sites: 'From the tumuli we derive evidence of things deposited with the dead . . . but the relics found in camps and dwellings are the things that were in everyday use, and, therefore, give us better insight into the social conditions of the people' (Pitt Rivers 1884a, 65). Like the great Worsaae (Daniel 1975, 48) he recognised the potential for retrieving information from the sherds of pottery and fragments of bone which most contemporary antiquaries would have discarded without a second glance: 'The value of relics, viewed as evidence, may . . . be said to be in an inverse ratio to their intrinsic value' (Pitt Rivers 1892, ix). Secondly the General recognised the importance of context. Whereas for most antiquarians it was enough to know which site an artefact came from, Pitt Rivers insisted that only by making an accurate record of the exact findspot and its relationship to structural features could the history of the site be reconstructed. Thirdly, though the analysis of archaeological finds had a respectable history, Pitt Rivers brought a degree of consistency and completeness to this aspect of archaeology. The best example of this is the measurement of modern animals and their bones for comparison with the animal bones found on excavations that he undertook for much of his Cranborne Chase work. He also undertook experiments, such as knapping flints and digging with bone and antler tools.

For Pitt Rivers all this scientific endeavour had one end. He was a fervent advocate of a gradualist Darwinian doctrine, of the law that nature makes no jumps, and he sought to apply this to human society. Evolution, not revolution, was the way forward. Through his publications and, more especially, through his museums Pitt Rivers sought to indoctrinate the people with this idea.

Before going on to discuss the character of this extraordinary man in detail it is necessary, however briefly, to sketch his family background.

PITTS AND LANE FOXES

In 1789 Marcia Lucy, youngest daughter of George Pitt, first Baron Rivers, married James Lane Fox of Bramham Hall, West Riding. While James Lane Fox came of stolid and traditional Yorkshire stock his bride was a member of a rather more volatile family. The lives of her elder sisters, Penelope and Louisa, are indicative both of the spirit and the tragic ill health of the Pitts.

Penelope had married in 1766 Edward, Viscount Ligonier of Clonmell, but they were divorced by Act of Parliament only five years later, the cause being her adultery with Vittorio Amadeo, Count Alfieri. Lord Ligonier accordingly fought a duel with the Count in Green Park, using a sword borrowed from a cutler in Bond Street. Lady Ligonier subsequently had an affair with a postillion, giving rise to the immortal couplet:

> But see the luscious Ligonier
> Prefers her post boy to her Peer.

In 1784 she married a man calling himself Captain Smith who, according to the *Gentleman's Magazine*, was a trooper in the Horse Guards (Cokayne 1929, 656–7). A very fine portrait of Lady Ligonier by Gainsborough used to hang in the dining room at Rushmore. Gray recorded that 'more than one West End dealer has offered the General several thousands for this notable work of art, but all to no purpose' (Gray Papers). Sadly some of the General's successors have been less scrupulous and the picture is now in the collection of the Huntington Library and Art Gallery, California.

Louisa was married in 1773 to Peter Beckford, a cynical fox-hunting squire with whom she had nothing in common. She fell in love with his selfish and eccentric cousin William Beckford of Fonthill and died in 1791 of tuberculosis

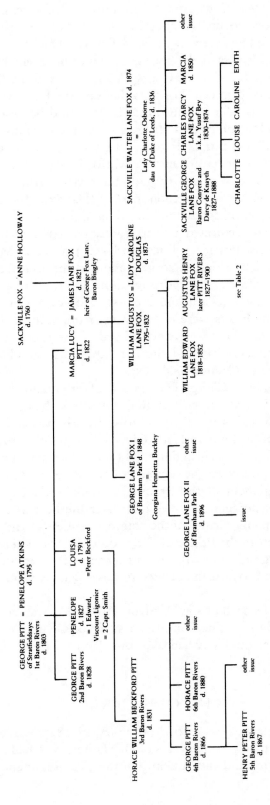

Table 1 The Pitt and Lane Fox families, *c.* 1750–1870: simplified genealogical table

and a broken heart (Mannings 1986, 303). Louisa Beckford bequeathed her poor health to her descendants who became the heirs of the first Baron Rivers and took his name. They were an ill-fated family. The three eldest sons of George, fourth Baron Rivers died at the ages of sixteen, seventeen and fourteen respectively. Only the fourth son, Henry Peter, survived his father but died unmarried at the age of eighteen. Lord Stanley saw the Hon. William Pitt and Henry Peter Pitt on his visit to Rushmore in 1858 and he described them as follows: 'I saw the eldest son carried out by a servant & put into a little carriage – he cannot walk at all & is not likely to live; they say the younger one is better than his brother, but I suspect not much' (Mitford 1939, 191). As if the early fatalities of the brothers was not enough their sister Alice was struck by lightning and killed on her honeymoon in 1865 (Hawkins 1982, 10).

The Lane Foxes were, on the whole, healthier and less imaginative than the Pitts. Their lives were dedicated to the traditional country pursuits of the squirearchy and to a reactionary political outlook. James and Marcia had four sons and a daughter. The eldest, George, inherited the Bramham estate, following the family tradition as the sporting squire and taking a great interest in agricultural improvement (Ward 1967, 64–5). However, for all their solid respectability the Lane Foxes were not immune from scandal. George's marriage failed and his wife went to live with Lord Chesterfield. When, in 1830, Lord Chesterfield suddenly married another lady, Mrs Lane Fox became the mistress of the Prince of Orange (*ibid.*, 65).

George Lane Fox's heir, George Lane Fox II of Bramham Park, was cast in the family mould. He was the perfect Regency Buck, being rusticated from Oxford because of his excessive devotion to sport. He was an inveterate race-goer and a member of the Four-in-Hand Club, he frequently drove the Tadcaster stagecoach and Glasgow mail and hunted four or five days a week. After his father's death in 1848, however, he calmed down and devoted the rest of his life to the careful management of the Bramham estate (*ibid.*, 66–71) though he remained an habitual pursuer of the fox. In later life he was regarded as the embodiment of the manly virtues of the country gentleman and sportsman by all levels of society, from the Prince of Wales down to his own tenants. Indeed so popular was George Lane Fox II with his tenantry that 'about the year 1856 the whole body came forward and offered to raise their rents for him' (Speight 1902, 407–8).

George Lane Fox I's second son, William Augustus, was born in 1795. In 1817 he married Lady Caroline Douglas, a sister of George Sholto Douglas, eighteenth Earl of Morton. They had two sons, William Edward, born in 1818 and Augustus Henry.

THE GENERAL

Augustus Henry Lane Fox was born on 14 April 1827 at Hope Hall near Bramham Park. When he was five years old his father, who had been an officer in the Grenadier Guards and subsequently in the 98th Regiment of Foot, died and his mother took him to live in London. Nothing is known of Augustus Henry's childhood until he entered the Royal Military Academy at Sandhurst in 1841 except that he read his father's letters from the Peninsula with interest (Constanduros 1953 unpublished) and that he had a toy boomerang. As he later recorded with some pride, 'I . . . acquired some skill in throwing it so as to return to me repeatedly, and also to pass behind me in its return flight' (Pitt Rivers 1883a, 457).

In adult life he was a large man and an imposing figure. His health was always weak however. He suffered from a bronchial condition and diabetes (Pitt Rivers Papers M1-10) which necessitated several visits to Carlsbad and other spas. He also suffered some affliction of his feet (*ibid.* App. 2, 24) though his grandson, Captain George Pitt Rivers, was later at pains to deny a local rumour that the General's feet had been frost-bitten in the Crimea (Constanduros 1953 unpublished). On occasions his physical weakness led to difficult and potentially dangerous situations. While lecturing at Salisbury Museum one evening he slipped on the platform and injured his leg and his hand, which smashed through a glass case. He insisted on continuing with the lecture but fainted and fell again. Having been revived by the Bishop of Salisbury and others he completed the lecture 'being seated whilst doing so' (Pitt Rivers Papers App. 2, 104).

The General was a man of fierce temper, not untinged with violence, of considerable energy and enthusiasm, unsociable with his peers, a domestic tyrant and yet approachable to his labourers; a dominant and aloof father figure in the grand Victorian manner, though possessing a dry sense of humour.

His temper was most evident in his relations with the members of his immediate family. His daughter Agnes recalled many unhappy incidents in her diary, most of them involving her elder sister Alice and herself. On 1 March 1882 the General 'swore like anything at Alice' (Hawkins 1982, 29). These incidents could turn to physical violence. At one time the General had forbidden his second son, St George, to enter the house or estate at Rushmore, but Alice arranged to meet him in the park. Mrs Pitt Rivers, who seems to have arranged a system of domestic espionage, employing servants to report her daughters' movements (*ibid.*, 32), told the General of this rendezvous. The General intercepted Alice crossing the hall on her return. He snatched her riding crop and slashed her across the face with it (Tomkin Papers).

Michael Pitt-Rivers has described his great-grandfather as having a 'powerful personality; cold, impersonal and serious, but never very human. He evidently inspired respect rather than affection; loyalty but not love' (1977, 23). The General dominated the lives of his children and of his archaeological assistants. Alice was driven into an unsuitable marriage with Sir John Lubbock because life under her father's roof was unbearable. The eldest son, Alexander, who never moved far from home, seems to have been totally overawed by his father. St George left home to pursue his own bizarre life in London while William escaped by joining the army.

The General seems to have had only three close friends. In the army there

2 Statue of Caesar Augustus, copied from an original in the Vatican. Caesar Augustus could have no direct historical connection with the Roman remains in Cranborne Chase, so the General's choice of this statue as a memorial is entirely due to the fact that he was the Emperor's namesake

was Colonel the Hon. Alexander Gordon, a fellow staff officer in the Crimea and godfather to the General's eldest son. Subsequently Professor George Rolleston, the Oxford anatomist, was the General's close companion; and after Rolleston's untimely death in 1881 Pitt Rivers found a kindred spirit in his fellow antiquary and Dorset landowner John Mansell-Pleydell. They regularly visited each other at home and Mansell-Pleydell was the General's most frequent correspondent. They shared a fear of the growing power of the radicals in the Liberal party. In October 1885 Pitt Rivers wrote to Mansell-Pleydell, 'If you go to Scotland on a Geological trip you will come back to find your park cut up into plots of 3 acres with a cow & a pigsty in each' (Pitt Rivers Papers M37b). Except for his relationship with these three men and his early attachment to his wife the General seems to have avoided emotional contacts. Feelings such as 'surprise,' 'delight' and 'satisfaction' were reserved for inanimate objects such as Egyptian boomerangs and medieval windows (Pitt Rivers 1883a, 454–5; 1890, 12). Although the General also maintained a regular correspondence with his old mentor Canon William Greenwell their letters are respectful rather than friendly in tone. The same may be said for letters from the General's other professional colleagues such as Sir John Evans and the man who was to become his son-in-law, Sir John Lubbock, later Lord Avebury. The General was a poor correspondent in any case, in the sense that he did not read the letters he received very carefully and often replied tangentially. His most persistant professional correspondent was J. H. Moule, curator of the Dorset County Museum at Dorchester. Amongst other subjects they discussed decorated pottery at length but on several occasions Pitt Rivers failed to answer Moule's remarks and questions (Pitt Rivers Papers L975, 977, 2184, 2186). Similarly Frederick James, who sent a skull to Pitt Rivers in 1898 to be measured in the craniometer, failed to obtain a reply despite making three subsequent applications for the information (*ibid.*, L2218).

One of the most striking characteristics of the General was his compulsion to collect and to order everything he collected, studying the objects in meticulous detail. By the late 1860s he had filled his house with ethnographic objects (Chapman 1985, 29) and thirty years later, though increasingly ill and close to death, he amassed the finest collection of Benin Bronzes in the world. Harold St George Gray, his secretary in the 1890s, described him as 'a voracious and omnivorous collector' (1905, xxxi). Not many people can claim to have created two major museums. The General's ethnographic collections were world-wide in origin but he had an extensive catchment area for objects of antiquarian interest as well. He was well known to dealers as far afield as Vienna, such as S. Egger and Co., who sent him the following charming letter in December 1882:

> Dear Sir, After much troubles it succeeded us to acquire a very nice Celtic sword, which we allow us to offer you. The last price of it is £20 and it is of an especially form and size. We request for a very soon answer, as we cannot reserve a price like that for a long time. (Pitt Rivers Papers B412)

The collections were put to use as tools for public education, Pitt Rivers' most cherished goal, but clearly not all the objects he obtained were meant for public display. In November 1888 Mr R. Alexander of the Indian Art Gallery, a firm with which the General had many dealings, wrote to him about objects that can only have been pieces of erotica:

> Sir, I beg to take the liberty of writing to ask if you would care to see two very exquisitely carved pieces of ivory of a certain character. I should not thus presume only that I had the pleasure of selling you two stone models which you may recollect. If you care to see them I should be glad of an appointment to show them as, should you call here I might not be able to produce them, as they are quite private, though at times I could, (*ibid.*, B423)

The General took great care to verify information connected with objects in his collections and was very proud of his ability to detect fakes (for example, Fox 1872a, 458), but he was not altogether proof against clever forgeries. Two objects from Farnham now in Salisbury Museum, a samian dish and mould (Acc. Nos. 3M 6B 8 and 3M 7B 3) are certainly not genuine pieces (Mark

Corney personal communication). The authenticity of the 'Pitt Rivers knife', an Egyptian antiquity, is also in question (James 1988, 86).

Although many of Pitt Rivers' interests and attitudes seem eccentric in the late twentieth century, he was a man of his time. One of the most positive aspects of his character was the incredible energy which allowed him to achieve so much despite almost constant ill health. This can be seen as an example of what Seaman has described as 'typically Victorian tirelessness' (1973, 50). His sense of personal moral responsibility, of duty and of respectability are all characteristic of the age in which he lived. He was extremely receptive to the new ideas of his age, to Samuel Smiles' doctrine of 'self-help' and to Charles Darwin's theory of evolution and he combined these ideas in his scheme of public education to support the ideology of the Victorian ruling class, 'designed to induce in the masses a docile acceptance of the tyranny of the capitalist entrepreneur' (*ibid.*, 6).

His racial views too are conventional in the light of Victorian modes of thought. Although they appear wildly extreme to a late-twentieth-century observer they were moderate in comparison with the established views of many of his contemporaries such as Sir Richard Burton, James Hunt and the continental craniometrists. Only in relation to the Irish did Pitt Rivers show a personal bitterness derived from his experiences in the 1860s. The attitude of the English ruling class to the Irish people was vindictive (Woodham-Smith 1953, 108–9) and this was reflected in the writings of many anthropologists (Stocking 1987, 63, 225) but the General abused the Irish not only in his overtly political speeches, accusing them of vicious crimes such as cattle maiming, which was certainly not confined to Ireland in the nineteenth century (see for instance Archer 1985), but also in his archaeological writings. His explanation for the existence of disc barrows is a case in point. He thought that they were unfinished monuments:

> The first idea of the mourners, when grief was poignant, may probably have been to erect a large monument to the deceased, and the ditch in such a case would contain a large area. In the course of a few days, however, the grief may have abated, and laziness supervened, in which case the arrested tumulus would assume the form described. The habit of all primitive people, including the modern Irish as a familiar instance, of lashing themselves up into a frenzy on the occasion of a death, and general excitability upon any common occurrence, followed by a speedy relapse, favours this hypothesis. (1898, 145)

The General's religious beliefs have been the subject of much controversy. He was accused of atheism in his lifetime and many people still believe this to have been true (for example, M. Pitt-Rivers 1977, 23). Certainly he was not a regular churchgoer, attending only at major religious festivals or at weddings and funerals, but he was scrupulous in allowing his dependants to worship as they pleased, and family prayers were held every day at Rushmore (Hawkins 1982, 17) at a time when the institution of family prayers was already in decline generally (Seaman 1973, 419–20). Furthermore the Larmer Grounds Sunday opening was certainly not an attack on the church as has sometimes been stated

3 The Jubilee Room, North Lodge, Rushmore Park: though built as a chapel the decorations are notably secular. It was provided by Pitt Rivers for his tenants and is typical of his picturesque park architecture

and several, though not all, of the local clergy approved of this form of innocent entertainment on the Sabbath (Pitt Rivers Papers M29g).

For a lecture at Whitechapel in 1875 on evolution and the Thames gravels, the General had written a revealing passage on religious systems but then struck it out and presumably it was not read. It affords some insight into his feelings about the Christian church:

> As we find in nature that there are some trees which throw their branches upward towards heaven and others the branches of which . . . droop downwards from the trunk . . . so in human institutions there are some which . . . develop upwards and become more perfect & more complex and others which have a tendency to deteriorate in their evolution. Of this latter class we may include all the religious systems of the world as seen under the influence of ritualistic degeneration . . . This is true of all religions but as it is always regarded as an act of grace to study the beam that is in our own eye let us test the truth of this observation by a brief survey of Christian ideas . . . Taking the existing altars of Christian sects as the

outward and visible signs of ritualistic degeneration and employing them as survivals to illustrate the evolution of Christian ideas in times past . . . we find that Christianity has been a drooping branch from the day when its founder suffered martyrdom upon the cross. His disciples forsook him and fled and the Christian churches in their respective ramifications have continued the flight with a velocity that has accelerated in ratio as the square of the times.

Commencing with the nearest existing representative of the simple supper table at which the early Christian sat or stood to commemorate the anniversary of his beloved master we may see this table at first removed and placed against the eastern wall, then railed off from the communicants who instead of sitting or standing at it kneel towards it as if it were a thing in itself to be revered we may then follow it as it gradually develops into an altar and by degrees becomes associated with all those emblems of fire and incense which in pagan times served to fix the attention of the worshippers . . . And side by side with this material development we may perceive the motive force which has been effecting this evolution is a gradual accession of the power of the priesthood who from having been originally the friends and councellors of the community have developed into the confessors and absolvers of sins and ultimately in some instances into the infallible & despotic rulers of human consciences . . .

What then if we do find that religion is subject to the same laws of evolution as all other human ideas. Are we to infer from this that we can see God in nothing, or may we not rather infer that we may see him in everything instead of peeping at him through the narrow chinks & crevices which have been prescribed for us during an ignorant age. (Pitt Rivers Papers P42)

This account of the evolution of religious systems echoes, to some degree, E. B. Tylor's view of religion (Stocking 1987, 195). Presumably this passage was struck out because of its potential to unsettle the minds of the 'tradesmen & working classes of the neighbourhood' who attended the lecture with regard to the established church, one of the pillars of society.

The General was open about his beliefs, motivation and aims to the point of being outspoken. There was nothing remotely furtive about his activities, which would throw suspicion on Thompson's notion (1960; 1977, 61–2) that he went to Brittany in 1878 and 1879 to practice field surveying in secret, even if there were not good evidence that his actual motives were quite different. Pitt Rivers' remarks about the labouring classes in both his political and archaeological works are extremely forthright: 'Hodge, though better off than he has ever been before, is in a lower condition, morally and mentally, than at any previous period' (Pitt Rivers 1891, 119). Despite this attitude Pitt Rivers was regarded by many of the labourers on his estate as a benefactor and a friend. He was approachable to them in a way that he never was to his social equals or to the intervening tenant farmer class. George Bealing recorded that ' . . . he weren't no sportin' man for shooting or nothing like that. No, his hobby were road making and tree planting and making ponds . . . He were a man you could talk to, you know. Nothing proud about 'n' (Constanduros 1953 unpublished). Frank Adams of Sixpenny Handley revealed how anyone could approach the General and converse with him at the Larmer Grounds: 'It was his greatest joy . . . to see the people there at Larmer . . . enjoying themselves; there was no question about that. That seemed to me to be his one aim – that was to make enjoyment for the other people . . . of this neighbourhood' (ibid.).

The origin of the General's personal interest in anthropology and archaeology will probably never be known for certain though speculation about his contacts with antiquarian members and connections of the Stanley family must be close to the truth. However, that he should have developed an interest in some form of scientific endeavour is barely worthy of comment given his professional and social status. The attitude of the military authorities to science is particularly relevant. The Staff College curriculum was extremely broadbased and aimed at the ideal of the gentleman amateur. Geology was taught, for instance, because it was hoped that officers on duty would actively advance geological knowledge (Harries-Jenkins 1977, 161–2). The Ordnance Survey's tradition of depicting antiquities stems directly from the military origins of the organisation and reflects the interest of General Roy, the first Director-General. The belief that the military profession has nothing to do with broad scientific knowledge (Bradley 1983, 2) is entirely a twentieth-century gloss. All branches of science were regarded as eminently fit pursuits for the ruling class in the nineteenth century, perhaps even more so than in the eighteenth century. The membership lists of later nineteenth-century archaeological societies illustrate this. Of the 248 ordinary members of the Royal Archaeological Institute in December 1897 no less than seventeen were peers of the realm. There were also two foreign noblemen, three MPs, two of whom had additional titles, three judges, a QC and ten baronets. The cloth was represented by an archbishop, four bishops, two deans, two archdeacons and thirty-eight clergymen, of whom one was also a baronet. There were two doctors of medicine, one of them knighted, fifteen military officers including a baronet and a knight, a Town Clerk, a Clan Chief and the 'Worshipful Chancellor' Ferguson.

This was the society to which the General gave his last major public address, at Dorchester, Dorset, in August 1897. He had driven from Rushmore in a carriage and pair with his secretary, Harold St George Gray, via Blandford where they picked up the General's friend John Mansell-Pleydell from his house at Whatcombe (Gray Papers). The General, an Honorary Vice President of the Institute, had been invited to give the Presidential address by the President, his wife's kinsman Viscount Dillon. Pitt Rivers used the occasion to review his long career in archaeology, touching on all his major discoveries and innovations. However, his closing words show an intellectual modesty which, though perhaps seemingly uncharacteristic, was certainly genuine: 'In conclusion, I have only to acknowledge my own shortcomings. Notwithstanding the care that I have taken to omit nothing, I am aware that my investigations fall short of what they ought to be' (Pitt Rivers 1897, 339).

2

Progress in modern musketry

Many writers on the General, mainly archaeologists themselves (e.g. Hawkes *et al.* 1947, 35), have tended to dismiss his military career with the word 'distinguished' before going on to discuss other aspects of his life. In a work of this length it is possible and it is fairer, both to the General and to his contemporaries, to place his military career in its context and attempt to make a realistic assessment of his contribution to military affairs.

The decision to serve in the army no doubt stemmed naturally from the tradition of military service in the Lane Fox family. A more personal desire for a military career may have been engendered by reading his father's letters from the Peninsula (Constanduros 1953 unpublished). His feeling for military glory is illustrated by the collections he amassed, which included not only many weapons but also objects such as two chairs believed to have belonged to Napoleon and Koer Singh's quilted coat, captured by Vincent Eyre during the Indian Mutiny (Pitt Rivers Papers M53, P178). The choice of the Grenadier Guards was also a matter of family tradition. Augustus' father, William Lane Fox, had served in the Regiment for seven years, during which he saw active service in the Peninsula, before transferring to the 98th Foot, and an uncle had also served in the Grenadiers.

In the mid-nineteenth century the army was still almost exclusively officered by the nobility and gentry and manned by the working class. The middle classes had little part in it at all (Harries-Jenkins 1977, 6). Augustus Lane Fox was typical officer material – the younger son of a cadet branch of a substantial gentry family with close connections amongst the nobility. He had spent only six months at the Royal Military Academy, Sandhurst. Of any other education which he may have undergone we know nothing. However, any lack of education or training would not have seemed amiss. The officer corps of the British army at this time was characterised chiefly by its amateur outlook and lack of interest in military matters (*ibid.*, 5). Only officers in the 'scientific' branches of the Artillery and Engineers were expected to possess any practical knowledge of their profession.

Fox was, therefore, a typical Guards officer, but within a few years of gaining his commission he was placed in a position to take up a specialised military interest outside his regimental duties. The army was undergoing a change in the basic infantry weapon. Except for the Rifle Brigade, the army was still equipped with the smooth-bore musket, Brown Bess, which had served it since the early-eighteenth century and now this was to be replaced by a more accurate rifled weapon. This was clearly a matter of importance and there were several types of rifles available. A committee was set up to experiment and report on the suitability of each type so that the higher command could make an informed choice. The Duke of Wellington was personally concerned and, following his death in 1852, his successor as Commander-in-Chief, Lord Hardinge, continued to take an interest in the matter.

A Grenadier officer, Studholme Brownrigg, was the president of this committee and Fox became one of its members, probably in 1851 (Hamilton 1874, xix). There is no apparent record of why he became involved but he seems to have taken an active part in the Committee's work. This was a crucial development for Fox because it led, directly or indirectly, to his collection of firearms and therefore to his later work on the 'evolution of culture', anthropology and archaeology. Some of the details of the committee's work show a foretaste of Fox's later scientific work: 'Diagrams were kept recording the result of each day's firing . . .' (ibid. xx).

When the experiments were finished the committee made its report and the French-designed Minié rifle was adopted for the army. Studholme Brownrigg and Fox were then despatched to Woolwich to instruct detachments from every battalion in the army in the use of the new weapon (ibid.).

In 1852 Fox travelled on the continent to study the systems of instruction in use in France, Belgium and Piedmont and drew up a code of instruction. This was first used by Fox himself in instructing the 2nd battalion of the Grenadier Guards and subsequently partly adopted for the whole regiment. Later in the same year Lord Hardinge sent for Fox and discussed with him the establishment of a School of Musketry for the army. He also 'desired him to revise his Regulations, so as to make them applicable for general purposes' (ibid., 153–4). Later criticism indicates that some officers considered Fox's system too complex (Fox 1858, 486–7; Thompson 1977, 26) and it may be that the partial adoption of the code by the Grenadiers and the revision desired by the Commander-in-Chief are due to this complexity. The revised code was given the title Instruction of Musketry. In April 1853 Lord Hardinge sent Fox to submit the proposed regulations to Colonel Hay who was to be the Commandant of the new School of Musketry at Hythe in Kent. Fox duly became principal instructor at the School. He was able to revise the Instruction of Musketry in the light of his experiences in that post and a published edition appeared in the following year (Hamilton 1874, 154).

Thompson remarks (1977, 17) that Hamilton's description of these events is important because Colonel Hay, having quarrelled with Fox, tended to minimise Fox's achievements at the School of Musketry. On the other hand, it must be admitted that as Hamilton was writing a history of the Grenadier Guards, he may have exaggerated the achievements of officers belonging to the

Regiment. Nevertheless it appears that Fox did play a substantial role in the development of the new system of musketry instruction and this duty gained in importance as war loomed upon the horizon.

In February 1854 British troops began to leave for the Mediterranean on the first step in the journey that was to take them to the theatre of war in the Crimea. Whether Fox travelled with the 3rd battalion of the Grenadiers or whether he travelled separately is not known, but he did supervise musketry training for the Brigade of Guards while they were at Malta. The intention was that Fox should form a school of musketry for the army in the field (Hamilton 1874, 163–4). This does not seem to have been fully achieved and, though musketry practice was taken very seriously, it was undertaken largely at battalion level.

Fox accompanied the Grenadiers when they left Malta for Scutari in April aboard the *Golden Fleece* (*ibid.* 165). At this point Fox is described by Hamilton as 'instructor of musketry for the army', implying that he was in charge of musketry training for the whole Army in the East.

In mid-June the army advanced from Constantinople to Varna on the Bulgarian coast. Here the troops were occupied building entrenchments and earthworks and with 'Musketry Instruction field-days' (*ibid.* 178) which were presumably Fox's responsibility. However Fox had by now gained other duties. On leaving Scutari he had accepted the post of Deputy Assistant Quartermaster General to the 2nd Division because 'the school of musketry was for a time partially suspended' (*ibid.* 181).

While in Bulgaria Fox suffered a number of minor disasters including the non-appearance of some of his personal equipment and the loss of his horses. 'I am so distressed at yr. losing yr. ponies & saddle', wrote his wife on 30 August; 'Surely the villain must have sold them . . . have you taken no steps about them or punished the servants is it Steele & the native . . .' (Pitt Rivers Papers App. 2, 25).

In September the army left Bulgaria for the invasion of the Crimea. Fox sailed in the *City of London* with General Sir de Lacy Evans and the staff of the 2nd Division, landing at Calamita Bay on 14 September 1854. On 20 September the allied armies reached the river Alma and the first battle of the Crimean war took place. The Russians occupied well prepared positions on the heights beyond the river Alma. The allied generals decided against a flank attack and flung their troops in a frontal assault across the river. Despite appalling losses the allied troops, by sheer determination and persistence, managed to reach the Russian positions, take them and force the enemy to retreat. Fox's exact role in the battle is not known. The 2nd Division was in the thick of the fighting and it was a staff officer's duty to expose himself to danger. This was amply demonstrated at the Alma by Lord Raglan himself who conducted the battle from a position far in advance of his own troops and practically within the Russian lines (Harries-Jenkins 1977, 15; Hibbert 1961, 74–5). Five members of the staff of the 2nd Division were wounded, including General Evans himself and Fox's immediate superior, Colonel Herbert, but Fox came through unscathed

(Thompson 1977, 25). As a result of Colonel Herbert's wounds Fox found himself doing the Assistant Quartermaster General's duty. Lord Stanley considered that this would 'be a good thing for him & now he is safe he will have all the credit & renown of having had the brunt of the battle to bear' (Mitford 1939, 90). The conviction that Russian resistance had totally collapsed after the Alma must account for his belief that Fox was now safe.

In the event the Alma was the only major action that Fox saw. The army continued to advance on Sevastopol but now, instead of making a direct assault on the town from the north the commanders decided on a flank march in order to take it from the south. By October the movement was complete, the allied armies were established on their bases at Balaclava and Kamietsch and the siege of Sevastopol had begun.

On 15 October a medical examination showed that Fox was unfit for service (Thompson 1977, 26). The weather had begun to turn noticeably colder about 9 October (Hibbert 1961, 114) and perhaps this had had an effect on Fox's bronchial condition. Fox was one of the few lucky enough, or privileged enough, to be invalided home rather than being subjected to the appalling conditions of the military hospitals in Balaclava and Scutari.

In assessing Fox's personal contribution to the war effort we can compare the awards he received with those of his brother officers in the Grenadiers. Of the hundred Grenadier officers who served in the Crimea all except fourteen, who didn't arrive until after the fall of Sevastopol, received the Crimean medal and Turkish war medal. Forty received further decorations. Of these forty, thirteen, including Fox, received only the Turkish Order of Medjidie, 5th Class. In addition eleven officers, including Fox, were promoted major by brevet. Fox was one of a group of five promoted on the same day, of which three were staff officers. This promotion was for distinguished service in the field (Hamilton 1874, xxi–xxxi).

Fox was also mentioned in dispatches by Sir de Lacy Evans. Thompson suggests (1977, 25) that staff officers were favoured in this respect by being more under the eye of their commanders than were regimental officers. In fact the situation was more extreme than that. Lord Raglan and his Divisional Generals in the Crimea followed the Duke of Wellington's practice in this, as in so many other fields. They never mentioned the names of officers other than those of generals and their staffs (Woodham-Smith 1953, 140–1). For the Duke, who had built up a small but efficient staff in the Peninsular campaigns (Keegan 1988, 132–8), there was some excuse for this practice. For Lord Raglan with his lamentably inept staff officers in the Crimea (Hibbert 1961, 15–16) the practice is harder to defend.

However, in one respect Fox had perhaps made a much greater contribution to eventual victory than these awards imply. At the battle of the Alma only a small proportion of the British infantry had been issued with the new rifles, but already the superiority of this weapon was apparent (Thompson 1977, 25). By the end of the campaign every infantry battalion was equipped with rifles and, presumably, had been trained in their use according to Fox's system.

Fox has left us little of his personal impressions of the war except for the brief and rather bald account of the battle of the Alma reproduced by Thompson (1977, 134–5). In this he does not mention rifles at all.

Fox resumed active service as soon as he had recovered from his illness. In 1855 he returned to Malta to continue musketry training. Before he left for Malta Fox went to see General Evans who had also been invalided home. As a result of this visit Evans wrote to the Military Secretary for the information of the Commander-in-Chief that 'He is very anxious as he is now a Field Officer to be an assistant on the General Staff rather than a Deputy Assistant. I can only assure you that he is . . . deserving of any consideration the rules of the Service may admit of . . .' (Pitt Rivers Papers A1). At no time in his life was Fox shy of asking for any advancement which he thought his due.

He stayed in Malta for two years. Johnny Stanley, his brother-in-law, was later to tell his mother, 'Many officers I have met who were at Malta under him have told me how ably and cleverly he managed the men' (Mitford 1939, 260). However, it was at this time that Colonel Hay, still in command at Hythe, criticised his methods fiercely. In his report on rifle instruction in Gibraltar and Malta, Colonel Hay made comparisons between the two to the detriment of Malta:

> Malta – At this station only three Battalions and two companies of the Corps of Royal Engineers have exercised through the prescribed course of Musketry Instruction out of the large force, viz. ten Battalions quartered here during the practice season for 1856–7.
>
> The cause for the non-training of so many Battalions at Malta may be entirely attributed to the system which was pursued, the worst that could have possibly been adopted where a large force had to be trained in a given time, by the officer charged with the supervision of the instruction and not to any local cause or defect in the authorised system of proceeding in this particular . . .
>
> The means available for Rifle practice at Malta have been ample . . . (Pitt Rivers Papers A1b)

This report was issued in October 1857. Fox had been promoted Lieutenant-Colonel, by purchase, in May 1857 and had returned to England in August. It is not clear what duties Fox undertook in the next three years. The quarrel with Hay did not prevent him from delivering a lecture 'On the Improvement of the Rifle' to the United Services Institute in June 1858. That this lecture was expected to be controversial in itself is shown by a letter to Fox from his friend Colonel the Hon. Alexander Gordon, advising him on how to deal with 'the enemy' (Pitt Rivers Papers App. 2, 47).

On 10 August 1857, Lord Stanley wrote to his wife,

> Fox seems of a discontented & querulous nature & expects some high post will immediately be offered to him & if not that he is ill used. I cannot see why he shld. not go back to his duty in the Regt., like many other officers who had higher staff offices than he has had & who did not consider it a hardship to do Regimental duty. (Mitford 1939, 152)

Deep in bitter argument with Hay and his staff at Hythe (Pitt Rivers Papers

4 Colonel Lane Fox

App. 2, 41–4, 51–7), Fox had reason to be discontented and querulous. Lord Stanley had little patience with his son-in-law, however. On 21 August he grudgingly agreed to use his influence on Fox's behalf and on 2 September asked his wife 'what does the discontented Field Marshal intend to do with himself? In the meantime I shld. prefer he does not go out shooting every day as I wish to keep some partridges for the use of the house' (Mitford 1939, 152, 154).

An enquiry into Hay's criticism does not seem to have been instituted until 1860. Sir James Lindsay, commanding the Grenadier Guards, wrote to Sir James Scarlett, Adjutant General, regarding Hay's report. Lindsay defended Fox against Hay's censure, suggesting that Hay had misunderstood the situation in Malta and quoting at length from Sir John Pennefather, who had been the General Officer Commanding in Malta at the time:

... the system carried out at Malta in 1856 by regiments instead of by detachments from each corps simultaneously was not carried out by Lt. Col. Lane Fox's
suggestion in any manner whatsoever but was entirely my own arrangement in
consequence of Nine Battalions being suddenly thrown into Malta from the
Crimea in an unsettled state after the War requiring constant attention to restore
discipline ... for whose Instruction in Musketry I may say I had only Col. Fox
and about 4 sergeants. The arrangement gave me a limited camp at St Georges
Bay for a Battalion, discipline being thereby much secured and my small
musketry staff being only sufficient for a small portion of the raw hands at any
time ... (Pitt Rivers Papers A1c)

Pennefather had notified Horse Guards of his plan and the Duke of Cambridge, Commander-in-Chief, had expressed himself satisfied with it as a
temporary measure. The regular system was reintroduced as soon as discipline
improved and resources became available. The proper complement of Instruc-
tors for ten battalions should have been ten officers and ten sergeants, Lindsay
pointed out:

There can be no doubt I apprehend that the effect of the Report has been preju-
dicial to the interests of Col. Fox. I believe I am correct in stating that he was
recommended to be recalled from Malta in consequence of his disobedience of the
Hythe regulations. Lord Hardinge had appointed him to Malta in consequence of
his having originated the principle of the system of instructing soldiers in the use
of the rifle ... Believing therefore that the terms of the Report convey an
undeserved censure upon an Officer serving under my command I trust that you
will have the goodness to investigate the circumstances connected with the
Report and take such steps as may seem meet to remove the slur which the
Report has cast upon him ... (Pitt Rivers Papers A1c)

Eventually Fox's name was cleared and on 30 January 1861 Johnny Stanley
wrote, 'I am glad to hear Fox has had justice done him at last' (Mitford 1939,
260).

In 1861 the '*Trent* Incident' brought further employment for Fox. The 1st
Battalion of the Grenadier Guards was one of the units sent to Canada in
December:

Previous to the departure of the Battalion, Lieutenant-Colonel Augustus Lane
Fox, of the Grenadier Guards, had, on the 2nd of December, been sent out to
Canada on 'special service', having completed which, he returned to England,
and in August of the following year was appointed Assistant-Quartermaster-
General to the Cork district. (Hamilton 1874, 321)

Hamilton does not tell us what this 'special service' was but presumably it had
to do with musketry training. The phrase 'particular service' had been used
when Lord Hardinge sent Fox to Malta to start musketry training before the
Crimean War. Nor do we know exactly how long Fox spent in Canada, but
the British forces did remain for several months and the Guards Brigade
received courses of musketry instruction while there in the summer of 1862
(*ibid.*, 327).

By August 1862, however, Fox had returned to the opposite side of the

Atlantic. In that month he took up his appointment at Cork. He held the post of Assistant Quartermaster General there for four years. This was an important appointment for his later career because his first archaeological fieldwork was carried out in Ireland at this time.

These were troubled times in Ireland. The Fenians were active and Fox was deeply involved in the Government's attempts to defeat them. His duties in this respect were wide ranging. For instance he was responsible for passing on the orders of the General Officer Commanding the Cork District to his subordinates regarding the disposal of troops in accordance with the wishes of the Civil Magistrates (Pitt Rivers Papers A7). He also acted as prosecuting officer at the Courts Martial of two British NCOs accused of aiding the Fenians (Pitt Rivers Papers A8; Thompson 1977, 30). He obtained convictions in both cases. Thompson also states (1977, 29) that Fox had responsibilities in Ireland for coastal defence, but this seems to be based only on Fox's possession of manuscript copies of reports of a committee on this problem which had sat in 1858 (Pitt Rivers Papers A5). His own involvement is not clear. Fox entered the academic debate on the causes of Fenianism. In a letter he stated that it had been part of his duty to investigate and report on the spread of Fenianism in Southern Ireland and supported the notion that Fenianism was essentially a racial, not a political, issue (Pitt Rivers Papers A8c).

On his return from Ireland Fox gave a series of lectures on 'Primitive Warfare' at the Royal United Services Institution (Fox 1867d, 1868b, 1869d). Fox's research on the history of arms and armour was exhaustive, as his surviving notes show. His reading covered classical and modern as well as prehistoric and ethnographic warfare and was concerned not only with weapons as material objects but with strategy and tactics (Pitt Rivers 'Arms Books' unpublished).

In July 1867 Fox received half pay, having purchased a Colonel's commission, and took no active part in military affairs for the next six years. The reason for the decision to free himself of military duties may have been the usual one of preserving the purchase price of his commission (Harries-Jenkins 1977, 70); it may also have been his poor health or an awakening archaeological interest which demanded more of his time. The fact that serving officers were positively encouraged to pursue their private scientific interests while on duty (*ibid.*, 162) should warn us against too easy an acceptance of the latter explanation, but it is noteworthy that his first experience of scientific excavation had been in April of the same year. He was to return to duty in 1873 when he was appointed to the command of the West Surrey Brigade Depot at Guildford, a post which he held until 1877. That he still took an interest in the soldiers' proficiency in marksmanship is demonstrated by a draft challenge which he issued from 48th Administrative Brigade HQ, Guildford, to any other Administrative Brigade for a rifle shooting match (Pitt Rivers Papers A9) but he was also giving attention to his anthropological and archaeological work at this time. His promotion to Major-General came on 1 October 1877.

Fox, after taking the name Pitt Rivers, finally retired in 1882, with the honorary rank of Lieutenant-General, though he remained on the active list until 1896 and was Honorary Colonel of the South Lancashire Regiment from 1893 until his death. His retirement in 1882 he attributed to ill health (Pitt Rivers 1887a, xi–xiii) but we must remember that this was only two years after his inheritance of the Rivers estates. It was not unusual for an officer who was heir to an estate to resign his commission on taking up his inheritance, in the belief that he could best serve his country by concentrating on the administration of his property and the other duties of a country gentleman (Harries-Jenkins 1977, 26ff).

In summing up the General's military career we find not a distinguished soldier in the sense that Lord Wolseley or Lord Roberts, his near contemporaries, were distinguished. He was, however, an efficient staff officer and administrator, and that was a rarity in his generation. General Pennefather, who had commanded one of Evans' brigades at the Alma and was later Fox's commanding officer in Malta, was fulsome in his praise:

> If my opinion of your bearing in the Field before the Enemy which was always cool & forward and effective, or your diligence zeal & intelligence as a Staff Officer can ever serve you, I am bound to give it in the strongest terms. If I were going on any hard work in war tomorrow, I know no man I should sooner have at my side than yourself. (Pitt Rivers Papers App. 2, 58)

This was written as a response to the dispute with Hay which must excuse the apparent exaggeration. General Sir de Lacy Evans, his chief in the Crimea, called him 'an extremely zealous hard working and meritorious young officer' and Sir James Lindsay, commanding officer of the Grenadier Guards wrote, 'he has considerable abilities [and] has taken great pains in self instruction . . . (Pitt Rivers Papers A1a, A1c).

Moreover, his efforts in the development of musketry instruction with the newly developed rifles in the 1850s may have been of crucial importance to the success of the British army for the rest of the century. On the other hand the theory of evolution as applied by Pitt Rivers was to have a dangerously inhibiting effect on the army in the very area where he had been most active, the improvement of weaponry. Pitt Rivers was not alone, nor indeed first, among military men in holding a belief in gradual change in all things (Chapman 1985, 16). There was no conception that the introduction of such modern weapons as the rifle and the machine gun would revolutionise European warfare (Harries-Jenkins 1977, 196). To what extent Pitt Rivers' own lectures to the Royal United Services Institution in the 1860s had contributed to this attitude, it is impossible to say.

3

Married life

COURTSHIP AND MARRIAGE 1845–65

Fox married Alice Stanley, eldest daughter of Lord Stanley of Alderley, on 3 February 1853 at St George's, Hanover Square. We do not know when or where he met her but the Lane Foxes moved in the same social circles as the Stanleys and several members of both families served in the Grenadier Guards. Alice's uncle retired on the same day that Fox joined the Grenadiers and her younger brother John Constantine Stanley served with the Regiment in the Crimea at the age of sixteen.

The Stanleys have been vividly described by their descendant, Nancy Mitford (1938, xxii–xxxiv). If they were rude, quarrelsome and lively then Fox probably fitted into their family circle quite well. The clearest picture of Fox we have at this time is from the acid pens of Alice's parents and her grandmother, Maria Josepha, Lady Stanley. He does not appear in a good light but the portrait is an interesting one, built up through the stages of his courtship and marriage to Alice. Alice was described by her mother as 'too short' but was pretty when in good health – which she did not enjoy at all times. She had a reputation amongst the family for miserliness (Mitford 1938, xxxiv, 117, 122, 124, 161, 238, 269, 297).

The first definite mention of Augustus Fox in the letters edited by Mitford is in August 1851, though clearly he had known the family well many years before this (Mitford 1938, 116; 1939, 11). Fox first proposed to Alice in 1849 (Mitford 1939, 50) but apparently her father refused his consent on the grounds that Fox's prospects were not good enough. Thereafter he was kept at arm's length as far as marriage was concerned. However, he remained a friend of the family. He was present on the occasion of Blanche Stanley's engagement to Lord Airlie, and 'the young Major & Alice laughed at each other's jokes' (*ibid.* 11). The family seem to have been in a high state of excitement and it must have been a rather difficult moment for Alice and the young Major, especially as Alice was older than Blanche.

Fox received a letter from his cousin Marcia Lane Fox regarding his courtship:

> I called on Alice but she was out & I cld. not persuade the Duchess [of Leeds] to go again afterwards – My advice to you is to go to the Ball this eveg. make a

distant bow to Lady Eddisbury one that will do for the *Trio* – take no further notice of Alice but dance with other young ladies in the same room where *she* is & after a short time go away *leaving her there*. This advice has been *well considered* I hope you will take it and Believe me Ever Your affect. cousin

M.

The conduct I wish you to pursue is perfectly *justifiable* under the circumstances & will teach her a useful lesson which she will not soon forget if she really loves & I still believe that she *does* as I can see no object in her *feigning* it to *me*.

I expect she will call here tomorrow if not I will go to her & write you the result. (Pitt Rivers Papers App. 2, 5)

This letter, which requires no further comment, is undated but must have been written before December 1850 in which month Marcia died.

Fox's elder brother, William, died on 13 June 1852. With this slight improvement in his prospects Fox felt that he could again ask for Alice's hand. He seems to have had information that Alice was still kindly disposed towards him, which in itself seems to have raised some family difficulties (Mitford 1939, 51; Pitt Rivers Papers App. 2, 4).

On 17 September 1852 Alice's mother, Henrietta, wrote to her husband:

I have just got a letter from Alice she is very much agitated & perplexed by Lady C. Fox's message; 'He will have 1000 easily & eventually 1500'. Alice says 'I wish to do what is right but I want yr. counsel surely that wd. be enough do you not think Papa wd. give me as much as he has given Blanche – I am not covetous nor do I care for anything great & *he* has no expensive habits. I never knew what Papa thought . . .' Write to her at once – I think you will consent. (Mitford 1939, 47–8)

However Lord Stanley did not think so and on 22 September she wrote again, 'I am very sorry you do not take Alice's affair more kindly, I am sure now it will break her heart if you refuse, Blanche says she is so very anxious & nervous . . . They [Lady Caroline and Fox] were hurt at the short way they were refused.' (*ibid*. 48–9)

Lord Stanley saw Alice and Fox and began to come around. On 26 September he replied to his wife,

Alice is in very good spirits & seems to amuse herself greatly with the young Major. I have said nothing positively as yet except that I must hear more positive particulars before I can definitely consent. If Major Fox has 2500 besides his commission it is probably not a case to refuse ones consent, i.e. supposing they both are really earnestly & sincerely in love & know their own minds, which by this time they ought to do. (*ibid*. 49–50)

By the end of the month Lord Stanley had given his consent and the news was communicated to Maria Josepha, Alice's redoubtable grandmother. On 1 October she wrote to Henrietta,

You may imagine how very happy your letter has made me to day – I am sure you must have been longing to tell me from the first dawn of the renewed affair & I fully understand you would not wish to say a word until you knew what Edward would say. We shall *all* rejoice equally that constancy has been rewarded & if he has no turn for expensive pleasures (we know *she* is very much disposed to

5 Augustus Lane Fox

be careful) . . . I cannot agree with you there is anything of a *bungle* in the business; *rudely* as he had been repulsed *once*, violently displeased as you were that he should have written to her, I think he could not venture to risk a second refusal before he tried to ascertain whether *she* was unchanged & whether there was a *chance* his renewed offer, not much increased in amount, would be listened to. (*ibid.*, 47–50)

The young couple's troubles were not yet over, however. At this juncture it was Fox's mother who introduced difficulties and tempers began to fray. On 10 December Henrietta wrote to her husband,

You will see by the enclosed note from Lady Caroline Fox that the marriage is put off indefinitely. I saw Lady C. yesterday & she was not cordial but said she wd. communicate when she thought the marriage cld. be. You see also she does not wish them to live with her – this Fox says is not the case but their statements rarely coincide. He has not dined here since you went. Alice has just gone to dine with Lady C. – they are odious people.

Three days later she was writing again that 'Nothing can be more touchy than

Fox & he complains of the silliest things – such as you never having said you were glad to see him. We are to hear in a few days when the time can be fixed – I shall not put myself to any inconvenience' (*ibid.*, 56–7).

Maria Josepha exerted a restraining influence on her son and daughter-in-law throughout and frequently put in a word for Fox and Alice. On 6 January 1853 she wrote to Henrietta, 'I hope you have been kind to poor Reynard which I have reason to say because you know you have written spitefully about him once or twice . . .' (*ibid.*, 61). Alice's eldest brother Henry was also an ally. He was apparently the only one of the family who really liked Fox though Johnny later wrote of Fox, 'I often think he has not been enough appreciated amongst us . . .' (*ibid.* xiii, 260).

Finally the marriage took place on 3 February 1853 (*ibid.*, 63). Mitford does not include in her selection any letters between 20 January and 2 May 1853. Perhaps this was one of the 'most tantalizing gaps' in the correspondence to which Mitford refers (Mitford 1938, xxvii).

Alice was soon pregnant, leading to her grandmother's quip that 'as they are poor, cubs will come thick & fast – don't tell Mr Reynard pray, as he don't understand a joke' (Mitford 1939, 63). Alice was delivered of a stillborn child in the barracks at Hythe on 19 November 1853. Apparently she was attended by no one but the barrack master's daughter. These circumstances were attributed by her family not to poverty but to 'silly obstinacy' which could have been avoided (*ibid.*, 70).

A few months later Fox was sent to Malta to make preparations for the forthcoming war with Russia. Alice was distraught at the parting. Some of her letters to Fox at this time have been preserved; they are long and written almost entirely without benefit of punctuation, rather in the form of a stream of consciousness. They are repetitive and extremely personal but they also contain material of wider interest. The first one, written on 29 March 1854, may serve as an example of the tone of the whole series:

> My precious dearest one my own Augustus I sent you a *long* letter yesterday by the Foreign Office in which I acknowledged the receipt of yr. 3 notes yesterday but I have been so miserable since thinking over yr. being ill & that I might have been with you that I have passed a most sleepless disturbed night Oh darling if you knew the yearning longing I feel . . . long for more particulars of yr. every day life & thoughts than you give How unsatisfying not to be able to follow you through the day not to know even where you are who you see what you do . . . if you wd. only write every night & always say how you are – this uncertainty of letters is awful & it must be dreadful for you getting so little authentic news. I cannot understand why you have not had more letters from me it is most provoking if they are lost the one you got must have gone out by the same ship you did darling I wld. not write so strongly about yr. letters to me only I feel it will be the only thing to keep me from utter despair I don't think you miss me as I do you . . . it was a mistake not taking me with you do you not feel it . . . I want consolation & you alone can give it me you used to write longer letters every day before we married & you did not love me then as much as you do now. I have just seen by the papers letters from Malta of the 24th so I hope I may get one from you

by the same mail & that you will have got several of mine. I wish I knew the best way to send letters. Southampton seems nearly as quick what do you pay for my letters 11d . . . it seems quite true that 5000 Russians crossed the Danube . . . I see they estimate their force at different places at 337,000 – the Turks are very anxious for the presence of the English & French there to aid them & say they must make haste or the Russians will come down upon Constantinople . . . they expect the fighting will take place in *Asia* at Kars wherever that may be . . . they mention nothing about yr. practice at Malta I hope you have got yr. own way at last. I suppose the other officers are conceited enough to think they cd. do as well without you – I daren't say I wish you had never gone you might reprove me but I may say what an everlasting regret I feel I did not go with you . . . Darling I do not wish to make you unhappy . . . I do pray for patience and strength but I have become so dependent upon you for all I did or looked or thought . . . Darling I hope you will answer all my questions exactly . . . who winds up yr. watch? What money do they use? English & have you got paid for yr. journey. I wonder whether you date yr. letters right for you know love you never knew what day month or even year it was at home Oh home that sweet word . . . There is a report this afternoon that Ld. Aberdeen has resigned as he says with one foot in the grave he cannot carry on the administration with war declared . . . I saw the Morning Post which had a letter from Malta in which you were mentioned as carrying on the practice with great energy but that it was most desirable Ld. Raglan shd. make his appearance soon or some directing spirit. Shameful indeed the way things are done . . . When I look back at the disappointment of my baby's death it seems to be so small a thing to what I now endure . . . I mentioned en passant [to Mrs Airey] that yr. appointment had not been put down with the others that she might mention it to Col. Airey . . . Darling promise you wd. send for me instantly if you were ill you must you shall I shall *never* forgive you if you don't . . . When shall I hear from you my own own love yr. poor little baby wife Alice. (Pitt Rivers Papers App. 2, 19)

One point in this letter deserves further consideration. The question about winding his watch may be a private family joke but the remark that Fox 'never knew what day month or even year it was' seems to be a factual statement. Nevertheless we might dismiss it were it not for the fact that several gross errors in dating his archaeological work are revealed in the Relic Tables which he published later in life. His excavations at Rotherley, for instance, are in some places attributed by him to 1885–6 and in others to the correct date of 1886–7 (Pitt Rivers 1888a, 67–110).

How Fox reacted to his wife's correspondence is not recorded except from the internal evidence of the letters themselves. The postal system was uncertain, several letters were lost and both Fox and Alice were inclined to blame each other for not writing often enough. She complained that his letters were short and he accused her of misdirecting hers. Several seem to have been delivered to his cousin, Charles Lane Fox (Pitt Rivers Papers App. 2, 33), who was at this time serving with Colonel Beatson's corps of Bashi Bazouks under the name Yusuf Bey (Russell 1855, 113).

A letter begun on 1 April opened with a tirade against politicans who, Alice thought, were abandoning the troops to their fate as war approached. This seems a curiously tactless thing to have written under the circumstances. More personal matters included the arrangements for sending out Fox's horses, which had caused a disagreement with Lady Caroline, and Col. Airey's assurance that Fox's appointment would appear in the *Gazette*. Alice resumed the letter the next day announcing that she would send it with the horses, presumably the ones which were later lost, and listing the items which Col. Gordon would bring out for him including 'the Turkish grammar, Camp book, List book, my picture, a pr. of boots & pr. of gloves 1 flannel shirt, card case, 2 sets mosquito curtains . . .' (Pitt Rivers Papers App. 2, 20).

Alice was living with Lady Caroline Fox, an arrangement which led to continual arguments, until later in the summer when she went to stay with her own family in north Wales.

Altogether this series of letters gives some intriguing insights to the characters of Fox and Alice. There is a certain candour in the way Alice reported on 5 April that a Mrs Scott 'told me she had told her brother Mr. Smith to tell me on Monday last at the ball in Dover St. he had seen you but as I was not at it I did not hear till today she said she had spoken to him about me, & he had said well she can hardly look more miserable than he does. Darling is it so? but that you were well and very busy . . .' *ibid* 21).

As the summer wore on her letters contained an increasing amount of religious sentiment. On 12 August she was quoting at length from the Book of Job and later in the month a boil on her face made her feel even more like Job. On 25 August she was still poulticing her face which 'made me think of your dear foot which I used to put a poultice on at night before you left' (*ibid.* 24). There are other vague references to his foot but the nature of the affliction is obscure. We also learn that he didn't like poetry but was fond of music (*ibid.* 25, 29). More than anything the letters demonstrate the degree of Alice's feelings for Fox, amounting to worship, at this time.

The few days after the Alma until the official despatches were published were particularly trying for Alice. Someone had mixed up the two Lane Foxes again and Alice received a report that Fox was wounded in the ankle (*ibid.* 32). On 9 October Henrietta, Lady Stanley wrote 'It has been an intensely anxious week, at the end it is a great comfort to find Fox safe & he is the only one for whom we are nearly interested . . .' (Mitford 1939, 90). Even at this juncture she did not refer to him by his Christian name.

Fox returned to England by the end of October 1954 and on 9 November Johnny Stanley reported to his mother that he had seen him in London and 'hardly knew him again he is quite sallow & had a beard – he looks rather seedy' (*ibid.*). Before going out to the Crimea himself the following Spring Johnny called on the Foxes at Chesham Place 'where he found everybody gone to bed, but he knocked up the whole house, alarmed Ly. Caroline Fox who thought the Russians had arrived & woke Alice & Fox . . . who told him to go about his business' (*ibid.*, 112).

On 2 November 1855 Alice was delivered of a son, Alexander, at Malta where she had gone with Fox when he returned to duty. The family were pleased but were scathing about the name. Lady Stanley wrote 'Alexander is not after the Emperor but Col. Gordon & Aug: wished it . . .' (*ibid.*, 126).

On 14 September 1856 the second son was born, also in Malta. The child's great-grandmother commented with typical frankness on the event. 'Two babies in a nursery under a year old is really too much happiness for the most ardent baby fancier. So they mean to call him St George, a very silly name & his schoolfellows will plague him about the dragon' (*ibid.*, 138). At no time did Lord Stanley show any affection for his Fox grandchildren. 'I thought you would find the Fox children miserable looking & the eldest seems to be lugged about everywhere & to be always with Alice', he wrote about the older ones in 1857 (*ibid.*, 152). The births of successive children were greeted with decreasing interest. On 30 August 1859 Lady Stanley told her husband 'Kate has sent over the letters as one announces Alice's safe confinement of a girl, only 2 hours illness & doing very well, I am glad she has a girl'. On 11 January 1861 it was Lord Stanley's turn to report 'Just had a note from Lady Dillon to say Alice had been confined of a girl both doing well'. Almost exactly a year later he was writing 'Alice was confined Saturday of a girl, doing well', but only after he had discussed the more interesting news that her brother Lyulph wanted a horse. On 9 September 1865 Lady Stanley told her husband 'I have heard Alice is again in the usual state, it was no surprise' (*ibid.*, 222, 258, 279, 310).

FAMILY LIFE 1865–1900

The passionate attachment between Fox and Alice did not last. An undated letter from Fox to his wife refers to their deteriorating relationship at some length. From internal evidence it was probably written in the late 1870s. This draft is incomplete and parts are quite illegible but the meaning is clear:

> I fear that you are *utterly without heart* . . . My reason for writing about it now is the hope that at a time when more amicable feelings exist between us you might be induced to listen to what I say but I have little hope however for us. Somebody said to me the other day about you 'You must be well aware that nothing which is said to Alice produces the slightest effect' and it is quite true. It is not my fault that I am not richer but there is no reason why poverty should be made such an *awful curse* as you make it . . . your temper is the cause of all the misery between us . . . for I do believe this – more stoney hard hearted woman never existed and that . . . you have never in your life known what affection meant . . . To me the loss of family affection is everything as I care but little for the society of strangers but by you it is little felt as your whole education and disposition has fitted you for society and not for family . . . I do hope also that you will avoid the evils of your own education in your children. They have most of them good feelings naturally and sympathy for others but I fear that cold blooded heartlessness has already deadened it in some of them . . . the last time you were at home you appear to have controlled your temper a little owing to my having kept as much as possible out of your way . . . I assure you that for the last four years now you have made my life a perfect curse to me . . . (Pitt Rivers Papers App. 2, 64)

Alice had taken a real interest in his military career, to the extent of making

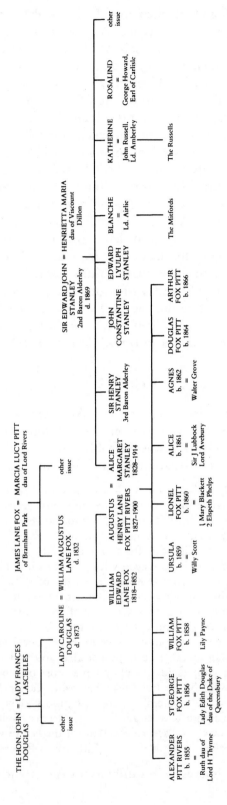

Table 2 The General's immediate family: simplified genealogical table

herself ill at the time of the enquiry into his conduct at Malta (Russell and Russell 1937a, 107–8), but she does not seem to have shared in the scientific pursuits which increasingly filled his time.

We know very little of their family life between the mid 1860s and the move to Rushmore following his inheritance of the Rivers estates and name in 1880. The rare references in Kate Amberley's letters and Journal are nearly all concerned with Augustus' bad temper. Sometimes there is no apparent reason for his ill humour, at others it is brought on by something Alice has done. When Alice went to Alderley to meet her new sister-in-law, Fabia, without his consent he was 'very angry at her having been, as he does not think it respectable & thinks it bad for his daughters . . .' (Russell and Russell 1937b, 280–1). It is only fair to Fox to say that most of the Stanleys felt the same, as there was some doubt as to whether Henry Stanley and Fabia were legally married.

The inheritance of the Rivers estates in 1880 made a substantial difference to the family. They moved from Earl's Court to the opulent Rivers town house at 4, Grosvenor Gardens and Lord Rivers' country seat, the architecturally undistinguished Rushmore, now became their home as well. Lord Stanley had visited Rushmore in 1858 and described it in a letter to his wife:

> This is, I believe, the only place in England 18 miles from a railway station. It takes as long to come from Salisbury as from London to Salisbury. The road is all over a down country & the house here is situated at the top of the highest hills on this high downy country, 800 feet they say above the sea. Immediately within sight of the house the country is bleak open downs, but below there is an immense extent of beautiful wild wood, the remains of old Cranborne Chase & rough ground with old thorns scattered on the open downs. The estate goes for 20 miles, with no neighbours, he [the 4th. Lord Rivers] is poor and gets comparatively a small income from the estate, but it is improving every day. (Mitford 1939, 191)

The estate consisted of about 27,000 acres (10,930 ha.) and in the General's time the annual income averaged a little under £20,000.

The few glimpses we have of life at Rushmore in the last twenty years of the General's life do not suggest a close or affectionate family. These glimpses come largely from the pen of Bertrand Russell, Alice's nephew by her younger sister Kate. He recalled 'Alice attempting to hold some function in the house. None of the guests arrived. Her husband, considering purely social activities to be frivolous, had, unknown to her, ordered all the park gates locked that day' (M. Pitt Rivers 1977, 25).

Russell was well aware of the General's interests:

> He spent every penny he could spare on excavating antiquities, much to the annoyance of his large family. My Aunt Alice – presumably as a result of his expenditure – practised petty economies to an almost incredible degree. There was never enough to eat, and if any of the bacon or eggs remained on a visitor's plate at breakfast, it was put back into the dish for the next comer. On one occasion, when a number of people had arrived unexpectedly for luncheon, I saw one of the sons have a tug of war with a lady visitor for the last plate of rice pudding; he won, and ate it up under her eyes . . . (Russell and Russell 1937a, 22).

6 Rushmore House with General Pitt Rivers in the middle foreground

7 The Gallery, Rushmore. The interior decoration of the house was largely entrusted to Morris and Co

As Thompson points out (1977, 89–90) Russell is incorrect in giving archaeological expenses as the reason for this lack of home comforts. The General's account books regularly show a healthy balance of income over expenditure and the 'petty economies' are more likely to be the result of Alice's characteristic miserliness which had been noted by her family much earlier in life. Russell was not alone, however, in believing that archaeological expenses were the cause of the problem. Agnes, the second daughter, confided to her diary in 1882 her belief that if it was not for the money the General spent on his archaeological staff the family would be considerably better off (Hawkins 1981, 141). She was quite wrong but the fact that she believed it to be true is significant.

Very occasionally a reminiscence from someone outside the family circle illuminates the scene. Thomas Hardy, a guest at Rushmore in 1895, wrote that it was a pleasant visit 'notwithstanding the trying temper of the hostess' (Hawkins 1982, 95). A local man, Henry Dennitt, remembered that the General and Mrs Pitt Rivers 'come to Larmer in two carriages – one in each carriage. They never rode together. I never seen them ride together . . .' (Constanduros 1953 unpublished). This is very different from the clinging relationship of their early married life.

There were nine children; six sons and three daughters. Alexander, the eldest, had artistic talents, perhaps inherited from the General, but was a weak character and possibly a disappointment to his father. The second son, named St George after one of the rifle ranges at Malta, was of a different character altogether, being independent, strong willed and generous though somewhat rash. He left home to become a businessman and inventor. Apparently Edison himself conceded that St George's invention of the carbon filament was a decisive factor in the commercial development of electric light (Hawkins 1982, 88–9). St George was for a long time on the Council of the Society for Psychical Research, which led indirectly to one of his many involvements in litigation when he slandered the novelist Radclyffe Hall, and was once fined for assaulting a fellow member of the Theosophical Society (Baker 1985, 122–4, 128–31). He held advanced political views which were anathema to his father, who partly disinherited him when he became vice-president of a Radical association (Thompson 1977, 89). Despite this St George and his father remained on speaking terms. St George was also described by Fabia Stanley as 'her dear nephew' in her first will in which she left him all her property. This will was subsequently shown to be null (Russell and Russell 1937a, 20). Willy, the third son, joined his father's Regiment and saw active service in the Zulu War of 1879 and in the Sudan. He reached the rank of Lieutenant-Colonel and was his father's favourite. It is presumably Willy that Bertrand Russell remembers as 'very smart and correct' coming down to breakfast late at Rushmore, though he refers to him incorrectly as 'the eldest son' (Hawkins 1981, 142). Willy was a friend of Baden-Powell (Pitt Rivers Papers App. 2, 91). The fourth son, Lionel, spent several years in Canada and returned in very ill health.

While Alexander took some interest in antiquities – he was elected FSA in

8 The General's sarcophagus in Tollard Royal church. The General was cremated at Woking, Surrey. He had forcibly expressed his desire that Mrs Pitt Rivers should be cremated as well with the words, 'Damn it, woman, you shall burn' (M. Pitt Rivers 1977, 24) but she outlived him by many years and is buried, as she wished to be, in Tollard churchyard

9 The Pitt Rivers at Rushmore: General and Mrs Pitt Rivers with Willy, Douglas, Ursula and three of the General's grandchildren

1883 – and Willy enquired politely after his father's 'diggings' in his letters it was only Lionel and Douglas, of all the children, who took an active role in archaeology. Lionel took part in excavations on Cyprus and seems to have considered working for the General as an unpaid assistant (Pitt Rivers Papers L90, L1981). The unsuccessful search for a career filled Lionel's life and he went back to Rushmore after the General's death to act as Alexander's secretary. Douglas, the fifth son, died at a very early age. He attended the Royal Agricultural College at Cirencester where his career was not a success. The Principal reported that he did 'exceedingly little work' (Pitt Rivers Papers M52). He subsequently attempted to settle as a farmer in South America but this too was a failure. On his return to Britain Douglas went to Acton Burnell and Stokesay castles drawing plans, elevations and sketches for his father, probably at the time of the excavations at King John's House, and he also exercised his artistic talents in the decoration of the open air theatre at the Larmer Grounds (Pitt Rivers Papers L1205, 1230, 1234, 2436). Arthur, the youngest child, born in 1866, suffered from ill health throughout his short life and died of tuberculosis in 1895, being buried at Tollard Royal (Thompson 1977, 89). In 1890 his mental health had also begun to deteriorate and in 1891 he voluntarily went into an institution. He subsequently tried to escape and was certified insane.

Ursula, the eldest daughter, born in 1859, married Willy Scott, a Stanley cousin, in 1880. A series of letters from Ursula to her father describe her attempts to buy ethnographic objects for him while on holiday in Switzerland (Pitt Rivers Papers L1338). The second daughter, Alice, married the General's colleague, Sir John Lubbock, later Lord Avebury. Though she was much younger than Sir John, and indeed younger than some of his children by his previous marriage, and did not share in his scientific interests at all, marriage to him was infinitely preferable to living any longer with her detested father (Grant Duff 1982, 15–16). Even the friendship between the General and Sir John did not prevent a row over Alice's trousseau, though the cause of the argument was Mrs Pitt Rivers' miserliness, as this letter from Lubbock shows:

> My dear General,
>   You may remember that last year I was obliged to apply to you with reference to some of the Bills for Alice's Trousseau which Mrs. Pitt-Rivers had not paid. To my great surprise the enclosed has been sent in again, & I have paid it as it was impossible to let Mr. Kenwall lose the money.
>   Mrs. Pitt Rivers admitted in the spring that she had authorised the dress being bought & took away the Bill, which of course we supposed was paid long ago.
>   I wrote to her some days ago, but she has taken no notice of my letter, so I am obliged to apply to you, as I cannot suppose you wish me to pay for Alice's trousseau. (Pitt Rivers Papers L280)

Agnes, the third daughter, who married Sir Walter Grove, is undoubtedly the best documented of the General's children. Not only did Thomas Hardy write a poem about her, 'Concerning Agnes', but Desmond Hawkins has written a biography with the same title (1982). Agnes had artistic and literary tastes. She knew not only Hardy but many other figures in the world of letters such as Hilaire Belloc and Thomas Hughes. She wrote four books, all of which were published and received considerable public acclaim. She had been educated at Oxford High School, showing that the General and Mrs Pitt Rivers followed the Stanley tradition of educating their daughters as well as their sons. Agnes was a strong supporter of Gladstone and spoke on the cause of Women's Suffrage and against vivisection. She rejected her father's politics in favour of those of her father-in-law, Sir Thomas Grove, a Radical Liberal MP. Her marriage to Walter Grove, after a wrangle over the settlement reminiscent of that which preceded her parents' wedding, was long and happy. Like many of the Lane Foxes she suffered from tuberculosis.

As well as his own children the General had two wards, Caroline and Edith Lane Fox, the orphaned daughters of his cousin Charles, who stayed at Rushmore or Grosvenor Gardens on occasion.

Despite the rather depressing picture of constant hostility within the family there are some faint signs of affection, particularly in the letters to the General from Willy and Ursula. Nevertheless the overriding characteristic of the letters from the children to their father is seen in repeated demands for money, in a variety of forms. From Lionel they are frequent and peremptory, from Willy rare and apologetic, from Agnes monotonous and insistent. The General seems to have paid up more often than not. Some of the family's financial dealings are quite inexplicable. In 1892 the General received a letter from Andrews and Pitblado, a law firm in Winnipeg, demanding payment of $49.20 for a lawnmower which Lionel had bought but failed to pay for (Pitt Rivers Papers B507).

After the General's death furious arguments broke out amongst the children over his will. They do not seem to have objected to the will itself so much as to the way in which Alexander handled it. There was litigation over the future of the Larmer Grounds and Farnham Museum. Lionel, acting as Alexander's secretary, tried to smooth things over. He commented that Ursula and Agnes were particularly 'unpleasant' (Pitt Rivers Papers App. 2, 88–90). Meanwhile Rushmore was let to a tenant. In 1903 Alexander decided to repossess the house, but the tenant was unwilling to leave. Eventually the tenant was forced to vacate the property but before leaving he wrote the words 'Blackguard Landlord' on the lawn with weedkiller so that they appeared mysteriously shortly afterwards. Alexander sued the tenant for libel and was eventually awarded damages of one shilling but rejoiced at bankrupting his opponent (Caverhill 1988, 35). Trouble with tenants was almost a family tradition but the General, unlike his sons, had always managed to avoid litigation.

INHERITANCE – PITT RIVERS AS LANDOWNER

Although he had been brought up in the landowning class of society Fox had no expectation of becoming a major landowner himself. When he was thrust into the possession of the Rivers estates in 1880 he had no experience of land

10 The gates of the Square, Rushmore, with the statue of Caesar Augustus and Temple of Vesta, designed by Romaine Walker, in the background. The General's initials are prominently displayed above the gates. The park was surrounded by a wrought iron fence painted in the Pitt Rivers livery colours of blue and gold

management, but the ideal of the duties of the landowner as understood in nineteenth-century Britain were very familiar to him.

The estate which he inherited, 27,000 acres, was one of the largest held by an untitled man in the whole of Britain and was considerably larger than those held by many noblemen. Indeed the General felt strongly that the title of Lord Rivers should have descended to him with the property and he petitioned two prime ministers, Gladstone and Lord Salisbury, to be granted a peerage. These petitions were in no way an appeal for recognition of any personal merit or endeavour but were made 'on grounds of family & position' (Pitt Rivers Papers App. 2, 70). Neither prime minister was anxious to have the General in the House of Lords.

The surviving correspondence and papers at Salisbury Museum give some idea of the General's activities as a country gentleman in the last twenty years of his life. The day to day management of the estates was largely left to Mr Creech, the agent, but the General himself kept a very strong overall control of his affairs. The worst side of the General's character is demonstrated in his business letters. We see him hectoring, bullying and bluffing his way through disputes with tenants, tradesmen and even the unfortunate Mr Creech himself.

The General's offhand treatment of businessmen included everyone from the baker at Woodcutts to the celebrated architects Philip Webb and Romaine

11 The General's traction engine, a Burrell, in the Carpenter's Yard, Rushmore. The General's name and address appear on a plate immediately above the manufacturer's nameplate

Walker (*ibid.*, B387, B541). Inevitably most of these incidents involved disputes over money, demonstrating that Mrs Pitt Rivers was not the only miser in the family. When Waller and Son sent in their bill for mending a burst water pipe in August 1894 Pitt Rivers wrote back refusing to meet the bill but offering them £1. With great forbearance Waller and Son agreed to accept £2, just enough to cover their expenses. Perhaps they had dealt with the General before and knew that it was better to cut their losses. If this were an isolated incident it could be dismissed but in fact it is only part of a more or less continuous stream of contentiousness. Pitt Rivers was repeatedly threatened with legal action in respect of unpaid bills, and small businesses often found it difficult to get payment for goods supplied (*ibid.*, B377a, B504, B508, B524, for example). Philip Webb, a more experienced businessman, found himself getting into increasing difficulties with the General. In reply to two letters of complaint from Pitt Rivers in January 1886 Webb wrote 'There is a complication of the British privilege of grumbling in them which I hardly know how to meet' (*ibid.*, B387). By July of the same year Webb had wound up the work he was doing for the General and gracefully backed out.

Even more disturbing than the seemingly endless refusals to pay tradesmen's bills are evictions of tenants. In 1887, against the advice of Mr Creech, the

General decided that he wanted the manor house at Hinton St Mary for his own use or for that of his eldest son. Mr Creech was therefore eventually forced to serve notice to quit on the tenant, Mr Harvey, though he managed to put off doing so for as long as possible. On receiving the notice in February 1888 Mr Harvey wrote to the General:

> I hope I may be permitted to address a few lines to you relative to the notice I lately received to quit the house in which we now reside, which has caused us so much pain and discomfort because I think the state of health both of Mrs Harvey and myself could not have been known to you at the time. As myself I am in my eighty seventh year and for the last two years I have been subject to chronic bronchitis and other ailments incidental to extreme age . . . My wife for the last five years has been suffering from sciatica and Rheumatism which has increased from bad to worse till at the present time she is perfectly helpless . . . Will you kindly take these facts into consideration and I hope the result will be you will permit us to remain where we are, and where we have resided the last thirty years . . .

The General, however, was adamant:

> I was extremely sorry to get your letter & to see how much you disliked leaving Hinton. To be brief I feel my duties to the property necessitate my occupying the house as soon as possible. It ought to have been done long ago as the position of an entirely absentee landlord under the circumstances is simply a disgrace . . . Nothing but a sense of duty in the matter would induce me to ask you to remove at your age & you are aware that there is no other house I could possibly occupy (*ibid.*, B272).

Despite Mr Creech's conviction that there was no need for the General to occupy the house at Hinton at all, the Harveys were duly removed later the same year and Alexander Fox Pitt installed in their place in 1895. There is no evidence that the General ever occupied the house in the interval. A similar case occurred in 1897 when the General bought 'The Rookery' at Burton Bradstock and evicted the tenant, Mrs Gillett, a seventy-five year-old invalid, though she had expressed a definite wish to live out her days there (*ibid.*, L1951).

The General also had trouble with tenants in a more exalted social position. In 1897 he let number 4 Grosvenor Gardens to Lord Wolseley, the Commander-in-Chief. When Lord Wolseley proposed to sublet it while he went to the seaside Pitt Rivers wrote to him in querulous tone, no doubt exacerbated by his ill health: 'As you have let the house for three months I think it will be best that that should stand as I don't wish to put you to any inconvenience but I don't think it is quite correct. However that can be gone into another time & I am not well enough to consider it now. Your letting the house is more inconvenient than I expected' (*ibid.*, L2026). Under the circumstances Lord Wolseley decided to give up his tenancy early (*ibid.*, L2031).

In view of the apparently arbitrary exercise of his rights over tenants it is perhaps surprising that the General enjoyed the reputation of a good landlord amongst many of the inhabitants of Cranborne Chase and his other estates. He created employment not only by his archaeological activities but also by road-building schemes which employed up to sixty men during the winter months. He saw himself as a friend to the poor, and some of the local clergy at least seem to have seen him in the same light (Pitt Rivers Papers B251). He was undoubtedly sincere in his belief that the concerned local landowner was the best friend the agricultural labourer could have. Like his close neighbour Lord Shaftesbury, the well-known philanthropist, he was generous in treating the symptoms of poverty at a local level but had no sympathy with movements for social reform which aimed to cure the disease itself (Seaman 1973, 24).

Too much should not be made, however, of the 'employment creation' factor in the General's archaeological work. He undertook excavation in the winter months not to create work at a slack season in the agricultural year (Hawkins 1948 unpublished) but because labour was not available at harvest time (Thompson 1977, 92) and because time in the summer had to be reserved for his official journeys as Inspector of Ancient Monuments.

Inevitably as a landowner Pitt Rivers became involved in local politics. His political affiliations were deliberately ambiguous and when he stood for election to the newly created Dorset County Council in 1888 it was as an independent. By upbringing and temperament he was a conservative but he had married into one of the great Whig families and many of his friends and colleagues were of a liberal frame of mind. The only political views which he could not accept were those of Radicals and Socialists. This must have caused him some pain as he was continually coming up against Radicals throughout his life. His chief in the Crimea, the intelligent and eccentric Sir George de Lacy Evans, was a belligerent Radical MP; his daughter Agnes married the son of another Radical MP, Sir Thomas Grove of Ferne House, whose views she adopted; finally his son St George espoused Radical politics in an active manner, causing the General great embarrassment at the County Council elections (Pitt Rivers Papers B217). The apparent ambiguity of his political beliefs allowed the General some latitude in petitioning prime ministers of different political colours for a seat in the House of Lords. To Mr Gladstone he wrote, '. . . my political opinions have always been those of a liberal . . . My eldest son holds the same views', while a year later he could write to Lord Salisbury with rather more truth, 'At the last elections I supported the conservative candidates in Wiltshire and the northern division of Dorset' (*ibid.*, App. 2, 68, 82).

The General had no success in politics. His surviving political speeches are naive. We do not know whether he had the oratorical ability to make them sound better than they read. In 1886 he addressed a Meeting of Friendly Societies at Handley. Pitt Rivers was well disposed towards Friendly Societies because they represented the doctrine of 'self help' which the General, with many of his contemporaries including Herbert Spencer (Seaman 1973, 296–7), believed to be the only road to social improvement. He made this point very strongly at the opening of this speech, alluding to what he saw as the demoralising alternative of 'state help':

Freedom & self help have hitherto been the robust characteristics of the Institutions of this country whilst foreign nations have relied more on their Govern-
ments to look after them but every year under the auspices of persons who
represent themselves to be the friends of the people our Institutions have tended
more & more to approach those of foreign countries until at last, if things go on
in this way the time will come when we shall open our mouths every day like
chickens to be fed by a Government Inspector. (Pitt Rivers Papers M37a)

Like his other political speeches this one is characterised by a series of sudden
jumps from one subject to another. On this occasion Pitt Rivers next turned his
attention to the proposed creation of County Councils which he said would
'only afford scope for busybodies . . . ever ready & anxious to distinguish
themselves by meddling in other people's affairs.' He then briefly derided the
previous Liberal government as thieves and time servers before moving on to a
bitter attack on the Irish nation:

The Irish live under exactly the same laws as ourselves, they speak the same
language, and as to race, all the best Ethnologists will tell you that there is little or
no difference of race. I never could understand how it is that whilst we in this
country are content to obey the laws and are very glad to have good laws to live
under the Irishman is not to be compelled to obey the law also, or why it is that
when they are punished for hamstringing cattle, shooting women in the legs and
other horrible crimes which would disgrace the lowest savages, any attempt to
punish the Irish for these horrible crimes is to be reprobated & called coercion.
How is the law to be maintained except by force. I trust that in this respect the
Irish may not only have coercion for 20 years as proposed by Lord Salisbury but
for 20,000 years . . . All laws rest upon a basis of physical force & we should none
of us obey the law where our interests were opposed to it unless we knew that the
policeman's truncheon would be down upon us if we infringed it. (Pitt Rivers
Papers M37a)

The General then turned his attention to the trade depression which he
attributed largely to two causes, the machinations of 'political agitators' and
'the lawlessness of the times', not an original phrase even in 1886 (Pearson
1983). Having thus dealt summarily with the main political issues of the
moment the General came to the crux of his speech:

One word about the much abused class of Landowners to which I belong. You
are told by some people to look at the inequality which exists. Inequality is a law
of nature & without it no progress could take place. One would really suppose,
however, to hear some people speak that a man who has invested his money in
land was suppose[d] to eat up the whole of his land himself with the products of it
& to leave nothing for others. In reality the amount that a wealthy man, whether
a landowner [or] a possessor of any other property, consumes himself, is very
little more than the poor man consumes and as regards the rest of his property he
is simply a distributor, he is bound by necessity to spend his money in wages &
the more he has to spend the better for those about him, the working classes are
the recipients of, rather than the sufferers by his wealth . . . who is it that has
borne the chief burden during the last few years of the agricultural depression,

> you all know that by far the larger proportion has been borne by the Landowner,
> next to him the farmer has suffered and the agricultural labourer least of all . . .
> (Pitt Rivers Papers M37a)

This argument was one which was frequently offered to agricultural labourers
at this time (Seaman 1973, 269). A statement of the General's own political
loyalty, if such it can be called, followed: 'In the old days when conservatism
meant the conservation of class privileges I was not a conservative, now that
conservatism means the conservation of our liberties & the maintenance of the
Empire & resistance to the dictatorship of a single man I am as staunch a
conservative as any Tory.' The distinction between the two types of conservatism, which springs from the thoughts of Herbert Spencer (*ibid.*, 296), was no
doubt more in the General's mind than in reality. He was an active member of
the Liberty & Property Defence League, an organisation which in 1896 claimed
that it had 'for thirteen years been vigorously combatting the pernicious and
predatory doctrines of Socialism and Socialistic Radicalism' (Pitt Rivers Papers
L1480) and which was in effect dedicated to the maintenance of the privileges of
the landowning elite at all costs. The General's political naivety is demonstrated by the anti-climactic closing remarks in his speech at Handley in which
he advises his audience to

> stick to your Friendly Societies & to the principles of British liberty & self help on
> which they are based, rely on yourselves & not on the state for advancement,
> don't marry too young or until you have earned a competence, keep sober &
> obey the law & then if bad times continue you have the colonies to look to . . .
> where a man can earn 5 or 6 shillings a day instead of 12 shillings a week . . . (*ibid.*
> M37a)

Dubious though some of the General's ideas may appear to us now they
were well regarded by at least some of the local populace. Ted Coombs of
Sixpenny Handley remembered him as '. . . a thorough gentleman . . . he
would try in every way to induce the younger generation to develop, . . . to
make strides like, for their own benefit' (Constanduros 1953 unpublished).

Pitt Rivers' campaign for election to Dorset County Council was inevitably
fraught with problems. In the first place he had originally agreed to support the
Hon. Humphrey Sturt, the son of his neighbour Lord Allington, but when he
was approached by a number of electors asking him to stand himself, he did so.
The contest was vigorously conducted and a great deal of active canvassing was
done. A rumour spread that the General was an atheist. Several local clergymen
rallied to his aid. 'If I have ever the misfortune to hear anyone call you an
Atheist, I shall at once discountenance the imputation, believing it to be grossly
untrue,' wrote the Rev. J. H. Ward. The vicar of Gussage All Saints did not
know 'who canvassed Mr King and told him that "you were an atheist" but I
rather think the expression used was "you were a Darwinite". It is very
probable that neither Mr King nor his informant knew what that meant' (*ibid.*,
M35). In his speech to the electors at Handley on 21 November 1888 the
General wisely refrained from making any overtly political statement and

concentrated on describing briefly the benefits he had brought to the neighbourhood by the creation of the Larmer Grounds and Museum and the employment derived from his road building schemes (Pitt Rivers 1888 unpublished). His opponent Mr Sturt, in a speech of his own, responded to the 'remarks made by General Pitt Rivers with respect to the Larmer Tree Museum and amusements. He thought the money laid out on such places would do more good if spent in providing good cottages for the labouring class' (Pitt Rivers Papers M35). The General was defeated. All his supporters agreed that he had done well nevertheless and Mr Creech reported that 'the General did not feel his defeat much' (*ibid.*, B321).

Pitt Rivers indulged in field sports rather less than most of his peers. In earlier life his persistence in shooting had caused his father-in-law concern (Mitford 1939, 154) but, despite the strong Lane Fox tradition, he did not hunt. He grudgingly subscribed a small sum to the South Dorset Hunt (Pitt Rivers Papers L87) and of his sons, Alexander and Willy at least seem to have been enthusiastic followers of hounds. His own shoots in Cranborne Chase were sometimes transformed into archaeological field days. There is a story, unfortunately not substantiated, that on one of the General's shoots at which both Lord Shaftesbury and Lord Pembroke were present Pitt Rivers found a flint arrowhead, stopped the shoot and made his guests search for flints (Constanduros 1953 unpublished).

4

Ethnology and anthropology

In 1851, when Fox began his scientific collection, ethnology was a study in its infancy. Borrowing from natural history, moral philosophy and a humanistic tradition stretching back into the eighteenth century, the ethnologists studied non-European mankind in order to understand their own society and as part of an older enquiry into the unity or diversity of mankind (Stocking 1987, 47–8).

The argument about the monogenesis or polygenesis of the human race was at the forefront of ethnographic and anthropological thought in the mid-nineteenth century, and in the period from 1850 to 1870 the polygenecists were in the ascendant (Leach 1982, 71) and challenging strongly the Christian orthodoxy of monogenesis. This debate was fuelled by data gleaned mainly from comparative anatomy but there were other sources of information open to ethnologists, notably European folklore, antiquarianism and philology. In the hands of its greatest exponent, Friedrich Max Müller, philology was firmly placed on the side of the monogenecists. Comparative anatomy, however, was a tool of the polygenecists. Although physical anthropology was not pursued in Britain at this time as strenuously as on the Continent or in America there were a number of polygenecist anatomists, such as Joseph Davis, John Thurnam and John Beddoe, working in the field. Davis collaborated with the archaeologist Thomas Bateman and used the human skulls from Bateman's collection as data for his argument that different skull forms were not transmutable between races (Stocking 1987, 66).

It has to be emphasised that both monogenecists and polygenecists held views which would today be regarded as offensively racist, but the polygenetic belief that mankind was divided into a number of distinct species is clearly more extreme in both style and impact. The ascendancy of polygenesis in the years after 1850 may be due in large measure to contemporary political events on the world stage. Stocking isolates Rajah Brooke's suppression of the Sarawak pirates in 1849, the Indian Mutiny of 1857–8 and the American Civil War of 1861–5 as particularly significant in this respect (*ibid.*, 63).

The debate between monogenecists and polygenecists was to some extent made redundant by the Darwinian revolution and the almost contemporaneous archaeological revolution which opened up an immensely long chronological span for human history, thereby bridging the gap between mankind and the rest of creation and making the evolution of mankind from an ape-like creature a feasible notion. Ethnology, which had for so long focused on the biological question of human unity, now turned instead towards the more cultural question of the origins and development of human civilization (*ibid.*, 70–6). The ethnologists of this generation saw human progress, in the gradualist mould, as a continuing increase in rationality with scientific thought replacing religious belief until myths and the supernatural would eventually be seen as illusory (Leach 1982, 108).

Victorian ethnology and anthropology were severely limited by the nature of their data. Apart from the evidence of physical anthropology and comparative linguistics the ethnologists relied, for their study of non-European groups, on information collected in a haphazard fashion by travellers, missionaries, soldiers and colonial administrators. There was no deliberate anthropological fieldwork. The data were therefore not only coloured at source by the prejudices and attitudes of the collectors but also frequently tangential or totally irrelevant to the needs of the theoretical ethnologists at home. Despite this, scientists in related disciplines who collected their own data, such as Darwin himself, accepted the theories of their armchair colleagues as equally valid to their own. From the 1850s onwards ethnologists were in increasing danger of being swamped by a mass of often contradictory information. In 1868 the Ethnological Society of London set up a Classification Committee to establish terminology and to design proformas for the collection, classification and mapping of data. The subjects emphasised by this Committee were not physical type or language but religion, folklore, sociology and material culture. Under the influence of Darwinism, or their own interpretation of Darwinism, the ethnologists, now sociocultural evolutionists, began to link their reclassified anthropological data with European folklore and new information from prehistoric archaeology to build a fuller study of primitive mankind (Stocking 1987, 102–9).

Sociocultural evolutionism, the new anthropological direction, appears superficially to have been born out of the union of Darwinian evolution and Spencerian sociology. In fact it is doubtful whether social Darwinism is really Darwinian at all (Gould 1980, 70–1) and Herbert Spencer's interpretation of Darwinism, which dominated amongst the sociocultural evolutionists, conflated Darwin's idea of adaptation with the notion of progress, a marriage that Darwin himself specifically rejected (Gould 1978, 36–7). Nevertheless the leading anthropologists of the later part of the nineteenth century – Sir John Lubbock, Edward Tylor and John McLennan – saw their subject as distinctly Darwinian. Lubbock, the great populariser of prehistoric archaeology, argued very strongly for evolution and against diffusion in tracing the history of mankind (Stocking 1987, 151–69). Ironically sociocultural evolutionism threw up a series of hierarchical and exploitative relationships, between educated British males and the rest of creation, which were at odds with the natural liberal tendencies of most of its practitioners. Evolution itself provided the answer to this paradox in that inequality was an inevitable part of the process of development. As the century progressed the liberal ideals of Lubbock, Tylor and others, including Fox, retreated in face of the possibility of mass democracy and the concomitant swamping of the educated middle classes by the mediocre masses (Lorimer 1988, 408) and were replaced by optimistic sociocultural evolutionism with its insistence on gradual progress in all things (Girdwood 1986; Stocking 1987, 231–2).

Meanwhile polygenesis and other traditional ethnological forms of enquiry had survived the Darwinian revolution. Clashes within the Ethnological Society of London between the largely nonconformist Christian Darwinists and a new generation of polygenecists led to schism and the foundation of the Anthropological Society by James Hunt in 1863. Although there continued to be much overlap of interests and even membership between the two Societies, there were distinctions. Hunt's anti-Darwinism and narrow interest in physical anthropology set the tone for the 'Anthropologicals' who also tended to be from established social backgrounds and tory in outlook. The 'Ethnologicals' on the whole were from nonconformist middle-class backgrounds and liberal in outlook. The explorer Richard Burton, who emerged as the flamboyant figurehead of the Anthropologicals, contrasts with the intellectual elite, Huxley, Lubbock, Fox, John Evans and Francis Galton, which was developing amongst the Ethnologicals. In effect the Anthropologicals were marginalised while the Ethnologicals eased themselves into the position of a new establishment, totally respectable despite their often advanced religious and social views (Stocking 1987, 245–53).

The hostility of the British Association for the Advancement of Science towards the Anthropological Society also kept them on the fringes and when, after several abortive attempts, the breach of 1863 was healed by the reunion of the Ethnological and Anthropological Societies in 1871 it was done to the distinct advantage of the Ethnologicals. The union, arranged by Huxley, Fox and four Anthropologicals, created the Anthropological Institute of Great Britain with Lubbock as its first President. By 1875 the term 'anthropology' had been absorbed by the Ethnologicals and had gained scientific respectability.

The first need for the new Institute was to improve the still chaotic data of its subject matter. In 1872, under the overall guidance of Tylor and with Fox as its secretary, a committee was established to draw up instructions for the gatherers of ethnographic and anthropological information. These *Notes and Queries* were published in 1874. Ironically, however, this effort was to bear little fruit because the Institute, dominated by prehistoric archaeologists, became increasingly concerned with European and even British matters (Stocking 1987, 254–61). The archaeologists continued to control the Institute until 1880, when it was in something of a decline, and the revival which followed in the early 1880s was led by a group of physical anthropologists, such as Francis Galton who had little interest in ethnography but was preoccupied with demonstrating the ascendency of heredity over environment in determining the potential of the individual (Lorimer 1988, 422). Archaeology and physical anthropology, for both of which raw data could be found in Britain and both of which were closely related to the central Darwinian subjects, biology and geology, had driven out the traditional ethnologists (Stocking 1987, 262).

Anthropology remained throughout the nineteenth century the preserve of amateurs despite deliberate attempts to establish it as a university discipline in the 1880s, notably by the creation of the Pitt Rivers Museum and the appointment of Tylor as lecturer in anthropology at Oxford in 1884. Likewise anthropology had little impact on public affairs, despite the wishes of its practitioners, indicated by Pitt Rivers' invention of the term 'applied anthropology' in 1881. Anthropology also remained totally divorced from its supposed subject matter, 'savage' man (*ibid.*, 272–3).

COLLECTION AND FIELDWORK

Fox began to collect firearms while he was serving on the committee considering the adoption of a rifle for the army. However, the fact that the development of firearms was his main professional preoccupation cannot, of itself, be taken as the reason for his desire to collect historic firearms. The initiative for the collection must have come from elsewhere, probably the Great Exhibition of 1851, the arrangement of which was so 'evolutionary' (Stocking 1987, 5) and which was an inspiration to so many Victorian men of science, or from the Stanleys and their circle of friends. The Lane Foxes were a family whose interests reached littler further than the traditional country sports and pastimes, so the Stanley circle must be seen as providing the intellectual stimulus for Fox's increasing scientific interests (Thompson 1977, 19). At the Stanley house he met not only the antiquary William Owen Stanley, Henry Rawlinson the Assyriologist and Alice's uncle Albert Way, Director of the Society of Antiquaries, but some of the most eminent scientists and social scientists of the day including the philosophers Herbert Spencer and John Stuart Mill and the geologist Joseph Prestwich.

Whatever the original reason for the collection, however, it was soon growing in size and scope. From firearms Fox branched out into different types of offensive and defensive weaponry, then into tools and implements, and thence to items of dress and ornament. On the title page of *Primitive Locks and Keys* (1883b) he states that he had been collecting locks and keys since 1851 so that the progression of his collecting policy may not have been so gradual or so straightforward as has sometimes been suggested. It is impossible to be sure how early Fox began to collect antiquities, for instance, because such evidence as exists is ambiguous (see for example Bowden and Taylor 1984). Chapman has traced the history of this collection from its origins to its final resting place at Oxford in 1884 in some detail (1984; 1985).

Interruptions such as overseas service were turned to good account as many objects seem to have been acquired by Fox personally on these occasions. He was not wealthy but at the same time an allowance of £1000 a year was not negligible. Though he relied on his mother to support him in major capital outlays such as his promotions (Thompson 1977, 30), he was very well able to afford the collection of ethnographic objects which could often be acquired at very little cost (Chapman 1984, 7). As his collection became well known gifts and bequests began to be added, such as the rare Egyptian boomerang which caused him such 'surprise and satisfaction' when it was left to him in 1883 (Pitt Rivers 1883a, 454–5). Until 1874 the collection was kept at his private London house, at first in Brompton Crescent and after 1867 in Upper Philimore Gardens. The collection filled the house from basement to attic with wall displays and cabinets in all the main rooms (Chapman 1985, 29).

Darwin's *Origin of Species*, published in 1859, had a profound effect on Fox. It was after reading this that he began seriously to classify his collection and to develop the theory which was to come into full fruition with his lecture 'On the Evolution of Culture' delivered in 1875 (Fox 1875a). He saw the development of material culture as being analogous to the evolution of natural forms which Darwin had described. This concept was central to Fox's thinking on material culture and was the starting point for all his anthropological and archaeological work. Darwin himself, it should be noted, was never convinced that social evolution was analogous to biological evolution (Howard 1982, v).

In 1861 Fox joined the Ethnological Society of London. It was probably here that he met Sir John Lubbock and Thomas Huxley (Thompson 1977, 33–4), both of whom were to have a great influence on his later career. Echoes of Huxley's ideas can be seen in Fox's works:

> Our reverence for the nobility of manhood will not be lessened by the knowledge, that Man is, in substance and in structure, one with the brutes . . . (Huxley 1863, 132).

> I cannot myself see how human conduct is likely to be affected disadvantageously by recognising the humble origin of mankind. If it teaches us to take less pride in our ancestry, and to place more reliance on ourselves, this cannot fail to serve as an additional incentive to industry and respectability. (Pitt Rivers 1887b, 276)

Lubbock's influence was concerned with archaeology, and particularly the preservation of ancient monuments, rather than with anthropology and ethnology. In the late 1860s the Ethnological Society began to take on a more archaeological flavour and as Fox was General Secretary of the Society at this time it is not unreasonable to infer, as Thompson does (1977, 34), that he was responsible for this shift in emphasis – though the continuing strong archaeological bias of the Anthropological Institute through the 1870s (Lorimer 1988, 411) suggests the influence of more than one man.

Fox's election to the Society of Antiquaries of London in 1864 shows that his interests were turning more towards archaeology, though his qualification for Fellowship stressed his 'attachment to ancient arms and armour', providing a strong link with the origins of his collection. One of his sponsors was Henry Christy, himself a collector of anthropological, as well as archaeological, objects (Thompson 1977, 32) and a friendly rival to Fox in the auction rooms (Chapman 1985, 25). By the 1860s at least Fox had begun to add antiquarian objects to his collection and in the 1870s this aspect of the collection grew in importance as his commitment to archaeology increased.

His return to active military service in 1874 prompted his decision to hand the collection over to a public body, both to rid himself of the expense and trouble of maintaining it and to make the collection itself, and his scheme of classification, available to a wider public (Chapman 1984, 8):

> The knowledge of the facts of evolution, and the processes of gradual develop-ment, is the one great knowledge that we have to inculcate, and this knowledge can be taught by museums, provided they are arranged in such a manner that those who run may read. The working classes have but little time for study. (Pitt Rivers 1891, 116)

The museum at Bethnal Green was a new venture, opened in 1872. It was a branch of the South Kensington Museum, deliberately planted in a pre-dominantly working class area of east London. This seemed to Fox the ideal museum to house his collection because 'as a new institution it seemed more amenable to his dictates' (Chapman 1984, 8). The collection was not to be a gift but rather a loan and Fox was determined to maintain a considerable amount of control over it. It was to be displayed according to his principles of classifica-tion (Fox 1874a) and he was to have the right to add to it and subtract from it at will. The Museum authorities accepted Fox's conditions and the display was set up in the spring of 1874. The published catalogue of the exhibition (Fox 1874b) gives a good idea of the extent of the collection at this time. There was an extensive display of human skulls, another of weapons and a third of other ethnographic materials. This third section also included practical demonstra-tions of various crafts (Chapman 1984, 9). Amongst other series in the display, not included in the catalogue, was that on early modes of navigation. This formed the basis for a lecture given that year (Fox 1874c) in defence of Huxley's racial views, which had been criticised by Richard Owen (Lorimer 1988, 412–13). Herbert Spencer saw the collection at this time and spoke with approba-tion of the typological arrangement (Gray 1905, xi–xii).

It was while he was commanding the Brigade Depot at Guildford that Fox, who was serving on the Anthropometric Committee of the British Associa-tion, undertook the scientific measurement of 477 men and officers of the 2nd Royal Surrey Militia. He was careful to explain in his report every detail of the proceedings including the information that, when taking chest measurements 'All the men were measured naked, except the officers' (Fox 1877a, 443–57). What the men and officers of the 2nd Royal Surrey Militia thought about the exercise was not recorded but it is unlikely that they were surprised by their depot commander's interest in physical anthropology. They served in an army whose Staff College taught geology, physics and chemistry in preference to the more obviously military subjects of strategy, transport and communications and whose officers were positively encouraged to make contributions to non-military science in the course of their duties (Harries-Jenkins 1977, 161–2). Fox was far from being the only officer who used his military position as an opportunity for pushing back the frontiers of knowledge. Many members of the Ethnological Society were military men (Thompson, 1977, 33) and no less a personage than Kitchener undertook surveys of archaeological sites while on active service in Palestine (Harries-Jenkins 1977, 162). Fox himself stated the situation clearly when he told the members of the Royal United Services Institution that, 'Owing to the wide distribution of our Army and Navy, the members of which are dispersed over every quarter of the globe, and have ample leisure for the pursuit of these interesting studies, this Institution possesses facilities for forming a really systematic collection of savage weapons, not perhaps within the power of any other Institution in the world' (1868b, 438).

Fox continued to add to the collection while it was at Bethnal Green. Groups of material arrived 'nearly every other month for the duration of the loan period', frequently delivered by Fox in person (Chapman 1984, 10–11). After four years the collection was moved from the branch museum at Bethnal Green into the main museum at South Kensington. This move was made in response to Fox's request at the time when he moved back to London from Guildford. South Kensington offered a better opportunity than Bethnal Green for the fulfilment of Fox's ambitions for his collection as an instrument for mass education. He continued to add items to the collection including objects from Brittany, presumably acquired during his archaeological trips there (*ibid.*, 11–12). Archaeological material from his own fieldwork came into the collection alongside objects bought from dealers.

Fox was combining archaeological and anthropological fieldwork as well. The report on his excavations at Dane's Dyke, Flamborough in 1879 contains an appendix on the measurements and racial characteristics of the local inhabitants (Pitt Rivers 1882a, 469–71). As well as adding to the collection Fox was trying to exercise control over it by advising the staff on changes to the display. The collection was, of course, still his property but established as it was within a public museum it was not under the direct control. This situation led to disagreements and in 1879 the museum authorities demanded that the position be clarified (Chapman 1984, 13). Either the museum would have to be given complete control of the collection or it would no longer be able to display it.

At this point the situation was changed entirely by Fox's inheritance of the Rivers estates. With his vastly increased wealth he declared his intention to extend the collection on a much more ambitious scale and demanded more room immediately, but he also hinted that the collection might be made an outright gift to the museum (*ibid.*, 13–14). A committee was set up to consider the situation and various proposals were put forward. Pitt Rivers continued to insist that he would have control over the collection in his lifetime though he made no stipulations as to what should be done with it after his death. 'If my system were accepted by men of science, it would be continued. If it were not, there would be no object in continuing it. Moreover, views become so much changed as knowledge accumulates that it would be mischievous to hamper the

FLAMBOROUGH WOMEN, OCTOBER, 1879.

MEASURED BY MAJOR-GENERAL PITT-RIVERS, F.R.S., P.A.I.

No.	Name.	Age.	Profession or Calling.	Race.	Height.	Chest.	Weight.	Shoulders.	Head.			Hair.	Eyes.
									Length.	Breadth.	Cephalic Index.		
					Ft. in.	Ft. in.	St. lb.						
1	Anne Nicholson	59	Fishwoman	P. Flamborough	5 1	3 5	13 10	broad high	7·3	5·7	73·0	Black	Blue
2	Mary Cross	49	Fishwoman	V.P. Flamborough	5 2	3 5	11 0½	broad high	7·3	5·8	79·4	Black	Brown
3	Mary Chadwick	55	Fishwoman	P. Flamborough	5 6½	3 2	12 11½	high	7·4	5·9	79·7	Black	Grey
4	Jane Woodhouse	48	Fishwoman	Flamborough	5 5½	3 1½	12 0	medium	7·5	5·8	77·3	Light Brown	Blue
5	Anne Oldfield	38	Fishwoman	V.P. Flamborough	5 5½	3 2	12 1	broad	7·4	5·8	78·3	Dark Brown	Dark Blue
6	Anne Chadwick	53	Fishwoman	Flamborough	5 2	2 11	10 8	broad	7·1	5·5	77·4	Red Brown	Grey
7	Mary Ann Traver	35	Fishwoman	V.P. Flamborough	5 7½	3 1	11 8	broad	7·6	6·0	79·0	Black	Brown
8	Anne Bellby	42	Fishwoman	V.P. Flamborough	5 8½	2 9	10 8½	medium	7·3	6·0	82·2	Black	Brown
9	Anne Gwin	66	Fishwoman	V.P. Flamborough	5 6	3 0	10 8	medium	7·5	5·9	78·6	Dark Brown	Blue
10	Mary White	34	Wife of Labourer.	V.P. Flamborough	5 6½	3 1	12 13	broad	7·4	6·1	82·4	Black	Brown
11	Sarah Colley	20	Fishwoman	V.P. Flamborough	5 2½	2 9½	9 9½	...	7·3	5·5	75·1	Red	Brown
12	Mary Cross	20	Fishwoman	V.P. Flamborough	5 4	2 10	10 10½	...	7·6	6·0	77·0	Brown	Grey
13	Anne Naggs	27	Wife of Fishwoman	V.P. Flamborough	5 3½	3 2	12 12½	...	7·6	6·1	76·2	Black	Brown
14	Anne Edison	67	Agricultural Labourer.	V.P. Flamborough	5 3	3 3	13 0	...	7·4	5·7	77·0	Formerly Black	Blue
15	Anne Major	33	Fishwoman	V.P. Flamborough	5 1	3 1	11 0	...	7·2	5·7	79·1	Black Dark	Dark Brown
16	F. Sawden	41	Wife of a Labourer	V.P. Flamborough	5 0	3 1	11 3½	...	7·1	6·0	84·5	Brown Dark	Blue Grey
17	M. Anne Cross	30	Fishwoman	V.P. Flamborough	5 3½	3 1	12 3½	...	7·3	6·1	83·6	Brown	Brown
	Totals	714	...	...	90 9	52 5	198·10	...	...	98·6	134·70	...	...
	Averages	42	...	...	5 4	3 1	11 9½	...	...	5·85	79·2	...	...

12 Part of the tabulated record of the physical anthropology of the inhabitants of Flamborough: the questioning required to obtain some of the information, such as the former colour of an elderly woman's hair, seems rather personal

future with ideas of the present' (quoted by Chapman 1984, 16). The committee expressed itself in favour of accepting the collection on the terms which the donor specified. As the committee was largely made up of long-standing associates of the General, such as George Rolleston, Augustus Franks, Sir John Lubbock and Thomas Huxley, this was perhaps a foregone conclusion, but the final decision of the Council on Education, which controlled the museum, was unfavourable. They were not prepared to accept the collection on the General's conditions. Pitt Rivers continued to place objects on loan at South Kensington until the autumn of 1881 when he was informed that the museum could accept no more loans from him and that more satisfactory arrangements would have to be made (Chapman 1984, 17–19).

It was at this point that Pitt Rivers began to think that a university might be the most appropriate institution to house his collection, given that his main desire was that it should be used for educational purposes. His choice fell on Oxford. He had a considerable respect for a number of Oxford scientists, especially his friend George Rolleston. It was perhaps Rolleston's early death in 1881 that finally decided him to give his collection to Oxford University as a 'gesture to Rolleston's memory' (ibid., 20–2).

The University accepted the collection in 1884 and the transfer was completed in 1888. On 30 June 1886 the degree of Doctor of Civil Laws was conferred upon Pitt Rivers by the University. This is best seen as a gesture of gratitude from the University to the generous donor of a magnificent collection of ethnographic objects. Certainly the award of this degree does not imply

13 General Pitt Rivers in his DCL gown

necessarily any recognition of academic achievement. It had been awarded to Lord Raglan not many years previously.

Pitt Rivers was, from 1884, prevented from exercising any control over the collection, which he regretted deeply (*ibid.*, 23–4). He quarrelled with E. B. Tylor, the lecturer in anthropology, and Henry Balfour, the assistant curator (Chapman 1985, 38). When Balfour published a paper on the composite bow (1889) Pitt Rivers replied with some stinging remarks in print suggesting that Balfour had plagiarised his own work and trusting that 'he will be encouraged to take up hereafter an original subject of his own . . .' (Pitt Rivers 1889, 250). An amplified and considerably more hostile version of these remarks exists in typescript in which the cause of the disagreement is made sufficiently clear: 'It is at all times desirable that young Gentlemen should acquire the habit of giving due credit to those who have preceded them, which is a part of good manners that might advantageously be taught at Oxford to those who need it' (Pitt Rivers Papers P62). Pitt Rivers continued to collect ethnographic objects however and many of these were displayed in his museum at Farnham along-side the archaeological and folklife collections. There is no catalogue extant recording all the objects at Farnham but we do know that the ethnographic collections were remarkably rich and varied.

The crowning glory of the General's ethnographic collecting came in 1897 when he purchased 240 works of art from Benin, Nigeria. In 1896 a trading expedition, travelling ill-prepared and virtually unarmed, against all advice and against the express prohibition of the King of Benin, advanced on the city and was ambushed. The expedition of 250 men was massacred, with the exception of only two who managed to escape. Within five weeks a punitive expedition

14 The Pacific Room, Farnham Museum

was mounted and in January 1897 the city of Benin was taken, the King captured and his territory annexed by Britain. The punitive expedition found the city in a state of bloodshed and disorder which they attributed to human sacrifices. They also found a remarkable collection of works of art in bronze, brass and ivory, chiefly in the king's compound and Juju houses. It was known that these were being made in Benin at least as early as AD 1700. These objects were brought away by members of the expedition and sold. The General tartly remarked that 'as the expedition was as usual unaccompanied by any scientific explorer charged with the duty of making inquiries upon matters of historic and antiquarian interest, no reliable information about them could be obtained' (Pitt Rivers 1900, ii). Nevertheless Read and Dalton in their book *Antiquities from the City of Benin* included considerable documentation obtained from members of the expeditionary force (Fagg 1976, iv).

The General obtained his collection of Benin bronzes through the antiques trade and placed them in Farnham Museum. He also produced an illustrated catalogue of the collection which was published only a few days before his death in 1900. Ling Roth, in reviewing the catalogue, said that Pitt Rivers had 'collected something of almost every phase, many of his articles being of the best' (quoted by Fagg 1976, iv). Only wealth was required to buy the best but the selection of items from almost every phase shows discrimination and a continuing desire to trace the evolution of culture. We do not know what classification scheme was employed to display the Benin bronzes at Farnham and work on their display was not completed before the General's death (Bradley 1989, 31) but it is certain that the classification employed would have been an evolutionary one. Sadly this collection, like nearly all the ethnographic material from Farnham, has now been dispersed.

THEORY AND IMPLICATIONS

Clearly the General was no mere dilletante collector of curiosities. What may have been little more than a hobby in the 1850s became a very serious business in the 1860s, as evolutionary theory was applied to the collection. The analogy between the evolution of culture and Darwinian evolution was seen by Fox to be quite exact and the application of a Darwinian evolution is clear in a great many of his works on both anthropology and archaeology. In his paper on the mere or pattoo–pattoo, a traditional weapon of New Zealand, he demonstrates by evolutionary theory how the pattoo–pattoo is derived from the axe rather than the club and is therefore a cutting or thrusting weapon rather than a bludgeon: '. . . nearly all the weapons of savages have derived their form from an historical development, and are capable of being traced back through their varieties to earlier and simpler forms, with as much certainty as the various forms of animal and vegetable life' (Fox 1870a, 107). Fox then carefully backs up the theory with anthropological evidence. 'The old Maories', on being closely questioned, confirmed that the pattoo–pattoo was a thrusting weapon used 'in prodding the enemy behind the ear with the sharp end' as Sir Charles Dilke graphically described it (*ibid.*). Fox also employed the language of Darwinian evolution. In his discussion of the flint implements found at Cissbury he says:

> . . . many ancient forms are retained during subsequent ages, and still survive amongst others that have sprung from them, so by a precisely similar process of *natural selection*, if we may apply that term, and I think we may, to the earlier stages of human art, many ancient types of tools and forms of ornament are in like manner retained . . . long after they have been superseded by others of more modern origin . . . (Fox 1869b, 70)

The General himself, though distinguishing between anthropology and archaeology, saw them working towards the same end. His interest in the latter developed quite naturally from his concern with the former. In writing of archaeology he frequently stressed its importance as an adjunct to anthropology and often used the term anthropology to cover the field of archaeology: 'As an old sportsman I commend flint hunting to all anthropologists who have not practised it' (Fox 1875b, 359). All the studies of mankind were, to the General, part of one great science perhaps best summed up in his well known remark that 'History is but another term for evolution' (Fox 1875a, 498).

Bradley has recently traced the intellectual development of the General (1983) and shown how his interests and the theoretical base of his anthropological and archaeological work progressed. Each stage in the General's scientific career led naturally to the next. There are no divisions between the phases and, moreover, he never really lost any of his early interests. New spheres of activity were added and came to dominate, but never entirely replaced, previous ones. His continuing concern with evolution and typology is demonstrated by his essay on chevron-decorated pottery (1898, 216–39) and his collection of Benin bronzes (1900) at the very end of his life. His interest in weaponry and primitive warfare was carried over into the excavations of Bokerley Dyke and Wansdyke (1892). Physical anthropology was very firmly in his mind when he measured the heads of some of his tenants in Cranborne Chase (1898, 122) and in all his excavations on the Chase, as the report on Rotherley makes particularly clear.

The work on primitive locks and keys (1883b) provides an example of the way in which Pitt Rivers combined his interests, relying as it does on the evidence of philology, mythology, history, anthropology and archaeology, all brought to the support of a theoretical evolutionary sequence.

Initially archaeological fieldwork was undertaken to benefit his anthropological studies by lengthening the sequence of material objects and constructions available for building typologies. The word 'typology', incidentally, appears to have been invented by the General (Pitt Rivers 1891, 116; Piggott 1959, 60). Archaeology was, in fact, to produce the long time scale necessary to establish an evolutionary sequence. That this was the principle function of his early endeavours in field archaeology is explicitly stated in the report on Cissbury (1869b, 70). Archaeology rapidly increased its hold on his time however and he was constantly urging the claims of archaeology to be seen as a crucially important branch of anthropological study to the Ethnological Society of London and subsequently to the Anthropological Institute. It is noticeable too that in his annual Presidential Addresses to the latter society the General was always able to list a larger number of papers in the Archaeology class than in any other branch of anthropology. To a large extent it was his own influence as President that brought this about. In time the roles of the different branches of anthropology were reversed in his perception and he was able to point to the usefulness of ethnography to archaeology. When discussing the use of unmodified natural objects as tools or implements, a use which would be archaeologically invisible, he says 'How much then is the prehistoric archaeologist indebted to the descriptive ethnologist who will observe and record such facts for our information' (1878, 446–7). From being the handmaiden of anthropology, archaeology has become an independent discipline.

The General was by no means the first to see the close links between archaeology and the other branches of anthropological study. As early as 1861 Bateman, who had collaborated with the physical anthropologist Joseph Davis (Stocking 1987, 66), had written in the Preface to *Ten Years Diggings* that 'The time has fortunately passed away in which it would have been needful to

introduce a book like the present by an apology for Antiquarian researches;
their importance as bearing on the ethnology and unwritten history of the
human race is now fully admitted by all who are competent to give an opinion
on the subject' (Bateman 1861).

As Chapman has pointed out Pitt Rivers was concerned with 'the interaction
of a variety of orientations toward several different anthropological issues'
(1985, 39–40) but cultural evolution remained the central focus of his work. To
the General gradual change was a natural law. If one exception could be found
to the 'evolution of culture' the whole edifice would collapse:

> If the principles which I have enunciated are sound, they must be applicable to the
> whole of the arts of mankind and to all time. If it can be proved that a single art,
> contrivance, custom or institution sprung into existence in violation of the law of
> continuity, and was not the offspring of some prior growth, it will disprove my
> theory. If in the whole face of nature there is undoubted evidence of any especial
> fiat of creation having operated capriciously, or in any other manner than by
> gradual evolution and development, my principles are false. (Fox 1868b, 435–6)

For Pitt Rivers evolution was not only a scientific truth, it was also a political
creed and a model for society. Social progress could only take place through
evolution, as opposed to revolution, and evolution could only take place
through education. Ultimately the theory of the evolution of culture justified
the existing social order, the expansion of the British Empire and supported a
dangerous form of racism. This was explicitly stated in the first lecture on
'Primitive Warfare.' Civilisation, he wrote, has always been 'confined to particular races, whose function it has been by means of war and conquest, to
spread the arts amongst surrounding nations, or to exterminate those whose
low state of mental culture rendered them incapable of receiving it' (Fox 1867d,
615). This justification of such episodes as the extinction of the Tasmanians
(Hughes 1988, 414–24) reflects in harsh terms the belief, widely held among
contemporary anthropologists, that as the Tasmanians represented a
palaeolithic state of society their extermination was inevitable and almost
necessary (Stocking 1987, 281–3).

This attitude is also clear in Fox's reaction to his Irish experiences which
'reinforced a typically stereotypical view of the Irish as socially and intellectu-
ally inferior' (Chapman 1985, 28). The anthropological literature of the later
nineteenth century, especially that part of it published by the Anthropological
Society of London (see Stocking 1987, 246–8), is full of value judgements
which are no longer acceptable and indeed were not acceptable to the General's
colleagues Lubbock and Tylor (ibid., 153, 159–60) though their own Euro-
centric attitudes appear racist today. However, we can now demonstrate that
Pitt Rivers' theory is incorrect, that cultural evolution is not analogous to
natural evolution (Gould 1980, 70–1; Thompson 1977, 43–4) and that gradual
change is not a natural law.

5

Early archaeological fieldwork

The intellectual and organisational background to later nineteenth-century archaeology has recently been reviewed by Levine (1986) and Chapman (1989) but the development of fieldwork has received less attention. Fieldwork in British archaeology had developed unsystematically through the work of a number of more or less gifted individuals from John Aubrey and William Stukeley onwards. There was therefore no school of fieldwork into which the General's career can be fitted.

By the beginning of the nineteenth century antiquarian fieldwork was a popular pastime for gentlemen of leisure such as Sir Richard Colt Hoare who, with his associate William Cunnington, carried out an extensive programme of excavation and survey, mainly of barrow cemeteries in south Wiltshire. The surveys, conducted by his steward Philip Crocker, were at small scale and the excavations were recorded minimally but Colt Hoare was at least able to distinguish between primary and secondary interments. He illustrated the finds but gave only the slightest attention to skeletal material, which was to earn him scathing attacks from later archaeologists including Pitt Rivers: '. . . in only one instance he describes a skeleton, saying that it "grinned horribly a ghastly smile" . . . No doubt the skeleton must have been laughing at him for his unscientific method of dealing with it . . .' (1887b, 264).

Archaeology continued to be practised by individuals but in the middle decades of the century it began to be seen also as a social activity, a development reflected in the rapid growth in numbers of county archaeological societies. The popularity of these organisations has been linked to wider social changes such as increased religious fervour and the birth of ecclesiastical movements, the influence of romanticism and a changing perspective among historians from the global and general to the local and particular (Piggott 1976, 171–95).

This social aspect of the local archaeology societies contrasts with the dramatic impact that prehistoric archaeology was making on the stage of world science at the same time. The acceptance, by the more progressive at least, of C. J. Thomsen's Three Age System in the 1840s, though it had perhaps been foreshadowed by earlier scholars (Rodden 1981, 63, 66), coincided with the discoveries of palaeolithic tools with animal bones by Boucher de Perthes in the Somme valley and by Godwin Austen at Kent's Cavern, Torquay. The vastly expanded timescale for the history of mankind thus revealed was one of the most significant and far-reaching scientific discoveries of the century and laid the foundations for the acceptance of Darwin's evolutionary hypothesis. Archaeology was established as a discipline independent of the classics and history and allied more closely with the sciences of geology, anatomy, zoology and botany. This change in orientation underlies the rift between Albert Way and Thomas Wright, leading to the separation of the Archaeological Institute from the British Archaeological Association, which was therefore more fundamental than the 'petty wrangle' described by Levine (1986, 69) though it is probably true that the argument resulted partly from a clash of personalities.

Having established the antiquity of mankind archaeology needed to develop a chronology for prehistory. Thomsen's Three Ages of Stone, Bronze and Iron provided a framework but the detail was to prove extremely elusive. The problem lay partly in the restricted range of sites studied by archaeologists. In 1865 Sir John Lubbock listed the sources of evidence available to prehistorians as burial mounds, peat bogs, Danish shell middens, Swiss lake dwellings, occupied caves and river drift gravels (1869, vi). This picture did not alter much through the following decades. In 1893 Pitt Rivers quoted Joseph Anderson's statement that not a single hillfort or prehistoric settlement site in Scotland had been securely dated and added that the situation was nearly the same in England (Barley and Barry 1971, 217).

By far the most extensively explored of the categories listed by Lubbock was the burial mound (Marsden 1974; 1978) but by the 1860s the barrow diggers had not been able to construct a relative chronology for their discoveries. This was due to the lack of any idea of context. While many archaeologists and collectors of antiquities appreciated the importance of provenance few thought it necessary to record more precisely the context of discovery. The name of the site was sufficient. At the same time different styles of funerary ceramics were seen as the result of differing functions or differential wealth, rarely as possible chronological indicators. Of those barrow diggers who thought the exercise worthwhile only a few, such as Canon Greenwell, W. C. Lukis, Charles Warne and John Mortimer, were able to make even the most tentative suggestions as to the date of the barrows they dug. Indeed the more definite chronological statements of Thomas Bateman and John Thurnam are the furthest from the findings of more recent research.

Standards of barrow excavation were so variable as to defy generalisation. The mid and later nineteenth century was a period of enthusiastic and unashamed treasure hunting frequently deprecated by serious archaeologists whose own digging was not much less destructive. Consistency was entirely lacking. Llewellyn Jewitt was a haphazard excavator who nevertheless recorded his curiously shaped trenches with skilful plans and precisely written reports (Marsden 1974, 77, pl. 20) while James Silburn excavated with extreme care but kept only brief and uninformative notes (*ibid.*, 97). A few men advocated and achieved higher standards, notable amongst them Bateman, Lukis, Edward Cunnington, Greenwell and his sometime associate the Rev. J. C.

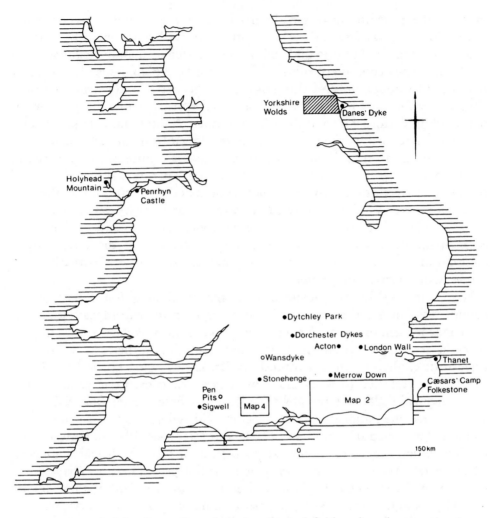

Map 1 Location of the General's early archaeological fieldwork and excavation in England and Wales and later excavations outside Cranborne Chase

Atkinson and the last great barrow digger, Mortimer (*ibid.*, 33–47, 54–7, 72–6, 91–4, 105–13).

Bateman and Greenwell ranged far and wide in the course of their researches but they were exceptional. Barrow diggers and the rare excavators of non-funerary sites, such as Steven Stone in Oxfordshire, the Rev. J. G. Joyce at Silchester and John Clayton on Hadrian's Wall, tended to restrict their activities to one locality.

The rather haphazard geographical spread of Fox's early fieldwork can be traced to two factors; his military postings and visits to the country houses of relations and friends. There is little in the General's early fieldwork which can be seen as the result of a deliberate research policy. Nevertheless there are certain themes which can be followed through the phases of early fieldwork, most of them stemming originally from ethnographic and anthropological roots. Primitive warfare and racial frontiers are well represented by surveys and excavations of hillforts and linear ditch systems, mainly in Sussex and Yorkshire. The evolution of culture and creation of typologies is very strongly represented throughout and this links with the need to construct a firmer chronology for early man in Britain, shown for instance in the report on his fieldwork in Oxfordshire and the Isle of Thanet. Another notable point is his use of accurate earthwork surveys which developed from an early stage in his archaeological career and which was to be a major feature of his later work. Other themes can be isolated, such as the use of experimental techniques and the study of river gravel deposits which came together so crucially in the Nile valley controversy. Significantly the excavation of barrows was not of such interest to Fox as it was to so many of his contemporaries and predecessors, even in the early stages of his archaeological career. Of the twenty-three episodes of fieldwork considered in this chapter only five are primarily concerned with funerary monuments.

Fox's early fieldwork coincided with the continuing florescence of the county archaeological societies which had begun in the late 1830s but he was quite independent of them. The only exception to this was the occasion in 1881 when he acted as adviser to the Essex Field Club during their excavation of a prehistoric earthwork called Ambresbury Banks in Epping Forest (Pitt Rivers 1881b). He preferred to work alone or with a few chosen companions. The work, if small scale, was privately funded but where greater financial outlay was required the national learned societies with which he was so intimately connected provided subscriptions. The labour force was either borrowed from the landowner, often a relation or acquaintance, or from the Royal Engineers. The General's avoidance of county societies at this period may also have much to do with the strongly Anglican and ecclesiological nature of these bodies noted by Piggott (1976, 175–82). Apart from his early association with Canon Greenwell the General had relatively little contact with the antiquarian clergymen who formed the backbone of the county societies. It was not until he became a landowner and therefore inexorably drawn into the realm of the Anglican establishment that he made significant contacts with clerics of an archaeological bent.

IRELAND 1862–6

Despite the General's statement that his first lessons as an excavator were received in Yorkshire under Canon Greenwell it is clear that he had been involved in digging of some description on his own account in Ireland in the 1860s. His work on raths and ogham stones certainly involved some excavation as well as field survey and observation.

His published report on Roovesmore shows that he dug down to the top of the souterrain chamber in order to be able to read the ogham inscriptions on the stones forming the roof and that, having done so, he considered that the structure was in danger of collapsing and therefore removed the stones (Pitt Rivers 1867a, 124–5). In the same report he recommends 'active exploration' if evidence about raths is to be gained before they are all destroyed (*ibid.*, 138).

Two points emerge from the Roovesmore report which have a bearing on his later career. In the first place he sent the oghams from Roovesmore to the British Museum (*ibid.*, 125), which contrasts with his later belief in keeping antiquities in their locality. Secondly we see the first evidence of his concern over the destruction of ancient monuments. His response to this threat is not preservation, which he later advocated so strongly, but rather 'exploration'. In effect his first response to destruction was 'rescue' and only later did he become concerned with conservation.

Fox dug into other raths in the south of Ireland. In 1864, the year before the exploration of Roovesmore, he had been studying raths near Cork with Richard Caulfield. Caulfield, as President of the Cork Cuverian Society, reported to that body on the work that he and Fox had undertaken at Kilcrea or Fahy's Fort and at Lisnahara Fort, and these reports were duly printed in *The Constitution* on 6 May and 20 May respectively. At Kilcrea they had merely observed the areas disturbed by the new railway cutting and Fox had taken some measurements. At Lisnahara, however, they had been more active:

> On Saturday 11th inst., with the assistance of a strong labourer and a long crowbar, soundings were taken in many parts of the fort to a depth of five or six feet [1.5–1.8 m] without any favourable result. The fort was then measured by Colonel Fox, and its centre found as nearly as possible. Here we had an excavation made six or seven feet [1.8–2.1 m] deep: bits of charcoal were met with, mixed with fragments of bones. Before leaving we had the place closed up. On Tuesday 17th inst., we renewed our operations, when, on sounding at the north part of the fort, the bar slipped down for about two feet [0.6 m]. As this indicated the presence of a crypt, we had the ground excavated, when, about five feet [1.5 m] from the surface, we found what turned out on further examination to have been the top of an arch, presenting the rudest elements of artificial work. It was constructed of small stones, placed lengthways into some sort of cement, quantities of which we discovered on the floor when clearing out: it was composed of fine clay, lime being largely used in its composition. Mixed with this cement we found charcoal and small pieces of bones. The evening brought our researches to a close. (Caulfield 1864).

Perhaps in retrospect the General felt that these unscientific proceedings were better forgotten. Certainly in later years he rarely referred to this phase of his archaeological work. This may account for his insistence that his earliest experience as an excavator stemmed from Canon Greenwell.

A draft account of Fox's excavation at Coolowen Farm, north of Cork, apparently never published, survives in the Pitt Rivers Papers. His concern with the evidence of animal bones is already apparent in this report, earlier than has been suggested (Thompson 1977, 46–7). After describing two standing stones he notes:

> Still further to the Eastward on the farm of Coolowen is another circular enclosure marked Shanatempleen on the ordnance survey containing within it

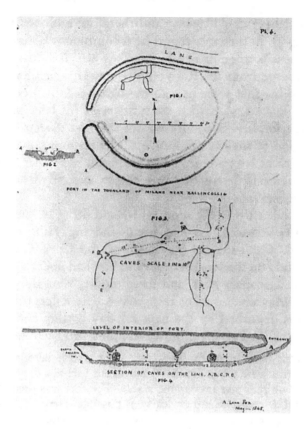

15 Sketch plans of a fort with a souterrain near Ballincollig, southern Ireland

traces of two quadrilateral structures & surrounded formerly by an uncemented wall parts of which have been recently disclosed by digging.

The place is held in great reverence by the people of the neighbourhood by whom as is usual in such localities marvellous events are said to have occurred within its sacred precincts, untold treasure of gold lays buried beneath the soil, the exact position of which has been put beyond question by the dreams of sundry old ladies in the neighbourhood, but who have been deterred from profiting by the revelation thus made to them by a wholesome dread ... here an inscription in ancient characters was discovered many years ago recording matters of import in the history of the country. The stone has unfortunately been destroyed but learned men not only from Dublin but also from France, America & other favoured places, like the Magi of old, have been attracted to this spot in search of it. finally it is said to have been a church & a grave yard but with what truth appears doubtful.

No spade had ever desecrated this ground until the other day when through the kind permission of Mr. McSwiney the owner, to the great consternation of the Inhabitants and notwithstanding the death of two calves which took place in the adjoining farm immediately the subject was mooted I commenced an excavation in a cavity at the top of a small mound forming the eastern extremity of one of the rectangular buildings above mentioned. The cavity was popularly supposed to have contained holy water and also to have served as a pulpit for preaching.

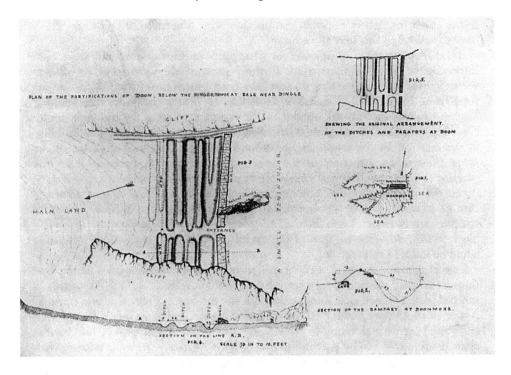

16 Sketch plans and profiles of promontory fort ramparts at Doon and Doonmore near Dingle, southern Ireland

Commencing at the bottom of the Holy water basin which was covered with grass & fern we removed a quantity of loose stones and earth and disclosed a pit 3 feet 9 inches [1.14 m] in depth and from 2 to 2, 5 [0.61–0.74 m] in circumference neatly faced with stone but not cemented or built in courses. towards the bottom some black earth was found which might have been buried turf, but there were no traces of charcoal. At the bottom of the pit running in the direction of the interior of the building a passage or 'Shore' as it is called by the Natives 1'9" [0.53 m] in height by 6'10" [2.08 m] in width and flagged over by two large flat stones was found to be completely filled with the bones of animals mixed with stones & earth. These on being submitted to Professor Harkness of the Queens College were pronounced to be bones of the Horse & the pig. there were no heads or teeth but principally bones of the ribs vertebrae & legs they were somewhat decayed in the interior but did not adhere to the tongue nor were any of them cut as if for marrow. Some were evidently young animals. Amongst these bones were also found small pieces of mortar or rather concrete in all of which fragments of sea shells were imbedded. No lime was found in this concrete. The Rubble of which it was composed appeared to consist of the old Red sand stone formation of the locality and even the fine sand on being disintegrated by acid appeared to have been formed of the same material.

The concrete lumps were exceedingly hard & firm. The absence of any trace of limestone about the place suggests the question whether the cementing material may not have consisted of burnt oyster shells. I am not aware whether there is any known process of making mortar by this means. But I have observed that oyster shells frequently occur in conjunction with mortar in the old forts that I have examined in this neighbourhood.

It is difficult to form an opinion for what purpose this building may have been intended. the first idea that struck all those present when the pit & its passage were exposed to view was that it must have been a small lime kiln. In a fort on the road from Blarney . . . I found a small kiln of nearly the same size opening however in this case on the outside of the rampart whereas the one now under consideration if such it was, must have been served from the rectangular building in the Interior. In the same neighbourhood there are several large kilns of the more modern construction in the banks of forts, always opening from the exterior & the parapets appear to have been partly cut away in the construction of them. the other rectangular building at Coolowen . . . has also a mound at the End of it and a circular depression on its summit seems to indicate a similar structure to the first. This is fortified however by a strong Fetish in the shape of a black thorn bush growing out of the cavity and it is doubtful whether any one could be induced to touch it.

One circumstance which I observed during this exploration may perhaps be thought worthy of notice at this time. Small urchins of from eight to ten years old jumped in and chased one another through the passage as soon as it was opened. A man of about thirty who I had employed to dig refused to go into it for a pound and altho I felt no inclination to put his prejudice to the test he proved his genuine disinclination to do so by picking up the stones laboriously from the bottom with that most antiquated of implements the long handled shovel of the country. While an old man of eighty his countenance quavering with emotion swore by the blessed virgin that not for fifty Pounds nor for any money I could give him would he lend a hand to such impiety and he warned me solemnly of the Calamities that would befall me in consequence. We see from this very clearly that the Fetish is dying out amongst the rising generation. Superstition like many other things which we call Evils has its uses in the Scheme of providence. It has preserved these Forts Dallauns & Tumuli to a time when Prehistoric Archaeology is beginning for the first time to be understood & appreciated. Its occupation is now gone, while that of the Archaeologist should commence in Earnest if he wishes to profit by these Relics of antiquity before they go. (Pitt Rivers Papers P5)

The final sentence was a prophetic statement concerning his own career.

LONDON WALL, OCTOBER–DECEMBER 1866

Fox's attention was drawn to the discovery of archaeological remains on a building site at London Wall by an article in the *Times* on 20 October 1866 describing the removal of twenty cartloads of bone from the site. He visited the site the same day and found a large excavation being made for an extension to a wool warehouse. He maintained a watching brief on the site for at least two months. A considerable depth of peat had been exposed overlying the gravel and throughout the peat were lenses of occupation material, piles, pottery and bones. Fox planned the positions of all the piles as they were exposed (Pitt Rivers 1867b, lxxii) and recorded the sections visible, remarking that 'the sides of the cutting shewed several admirable sections in which the history of the growth of the peat has been faithfully recorded' (*ibid.*, lxxiv) and he names two 'witnesses', Carter Blake and the Rev. D. I. Heath, who will speak for the accuracy of his section drawings, foreshadowing his later statement that archaeological evidence should be strong enough to stand up in a law court (Pitt Rivers 1883c, 436). He was able to demonstrate that the area was inhabited throughout the time that the peat was in process of formation and that this fell within the limits of the period of Roman occupation because Romano-British pottery was found from top to bottom. He was not apparently able to identify the pottery himself, but submitted it to Augustus Franks at the British Museum (Fox 1867b, 62–3). This limited timescale caused a problem: 'It is certainly difficult, if not impossible, to reconcile this enormous rise of seven to nine feet [2.1–2.7 m] of peat during the four centuries of the Roman occupation with anything that has hitherto been conjectured respecting the growth of peat on the continent' and this led to a lengthy but inconclusive discussion on fluctuating water levels (Fox 1867c, lxxv–lxxvi). Fox tentatively suggested that the piles and occupation layers represented the remains of a Late Iron Age lake village which had continued undisturbed through the Roman period: 'Savages in all parts of the world appear to have had an affection for swampy ground, and it is not unlikely the Romans may have left them in undisturbed possession of it' (Fox 1867b, 63). In the paper which he read to the Anthropological Institute on 18 December he went further, suggesting that this was the site of Cassivellaunus' capital because Caesar described that as situated amidst woods and marshes and Fox considered that 'A town situated in the midst of marshes could have been built on nothing else but piles' (1867c, lxxviii).

A small number of human skulls was also discovered on the site, which excited Fox as a physical anthropologist. Two of these were found at the bottom of the peat formation:

> One of these skulls is a remarkably fine one; the other quite the reverse, very small in the frontal region, large in the parietal and cerebellum, and somewhat pointed and low in the crown. Such a skull might very possibly have belonged to a savage, but no sound theory can be based upon it, as the Roman legion with its auxilliaries was such a heterogeneous body composed of different nations, that skulls of almost any description might be found amongst them (*ibid.*, lxxvii)

Fox concluded this address to the Institute with an appeal that the matter should not be allowed to rest:

> Thus while the remotest parts of Europe are being searched for the vestiges of lake dwellings, and the most valuable reports on the same subject are received from the four quarters of the globe, similar remains are in daily process of destruction at our own doors by persons who are ignorant of their meaning and of the importance that attaches to them. This certainly ought not to be. (*ibid.*, lxxix)

It was a theme to which he was to return repeatedly throughout his life.

Nothing seems to have come from this appeal in the way of support from other members of the anthropological world but Fox himself was not prepared to allow the opportunity to slip. After reading his paper on 18 December he stepped up his activities on the site, watching 'the workmen for four and five hours together during several successive days while they dug from top to bottom, commencing with the superficial earth and passing through the peat to the gravel below' (*ibid.*, lxxix). It was at this point that great quantities of shoe leather were discovered in the peat suggesting

> at first sight, the question whether this spot may have been devoted especially to the manufacture of shoes, but the whole of the specimens obtained were fragments of worn or made shoes. I found no pieces of unformed leather, which would certainly have been the case had this been a quarter for shoemakers. (*ibid.*, lxxix)

It was a nice point of interpretation for the budding archaeologist.

YORKSHIRE WOLDS, APRIL 1867

> My very first lessons as an excavator were derived from Canon Greenwell, during his well-known and valuable exploration in the Yorkshire Wolds, in the course of which I obtained a large amount of useful experience that has been a constant source of enjoyment and interest to me ever since. (Pitt Rivers 1887a, xix)

We do not know much more about Fox's experience with Greenwell on the Wolds than that which is contained in this statement. The two had been introduced to each other by Albert Way. Fox probably assisted Greenwell with his barrow excavations on Willerby Wold and Ganton Wold (Kinnes and Longworth 1985, 12–13) but his main task was a study of the linear ditch systems of the same area. Fox does not appear to have published the results of this work except, briefly, in his Dane's Dyke paper (1882a) but part of a manuscript description, entitled 'Notes on the Entrenchments at Folkton, Willerby, Binnington, Hunmanby, Ganton & Sherburn Wold on the South of the Vale of Pickering near Scarborough' survives (Pitt Rivers Papers P12). These notes, or the surviving portion of them at least, contain very little interpretation, however Canon Greenwell himself recorded Fox's views on the function of these ditches:

> These lines of fortification . . . have been very carefully surveyed by Colonel A. Lane Fox, FSA. His opinion is that these earthworks and their arrangement for defensive purposes are only to be explained on the supposition that they were made by a body of men advancing from the East, and gradually entrenching themselves as they extended their progress towards the West. If this view is correct, and the evidence of these arrangements considered strategically is certainly strongly in its favour, it appears to necessitate the occupation of the wolds by a people who, coming oversea, had landed upon the adjoining coast. (Greenwell with Rolleston 1877, 123–4)

Greenwell rejected the notion that these people could be identified with the Angles because of the lack of similar entrenchments in their homelands. The

Dannewerke, he says, 'if in later times it was ever anything more than a divisional or boundary work, it seems probable it represents a line of defence constructed at a time antecedent to the Scandinavian occupation of Denmark' (*ibid.*, 124). Here then is the reason for Fox and Rolleston's later excavation on the Dannewerke and for Fox's work at Flamborough Head. They needed to date these earthworks in order to test their relationships. They did not, however, excavate any of the earthworks on the Wolds themselves.

Greenwell's association with Fox continued intermittently until the death of the latter. Fox was undoubtedly greatly influenced by the Canon. Greenwell's statement that, 'It is impossible to reprobate too strongly that ignorant and greedy spirit of mere curiosity-hunting which has done – and alas! is still doing such injury to proper investigation of our ancient places of sepulture' (Greenwell 1865, 241) was one which Fox took very much to heart and which was to become one of the central tenets of his archaeological practice.

Of the other great Yorkshire barrow excavator, Mortimer, there is scarce mention in the General's works or papers. Fox must have met Mortimer, if not at this time then certainly later. That he admired Mortimer's work is shown by his highly favourable review (Pitt Rivers 1882b) of 'Discovery of Ancient Dwellings under Barrows' but the fact that he regarded Mortimer's work as a 'supplement' to that of Greenwell suggests that he adhered to the Canon's side in the Greenwell-Mortimer rivalry (Marsden 1974, 100–1). Doubtless social intercourse was easier between the Colonel and the Canon than it would have been between the Colonel and the corn chandler.

SUSSEX HILLFORTS, SEPTEMBER 1867

On 6 July 1867 Fox took half pay. Whatever his reason for doing so, the freedom from military duties allowed him to make an extended study of the hillforts of Sussex in the late summer of that year. The results of this survey were published in a substantial paper in *Archaeologia* (Fox 1869a), the first of a series of papers by him in that journal on the subject of early fortifications. He claimed to have examined nearly all the hillforts between Beachy Head and Chichester while staying in Brighton during the month of September (*ibid.*, 27) and recorded them by 'rough sketches from measurements taken on the spot, either by pacing, or by means of a tape and pocket level' (*ibid.*, 32). This is the first description of any type that we have of Fox's field surveying techniques. Unfortunately only a few of these sketches were ever published.

In studying these earthworks Fox had three principal concerns: to show that they were defensive works, that they were pre-Roman, and that they were isolated forts and not part of a system of defence. The first of these concerns arose out of the opinions expressed by earlier writers that the hillforts were principally religious sites. Fox quoted General Roy's comment that 'With regard to the military antiquities, it seems to have been a misfortune that few of the commentators who have treated on this subject, however well qualified in other respects, have been military men.' Roy had been talking of Roman

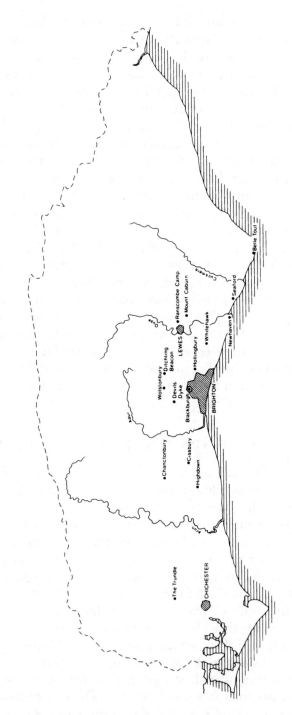

Map 2 Location of the General's fieldwork and excavation in Sussex

military sites but Fox was determined to apply the same argument to the hillforts which he believed to be pre-Roman. He was able to show on site after site that in his opinion, as a student of military science, the ramparts were laid out with a view to defensive capability. Of Mount Caburn, for instance, he wrote that its circular form, attributed by earlier antiquaries to its function as a temple, was

> attributable to its following the outline of a circular hill, in conformity with the recognised principles of castramentation observable in all the other intrenchments of the neighbourhood . . . The double vallum . . . is double only on the northern or weak side of the hill, from which point alone, with the then existing features of the country, a hostile attack could have been anticipated, and on which side the slope of the ground outside is more gentle than on the southern half of the fort where . . . there is only a single parapet . . . This is in precise accordance with the principles of defence which I shall have occasion to point out in several other works upon the downs . . . I have frequently observed the same peculiarity in the dikes upon the Yorkshire Wolds . . . (ibid., 36).

Fox's belief that the hillforts were of pre-Roman date was based originally on his observation that the hillforts were totally unlike known Roman forts in form and location and that the interiors of many of them were strewn with struck flints. He was forced to admit that these flakes 'afford the only evidence of British origin that I have discovered in most of the forts . . .' (ibid., 33) but the limited excavations which he made brought to light 'a large number of flint implements, all without exception of the chipped and unpolished kind and unaccompanied with any trace whatever of metal' (ibid., 50). Nowhere does he describe these excavations in detail, but the implication is that they were all in the interior of the forts or in suspected outworks. He does not seem to have excavated the ramparts or ditches at all. He found some pits in the interiors, which he regarded at this stage as habitations, another demonstration of pre-Roman date (ibid., 50). This dating, more or less correct for the wrong reasons, was not improved upon until his second series of excavations in Sussex in 1875. The third line of argument, again suggested by the need to counter the belief of earlier writers that the hillforts had been located with a view to the general defence of the Sussex coast, relied on geological evidence. Fox was convinced that the four river valleys which divided the downs had once been inland arms of the sea, for which evidence was found in the form of clay deposits, and that the Weald was an impenetrable barrier (ibid., 27–30). The hillforts, therefore, occupied isolated blocks of downland and Fox found nothing 'incompatible with the hypothesis of their having been isolated works, erected by several distinct tribes as a protection against the incursions of their neighbours. Such a state of society is more in accordance with what we find to be the early condition of savage life in every part of the world . . .' (ibid., 51). He was able to refer back to his own previous fieldwork to show that in this respect the Sussex hillforts differed from the dykes of the Yorkshire Wolds but resembled the Irish raths.

CISSBURY, SEPTEMBER 1867 AND JANUARY 1868

The paper dealing generally with the Sussex hillforts was immediately followed in the pages of *Archaeologia* by another dealing principally with Fox's excavations at Cissbury, a large univallate hillfort (Fox 1869b). At the outset Fox laid down his reasons for digging there:

> I determined to make a series of excavations, in order to determine whether the indications of the stone age observable on the surface corresponded with those of the implements found in the soil; and if so, whether the positions in which these implements were found were such as to afford evidence of their having belonged to the people who constructed these forts. (*ibid.*, 54).

Cissbury was chosen because of its size and the clear indications of numerous pits as well as the quantity of flakes on the surface. He opened thirty pits in the two seasons, which he decided were dug for flint extraction, and also examined some rectangular enclosures within the fort which he decided were probably Roman or later.

Fox was also concerned by the 'still more interesting question whether the intrenchment was coeval or subsequent to the pits' (*ibid.*, 73). Having decided that it was possible, though unlikely, that the pits might pre-date the ramparts he wished to test this: 'I therefore caused a trench to be dug 33 feet [10 m] long and four [1.2 m] in width, in that part of the bottom of the ditch which was nearest to the pits' (*ibid.*, 74). He found a quantity of worked flints on the bottom of the ditch and concluded that the fortifications were probably contemporary with the flint workings. Throughout these excavations at Cissbury he was dating by the typology of objects found in negative features. It does not seem to have occurred to him at this time to excavate part of the rampart to find objects in a more secure context or to see whether any pits were sealed by the earthwork.

As this was the first major excavation that Fox undertook it is important to assess his motives. It has become the accepted view that Fox's interest in archaeology at this time was merely as a source of objects to build up typologies (Bradley 1983, 4; Thompson 1977, 48). This view is not unreasonable given Fox's own statement that:

> Notwithstanding the great difficulty of collecting the necessary materials for displaying a connected series of such forms, a difficulty fully equal to that which the geologist experiences in arranging his palaeontological sequence, this fundamental maxim is nevertheless capable of clear demonstration in any well-assorted collection of early and savage implements, and embodies, I believe, the pith and marrow of pretty nearly all that can be extracted from the study of prehistoric and comparative archaeology. (Fox 1869b, 70)

It is also supported by the very lengthy and detailed discussion of flint types included in the Cissbury report and by the fact that the report is illustrated by a double plate of flint drawings but no site plan or any other plan or section drawing. On the other hand there are indications that Fox was digging out of a genuine interest in the archaeology of the site itself, and not just as a means of collecting flints. In the first place there is his own statement on the aims of the excavation, quoted above, in which attention is to be paid to the precise location of finds and the bearing which this might have on the history of the fort. Secondly there is a fairly detailed description of the pits excavated with a discussion of their function and date as well as the 'still more interesting question whether the intrenchment was coeval or subsequent to the pits' (*ibid.*, 73). Thirdly, his previous fieldwork on the Sussex hillforts and elsewhere had tended to advance general archaeological knowledge rather than artefact typology because site survey had been at least as enthusiastically pursued as surface collection or excavation. Finally, there is the influence of Canon Greenwell to be considered. Greenwell had come to dig with Fox at Cissbury during the January 1868 season (Fox 1875b, 361). Greenwell clearly believed in a wider application for archaeological fieldwork than the collection of objects. The resolution of this apparent contradiction in Fox's aims at this time probably lies in the wider interpretation of the term 'typology' to include not merely portable objects but also earthworks and monuments and, by extension, the building up of a secure chronology for all aspects of human history. Following from this, Thompson is incorrect in suggesting that Fox could not, or did not, attempt to interpret the pits he dug at Cissbury and that it was only after Greenwell's lecture on Grimes Graves in 1870 that he realised that they might be flint mines (1977, 48, 50–1). On the contrary, Fox approached the matter of the pits very firmly: 'For what use then were they formed? I am inclined to think for the purpose of obtaining flints . . . This would account for the great depth to which some of the pits had been sunk and I am much confirmed in this opinion by finding that Mr Evans, from a description given him of the place, had arrived at precisely the same conclusion that I had formed on the spot' (Fox 1869b, 73).

OXFORDSHIRE AND THE ISLE OF THANET, APRIL AND SEPTEMBER 1868

In April 1868 Fox was staying at Dytchley Park, the home of his wife's uncle, Lord Dillon. He later reported to the Ethnological Society 'some evidence of the Romanised Britons that I happen to have stumbled upon . . . the tendency of which is to prove that there must have existed, during the Roman period in this country, a class of people who employed flint tools . . .' (Fox 1868a, 1). He apologised for bringing such an apparently uninteresting subject to their attention but said that 'our knowledge of prehistoric times is so scanty . . . that almost any evidence calculated to add to our information upon these subjects seems to be worthy of record' (*ibid.*, 2), an early example of his appreciation of the importance of unspectacular evidence to archaeology. While staying at Dytchley he had examined the country between Kidlington, Charlbury and Woodstock, an area bounded to the north and east by Grimes Dyke. True to his interest in linear earthworks, he described the dyke before going on to discuss the results of his fieldwalking. 'It is not merely a boundary, but without doubt a fortification, for its commanding position, its adaptation to the features of the ground, and the situation of the ditch, are points which, viewed tactically, are sufficient to determine it to be a work of defence' (*ibid.*, 3). He considered its similarity to the Yorkshire dykes but concluded that its relationship to Roman sites suggested that it was contemporary with them. He then went on to describe briefly the sites which he had studied. At Callow Hill he found Roman pottery and tile fragments with flint flakes and scrapers but the limits of both flint and pot scatters being coterminous afforded 'very strong presumptive evidence for associating the flints and pottery together in point of time' (*ibid.*, 4). The same discovery was made at Devil's Pool where he not only made a surface collection but also excavated a small area and found 'part of a Roman floor . . . Immediately to the north, adjoining this structure, about an acre of ground was covered with the *debris* of flint manufacture' (*ibid.*, 4–5). Here again he examined 'a considerable tract of country to the north, west and south of the area which is contiguous to the pavement, without discovering a single flint . . . we may perhaps be allowed to conjecture that the flints . . . may mark the residences of British slaves, who dwelt . . . in the immediate vicinity of their master's house' (*ibid.*, 5–6). Fox was not entirely happy about the attribution of flint technology to the Roman period, however, and he stressed that 'it is necessary to bear in mind that as all these remains were found on the surface, there is always a possibility of their having belonged to different periods, notwithstanding the circumstances which in this case appear to warrant us in associating them together' (*ibid.*, 6).

The problem of the association of flintwork and Roman remains arose again later in the year when Fox spent some time in east Kent. He examined an extensive area around Margate, Ramsgate and Broadstairs in which he found three flint scatters. He did not record their location. At the same time some labourers digging for brickearth between St Peters and Reading Street had discovered some pot sherds and a large pit. Fox 'determined to have it dug out' (*ibid.*, 8–9). They found flint implements, nails, animal bones, shells and Romano-British pottery throughout the fill 'in such a manner as to leave no doubt that both the flints and the animal remains must have been deposited at the same time as the pottery' (*ibid.*, 10). This pit, like those at Cissbury, he interpreted as a flint mine. The flints in the pit he saw as 'survivals' of earlier tool forms that had continued in use into the later, Romano-British period. Now they would be treated as residual material.

Fox made no attempt to locate any of the findspots or excavation trenches accurately in this report and he published no maps or plans. More significantly he did not, by written description or by illustration, record the tessellated floor at Devil's Pool. This is in striking contrast with much of his later work and shows how little he appreciated the need for precision in recording at this time. On the other hand these two pieces of fieldwork do illustrate two increasingly important aspects of Fox's work, his wish to create a more solid chronology for British prehistory and the Romano-British period through typology, the only means available to him, and his realisation of the crucial significance of the apparently mundane in the study of archaeology.

Between these two episodes of fieldwork Fox was busy with the International Congress of Prehistoric Archaeology, which met that year at Norwich and London from 20 to 28 August, and of which he was General Secretary. His archaeological fieldwork had been comparatively limited up to this time and his appointment as Secretary to the Congress owed much to his acquaintance with the leading British archaeologists and men of science and to a reputation for organisational skills connected with his work for the Ethnological and Anthropological Societies (Chapman 1989). Apart from the number of names distinguished in British and European archaeology listed as delegates to the Congress it is noteworthy how many family connections of Fox's wife were in attendance, among them Lord Stanley of Alderley, William Owen Stanley, the Dean of Westminster and the Hon. Charles Howard MP. Contributors of papers included many close associates of Fox, such as Tylor, Lubbock, Huxley, Boyd Dawkins, Evans and Franks. The Committee had issued a list of twelve topics which they suggested as general themes for the Congress, of which three particularly seem to bear Fox's stamp; 'Intrenchments, and Implements of War', 'Existing Customs and Implements as Illustrators of Prehistoric Times' and 'Indications of Continuous Progress in Arts and Civilisation During Successive Prehistoric Periods' (International Congress 1869).

HOLYHEAD, AUTUMN 1868

In 1861 Alice Fox's uncle William Owen Stanley of Penrhos, a keen antiquarian (Smith 1984), had excavated three unenclosed hut circles at Ty Mawr on Holyhead Mountain. A report, including detailed measured drawings, ethnographic parallels and a finds report by Albert Way, was duly published (Stanley 1867) and in 1868 Stanley returned to the site to excavate nine more hut circles. On this occasion he was accompanied by his nephew Fox. The more systematic approach and more detailed recording carried out in this second campaign may have been due to Fox's influence (Smith 1984, 87) though it is equally possible that some experience was passing in the other direction, especially in view of the concerns shown by Stanley in his first report which are echoed in so much of Fox's later work.

THAMES GRAVEL TERRACES, JANUARY–JUNE 1869

At the beginning of 1869 Fox was using his own house in Phillimore Gardens, Kensington as a base for fieldwork in the area around Acton. The relatively recent vindication of Boucher de Perthes' work in the Somme valley by Lubbock, Evans and others caused him to turn his mind to Palaeolithic matters. There is some doubt as to whether Fox chose this moment to study the gravel terraces at Acton because building work was being carried out there or whether that was a happy coincidence. He described his discoveries to the Geological Society (Fox 1872a) and again as part of a longer lecture at the Whitechapel Foundation School in 1875 (Pitt Rivers Papers P42).

The audience at this lecture consisted, according to a note by Fox at the head of the draft, 'partly of the members of the literary & scientific society there & partly of tradesmen & working classes of the neighbourhood'. It was evidently difficult for him to pitch the lecture so as to hold the interest of such a heterogeneous audience but he attempted to do so by referring frequently to everyday experience. In the course of the lecture he explained that he was introducing the subject of the gravel terraces because 'as it relates to the valley of the Thames at Acton, close above London, the locality may possibly be known to some of those present.' He had already described cultural evolution in terms of the experiences of a railway passenger and now he fixed the attention of his audience on the new subject by saying, 'The River Thames, as most of those are aware, who have been up to Richmond by the steam boat, makes several broad bends in the comparatively flat bottom of the valley between Richmond and Battersea.'

After describing the geology and topography of the terraces he explained the nature of his discoveries and the conclusions which he drew from them. House foundations were being dug in the high terrace at Acton and as this terrace was similar in appearance to the one in which de Perthes had found Palaeolithic implements Fox determined to watch the excavations. He found nothing for 'some months of constant watching' but then his patience was rewarded by the discovery of several implements and an elephant's tooth within stratified seams of sand and gravel '80 to 100 feet [24.4–30.5 m] above the present river mean tide.' Fox then described the animal remains he had found at the middle terrace level, including elephant, rhinoceros, hippopotamus and various types of extinct deer. Finally he described the Neolithic and Bronze Age discoveries that had been made in the river itself, showing that

> the river ran in its present winding course at that time and probably much earlier and this gives us some idea of the great length of time it must have taken to erode the whole valley . . . for in doing this it must not only have shifted its course over every portion of the valley, which is here 4½ miles wide, but it must have gone over the same ground repeatedly at different levels . . . and yet we see that the course of the river changes so slowly that it has certainly run in its present course 2000 years or more. (Pitt Rivers Papers P42).

The paper presented to the Geological Society was more technical and detailed and was accompanied by a report on the animal bones by George Busk. Fox also describes in this paper how he offered rewards to the workmen for every implement or animal bone found (1872a, 453) and how careful he was to verify the findspots, something which had concerned him ever since his Irish experiences:

> In all cases . . . I took particular care to test the accuracy of the statements of the workmen as to the exact positions of the implements, and I have no doubt of their

correctness in each case. Shortly after I commenced my visits to Acton, some rather ingenious attempts at forgery were foisted upon me, by chipping, varnishing, and, when dry, burying the flints thus prepared in the ground. (*ibid.*, 458).

When he demonstrated that he was not to be taken in by such forgeries the practice stopped.

NORTH WALES, OCTOBER 1869

The Autumn of 1869 found Fox visiting his maternal uncle, Lord Penrhyn, at Penrhyn Castle near Bangor. On this occasion Fox undertook one of his rare barrow excavations, opening two cairns on Moel Faben near the Castle. The decision to do this work was clearly taken on the spur of the moment: 'The cairns . . . stand out so conspicuously upon the hilltop, that I was unable to resist the temptation of examining them . . .' (Fox 1870b, 307) and this episode, more than any other, demonstrates the 'country house weekend' setting of Fox's fieldwork at this time: '. . . on 16th. October 1869 I ascended the hill, accompanied by three gardeners whose services Lady Penrhyn had kindly placed at my disposal' (*ibid.*). A broken urn was discovered and restored, 'an operation which was kindly undertaken and efficiently executed by one of the ladies in the house' (*ibid.*, 307–8).

However, this should not detract from the serious purpose with which the work was invested. Having thoroughly investigated the cairns Fox examined some nearby hut circles and noted the presence of 'lines of cultivation'. The report concludes with a lengthy discussion of finds from barrows and cairns in Wales and the west of England, distinguishing those containing bronzes from those containing flint only and those containing worked stone, and commenting on the almost infinite variation in style of cinerary urns. His concern was the creation of a relative chronology for these differing deposits. He would give no firm opinion as to the date of the cairns he had opened though he felt that they were probably of the Bronze Age: 'To future explorers must be left the credit of determining this point, I would only suggest in conclusion, that it might be worth while to re-examine, with this object, some of the cists in which bronze weapons have been previously discovered (*ibid.*, 320).' The report is therefore more than a record for posterity; it is the statement of a particular problem and offers a research strategy for approaching it.

PROPOSED EXPLORATION OF STONEHENGE, 1869

The British Association formed a Committee to undertake excavation and restoration work at Stonehenge with Fox as a prominent member. The landowner, Sir Edmund Antrobus, was able to ensure that the excavations never took place (Chippindale 1983a, 61) but Fox did some fieldwalking in the vicinity. His report to the Ethnological Society reveals that he had already acquired a firm grasp of the conditions required for surface artefact collection: '. . . I was able to examine a field close by that had been ploughed, rolled, and subsequently washed by rain, and which was therefore in the best possible condition for finding the flints, had there been any' (Fox 1869c, 3).

DORCHESTER DYKES, OXFORDSHIRE, 1870

On 21 June 1870 Fox read a short paper to the Ethnological Society on the subject of the hillfort on the Sinodun Hills and the earthworks on the north bank of the Thames at Dorchester. The reason for this was his concern over the destruction of the Dorchester Dykes as they were flattened in order that the land could be brought under the plough. He gave a brief description of both the hillfort and the Dykes, which he believed to be a connected series of earthworks. He had collected material from the Dykes but it is not clear whether he had undertaken any excavations. He mentions a 'fresh cutting' through the northern rampart but does not specify whether this was an archaeological investigation or part of the destructive works (Fox 1870c, 413). St George Gray certainly believed that Fox had excavated the Dykes himself (1929a, 20).

Fox visited the landowner personally and was able to persuade him to cease the levelling 'for the present'. However, he 'could obtain no assurance that it would not be continued at some future time' (Fox 1870c, 415). Some of Fox's frustration and disappointment is apparent. It is greatly to his credit that he undertook personally the attempt to save these earthworks from destruction in the absence of any formal action by public authorities or by archaeological and scientific societies, and his experience at Dorchester must have had a bearing on his later work as Inspector of Ancient Monuments. It is remarkable that he did not advocate excavation as a form of 'rescue' in this case. He may have felt that his own brief fieldwork had recovered all that could be expected in terms of information from the site. Alternatively this approach may represent the transition between his support for 'rescue' excavation in Ireland and his later advocacy of total preservation wherever possible.

It is perhaps also notable in this context that 1870 was the year in which Fox's colleague, Sir John Lubbock, began the work which was to culminate in the Ancient Monuments Act of 1882.

BLACKBURGH TUMULUS, AUGUST 1872

On a previous visit to Brighton Fox had noticed the round barrow by the Dyke Road 'known to the peasantry of the neighbourhood from time immemorial as the Black Burgh' (Fox 1876a, 280). He took the opportunity offered by the meeting of the British Association at Brighton in 1872 to open the barrow.

He began by drawing a profile of the mound from north to south. The detailed recording of the surface morphology of a monument before excavation was a matter which Fox had not always attended to previously, but it was to become increasingly important to him. A wooden three-dimensional model of the Blackburgh Tumulus in the Salisbury Museum may be the earliest in the series of archaeological site models. It appears to show a simplified surface morphology, presumably based on this one north-south profile. Later models were made from detailed contour surveys. Fox drove a trench 20 feet (6.1 m) wide from the southern edge of the mound towards the centre in traditional antiquarian style, but he recorded the results with considerable thoroughness. He found postholes and stakeholes sealed beneath the mound, a phenomenon he had come across before on the Yorkshire Wolds. He was to find them again at Merrow Down and he mentions 'a number of them in a tumulus opened by me near Aldborough, in Suffolk' (*ibid.*, 281) which is otherwise apparently unrecorded.

Below the turf the top of the mound was covered with a fairly dense scatter of waste flakes and scrapers. Towards the centre of the mound was a two inch (5 cm) thick layer of oak charcoal. Fox also found animal bones, pottery and a modern iron shetlink. All this was carefully recorded. A central grave contained a crouched inhumation accompanied by a bronze knife-dagger and awl, an accessory cup of unusual form and a number of shale beads. Several sherds of medieval pottery, thought by Fox to be Romano-British, were discovered in the mound and may relate to a grave robbing episode. Fox recognised the cut of this robber trench in the section but interpreted it as a secondary interment (*ibid.*, 285).

Fox concluded his report with an early example of the characteristic homily on the subject of archaeological recording and publication:

> I trust that the minute details of measurement that I have given will not be found very tedious . . . comparatively few of these barrows are now left to be explored, and upon those who dig into them devolves the duty of recording carefully what they find. In our present state of ignorance concerning them we cannot tell upon what points of detail theories in after ages may be made to turn . . . If we must err, therefore, it is well that it should be on the side of accuracy. (*ibid.*, 286)

The importance of recording techniques is firmly related to theoretical requirements, lending force to Bradley's argument (1983, 9) that the General was not merely an 'unreflecting technician.'

CISSBURY, APRIL AND JUNE–SEPTEMBER 1875

In 1873 and 1874 Fox appears to have undertaken no fieldwork, except for brief participation in William Owen Stanley's excavation at Ynys Lyrad (Smith 1984, 87), perhaps because of the increased pressure of military duties consequent on his new post at Guildford. A number of considerations, however, led him back to a re-examination of Cissbury in the Spring of 1875. As he remarked, the increase of knowledge about Cissbury, and about flint mines, had been 'a work of slow and gradual development' (Fox 1875b, 357) but in the few years since his previous excavations there the tempo had increased.

Unknown to Fox flint mines had been discovered in Belgium before his excavations at Cissbury in 1868. These mines, at Spiennes, were first discovered in 1847 but were not fully explored until the 1860s when mining and railway building uncovered large numbers of shafts. Fox described them in some detail in his second Cissbury report (*ibid.*, 361–3). Secondly, in 1870 Canon Greenwell had carried out his remarkably successful excavations at Grimes Graves, Norfolk. The fact that drove Fox back to Cissbury, however, was that other people had been excavating there in the interval. Mr Tyndall of Brighton excavated one of the Cissbury shafts but 'unfortunately died before he could make a proper record of his excavation' (*ibid.*, 364) and Ernest Willett dug another with spectacular results, finding galleries similar to those at Grimes Graves.

Fox began his second campaign at Cissbury in 1875 by reopening two of the large pits, one previously excavated by himself and one by Canon Greenwell. He immediately came to the conclusion that they had not bottomed the pits and that they were considerably deeper than they had supposed. Having established that the pits were in fact the shafts of deep neolithic flint mines he approached the 'question of still greater anthropological interest' of the relative ages of the flint mines and the hillfort: 'Valuable as previous discoveries had already been, the opportunity thus afforded of establishing a sequence between these two distinct classes of prehistoric remains appeared to exceed them all in interest and importance' (*ibid.*, 365–6). Accordingly he opened another trench in the ditch. This trench he called a section though it ran along the length of the ditch rather than across it, as a modern section would. His description also indicates that it was dug in spits and not by stratigraphic layers. The finds from the ditch confirmed the pre-Roman dating of the earthworks already established but failed to give a firm relative chronology with the flint mines. Fox's description of the ditch indicates that it had been recut, though he did not note the fact himself.

Fox still needed to find a flint mine shaft in direct relationship with the hillfort rampart to establish their relative dates but his limited resources were already fully stretched and he now decided to approach the Anthropological Institute for assistance. With a subscription of £30 from the members of the Institute and, with the assistance of Mr J. Park Harrison, Professor Rolleston and Sir Alexander Gordon amongst others, Fox continued his explorations. He now cut a trench in the south-west corner of the hillfort, the only point at which flint mine shafts could be detected outside the ramparts as well as within. Having excavated the two shafts nearest the ramparts to ensure that they were in fact flint mines he began to excavate the adjacent section of hillfort ditch. At last Fox found what he had been seeking, a backfilled shaft cut by the hillfort ditch. He excavated the shaft and its radiating galleries. Subsequently he found a shaft sealed by the counterscarp bank and another sealed by the main rampart. A fourth shaft was discovered:

> As we had destroyed the evidence of the relative antiquity of the two works afforded by No. 1 escarp shaft, it was determined to preserve a section of this shaft, which might be seen by any geologists who might visit the diggings; accordingly we excavated only the half of this shaft which was nearest to the other, leaving a vertical section of the *filling* and *silting* across the middle. (*ibid.*, 373)

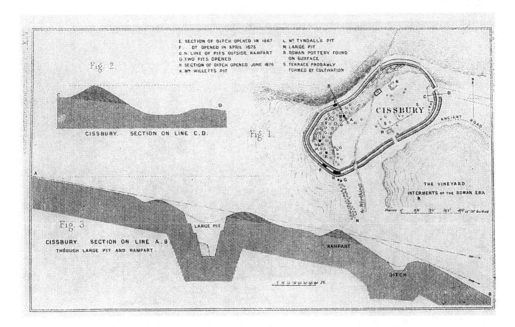

17 Plan of Cissbury with profiles of the ramparts

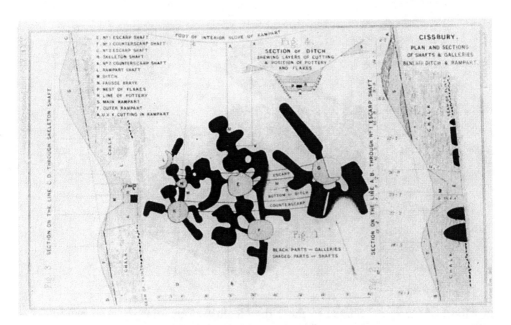

18 Plan and sections of the ramparts and flint mines, Cissbury

This section, of which a drawing was published (*ibid.*, pl. XVI), was in fact seen by Joseph Prestwich, Godwin Austen, John Evans and George Rolleston amongst others.

In following the galleries of the first shaft Fox made another exciting discovery when he found the bottom of another shaft:

19 Perspective drawing to illustrate the relationship between flint mine shaft and ramparts, Cissbury

20 Model of Cissbury, hinged to show the Neolithic flint mine galleries below the hillfort ramparts; carved wood. This is one of the General's earliest models

Presently a well formed and perfect lower human jaw fell down from above, and on looking up we could perceive the remainder of the skull fixed . . . between two pieces of chalk rubble. When I saw this I hollowed out so loudly that Mr. Harrison, who happened to be outside at the time . . . thought that it [the gallery] must have tumbled in, and came with a shovel to dig us out. It was some time before I could make him understand that we had added a third person to our party. (*ibid.*, 375)

The skull proved to be part of the complete skeleton of a woman buried in the shaft with the remains of several animals.

Only when he had explored six shafts and their galleries did Fox turn his full attention to the hillfort ramparts. He dug a section through the main rampart above his ditch section in the south-west corner of the fort. He identified a buried soil under the rampart, a turf stack at the front, the main body of the rampart formed of chalk from the ditch and no less than seven 'successive layers of turf and rubble' (*ibid.*, 379).

The excavations were concluded by the digging, in half-section, of another large mine shaft in the interior of the fort. This was abandoned due to the collapse of the fill after wet weather.

Throughout the excavations finds had been relatively scarce but all were carefully recorded and described, from sherds, pieces of worked chalk and flakes to snail shells, charcoal fragments and animal bones which were discussed in an appendix to the report by George Rolleston.

Fox's second campaign at Cissbury is significant for several reasons. First, it enabled him to make an important contribution to the study of flint mines, clearly a fashionable topic of archaeological research in the 1870s. More importantly it illustrates certain advances in his field techniques. Digging in spits rather than by stratigraphic contexts is the one serious weakness that can be isolated and it is one that remained to the end of the General's career (Pitt Rivers 1898, 26). The orientation of his ditch sections differs from his later practice and more recent orthodoxy but as the primary function of these trenches was to locate the mouths of mine shafts it is understandable. The greatest advance was in the recognition of stratigraphic relationships between different features and the use of the vertical section to demonstrate separate episodes in the filling and silting of features. The isolation of filling and silting as two distinct processes, one the result of human agency and the other entirely natural, also seems to originate from this excavation.

Finally the experimental work which Fox carried out while at Cissbury in 1875 should not be forgotten:

> In order to ascertain the exact mode of working the chalk by the prehistoric men, I made a set of deer-horn tools similar to those turned up in the diggings. Out of a pair of antlers I made two picks, one mandril, two wedges, and five tine punches. Cutting off the tines took me from five to ten minutes, and the best mode of making the wedges was found to be by grinding them on a wet sandstone. Commencing with a surface of hard, smooth chalk, and taking the work turn about with one of the men, I found that we had made an excavation 3 feet [0.9 m] square and 3 feet deep in an hour and a half, consequently, by continuous labour, and sufficient reliefs, it would have taken us twelve hours to form the longest gallery found, viz. 27 feet [8.2 m] . . . (Fox 1875b, 382)

SEAFORD CAMP, 1876

The excavations at Seaford were undertaken for both research and 'rescue' reasons. Fox had been less sure of the dating of this hillfort than of the others he had examined in Sussex because of the apparent angularity of its ramparts and because he could find no worked flints in or near it. There was in his mind the possibility that it was a Roman fort, though this possibility was much weakened when John Evans told him that he had found a few flakes there in 1867. This chronological question needed to be resolved so when it was reported, incorrectly as it turned out, that the cliff on which the fort stands was to be destroyed to form a breakwater Fox agreed to undertake the excavations on behalf of the Anthropological Institute (Fox 1876b).

The form of the ramparts occupied Fox's attention primarily but he restricted his efforts initially to careful reconnaissance and survey work. In his view 'The most characteristic feature of a British earthwork . . . consists in its conforming to the outline of the hill' (*ibid.*, 12) with the rampart placed so as to leave no dead ground. At Seaford, however, there were sections of the northern rampart where dead ground had been left so that '. . . the spectator from the rampart is unable to see . . . how much cover it might afford to an advancing enemy' (*ibid.*, 13). This problem was resolved to Fox's satisfaction by drawing a profile of the hillside and overlaying on it a 'line of vision' which showed that the rampart would have had to be five feet (1.5 m) higher in order to eliminate the dead ground. When he later discovered that the ditch contained seven feet (2.1 m) of silt he mentally transferred five feet of it to the rampart and concluded that the rampart of Seaford 'does actually fulfill the condition of a British camp' (*ibid.*, 14).

Before excavating the ditch, however, Fox had turned his attention to a mound within the fort which might have been either a barrow or part of the gateway defences. His description of the mound's shape implies that it may have been opened previously. Fox found no human remains but several sherds of 'British' pottery and a number of flint axes, axe fragments, hammerstones, flakes and a barbed and tanged arrowhead. One of the axes had clearly been deliberately broken on site and part of it deposited in a large hole below the barrow. For the first time Fox explicitly uses an anthropological parallel to explain an archaeological phenomenon:

> For what purpose could this breaking up of an implement over the grave of the deceased have been practised? We are reminded of the superstitious rites of some tribes of North American Indians, who break or otherwise destroy all the weapons of the deceased warriors before placing them in the graves, under the supposition that it is the soul of the defunct weapon which accompanies that of the defunct warrior into the happy hunting grounds of the life to come. (*ibid.*, 16)

A section was next cut in the ditch in the north-west part of the hillfort close to the cliff edge with the purpose of obtaining dating evidence. The upper filling or 'mould' contained medieval and Romano-British sherds, the primary fill contained nothing but a few sea pebbles, possibly used as sling stones. A cutting through the rampart yielded only two flakes.

The Prices, who owned the land, were meanwhile digging in the Roman cemetery to the north of the Camp and Fox himself opened a small trench there. The fact that he found flint flakes and a scraper in apparent association with the Romano-British cremation deposits tended to confirm him in the opinion he had formed after his fieldwork in Oxfordshire and Thanet and he referred to similar discoveries by Boyd Dawkins at Hardham, Sussex, but his mind was still open: 'The further excavations of the two Messrs Price will be of interest, however, in determining whether this cemetery contains any relics of an age prior to the Roman to which the flint flakes may have belonged' (*ibid.*, 20).

The question of whether Seaford Camp itself was of Roman or earlier date remained unsolved by direct artefactual evidence but Fox now believed it to be pre-Roman on morphological grounds.

BARROWS NEAR GUILDFORD, OCTOBER 1876 AND MAY 1877

Fox had bought a house at Merrow near Guildford when he took up his post as commander of the West Surrey Brigade Depot in 1873. At some time during the first three years of his residence there he noticed six small barrows near a neighbouring house on Merrow Down and in October 1876 he excavated them, though 'in doubt when he commenced whether they would turn out to be graves' (Fox 1877b). This excavation was reported but never fully described by Fox and it was not until his original notes and drawings (Pitt Rivers Papers, P40 and R7) came to light that a full account was published (Saunders 1980). The first three barrows contained cremations, the third accompanied by a knife which, Fox claimed, 'determines the whole cluster to be of the pagan Saxon period', dating which has been confirmed by modern scholarship (*ibid.*, 74). The remaining barrows yielded nothing and Fox's record of them is scanty. It is possible that further notes may have been made and subsequently lost but the discrepancy between the appeal for detailed recording at the end of the Blackburgh report and this apparent lack of recording at Merrow, and presumably at Aldborough, is noteworthy.

In the following May the General opened a further two barrows on Whitmore Common. Again the results of this excavation were only briefly reported (Fox 1877b) though the General's intention to publish more fully in this case is demonstrated by the existence of a printer's proof of the excavation plans and sections, eventually published by Gardner (1924). Both barrows contained Earlier Bronze Age urns containing cremated bone. The published plans show small trenches, in the case of Barrow 1 apparently circular, in the centre of the mounds. Barrow 2 had a ditch visible on the surface but no attempt was made to examine this or to look for a similar feature in the case of Barrow 1. The surface morphology of the barrows appears to have been recorded from a

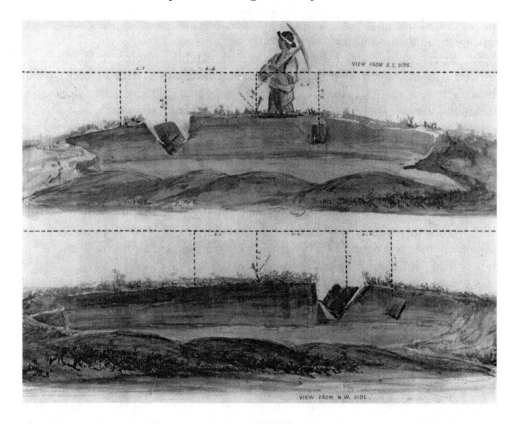

21 Watercolour sketch of the opening of one of the barrows on Merrow Down, Guildford

single transect, though some rather unconvincing contours have been added to the plan of Barrow 1.

SIGWELL, SOMERSET, JULY 1877

The excavation of three round barrows at Sigwell was a joint project carried out by Fox with his friend Professor George Rolleston. In fact it was much more than a simple excavation, for while Rolleston supervised the digging Fox's particular function was to undertake a survey, both of the site itself and of its surrounding landscape, and some fieldwalking.

The 'twin' barrows were excavated first, then the outlier, each barrow taking two or three days to dig with a team of about seven men. In the first barrow they found nothing, in the second a cremation and a bronze dagger in a bark container and in the third a cremation with sherds, flints, signs of burning and stakeholes in the buried soil. In the discussion (Rolleston and Fox 1878) three questions were raised: the variety in modes of burial in the Bronze Age, the smallness of the burial deposit in proportion to the size of the barrow (this as a caution to careless excavators rather than as an archaeological observation) and the relative position of the third barrow to a 'British camp' which they considered was earlier than the barrow. The report concluded with an anthropological description of the amount of fuel and length of time required to cremate a human body and Fox's interpretation of Sigwell camp as an outpost of the hillfort at South Cadbury which 'affording as it does some insight into the social condition and military organization of the inhabitants of this district at a very remote period, may be regarded as being of some interest to anthropologists' (ibid., 191).

This project is of interest mainly for its appreciation of the barrows as part of a historical landscape and also for the attempt to create a two-way traffic of information between archaeology and other branches of anthropology.

MOUNT CABURN, SEPTEMBER–OCTOBER 1877 AND JULY 1878

Mount Caburn is a small but impressively sited hillfort on a summit of the South Downs overlooking Lewes. This, perhaps the General's best known early excavation, was undertaken with a workforce of between three and five men over two short seasons. A number of pits within the hillfort were excavated and their use for grain storage discussed (Pitt Rivers 1881a, 449) and the ramparts and ditches sectioned. The ramparts of the neighbouring site called Ranscombe Camp were also examined.

This episode reveals many of the weaknesses and strengths of Fox's methods. On the debit side must be placed his continued failure to make the most of the stratigraphic section for proving the relative chronology of features, underscored by his statement that he had 'no means of determining' the relationship of two intercutting pits (ibid., 440). Similarly ditch fills were still dug in spits and no section drawing of the ramparts of Mount Caburn was published though one of Ranscombe Camp was. On the credit side must be set the discovery of small features, such as stakeholes, the noting of snail shell evidence, the intelligent interpretation of both pits and defences and the attempt to conserve badly preserved animal bone by soaking in size (ibid., 431, 453, 462–4).

Fox's continuing commitment to evolutionary schemes is demonstrated by a lengthy discussion of bone combs and dot-and-circle decoration (ibid., 431–4, 436–7) while the essentially gentlemanly aspect of the exercise is recalled vividly by his description of the wattle impressions in daub found in one of the pits: '. . . the osiers were exactly one third of an inch in diameter, exactly the size of those of a large hamper I happened to have by me' (ibid., 456).

Mount Caburn also shares with Caesar's Camp the distinction of being the first site for which a Relic Table was published. The Relic Table, which was to become one of the hallmarks of the General's later work, was a tabulated record of every feature excavated, giving the date of excavation, artefacts recovered and dimensions, and in a sense represents the pinnacle of the General's 'scientific' recording techniques.

CAESAR'S CAMP, FOLKESTONE, JUNE–JULY 1878

The excavation at the supposed hillfort Caesar's Camp ran more or less concurrently with the second season at Mount Caburn and though the actual digging only occupied just over two weeks with a workforce of between eight and ten labourers a good deal was achieved. The supposed topographical similarity of Caesar's Camp to Mount Caburn was the starting point of the excavation, the idea being, according to the published report, to 'see to what extent we are justified, if at all, in forming an opinion upon the date of an entrenchment by its external appearance' (Pitt Rivers 1883c, 429). Caesar's Camp does not, in fact, very much resemble Mount Caburn, expt in topographical siting, and it was perhaps no great surprise to the General that Caesar's Camp proved to be not a prehistoric hillfort but a medieval castle.

He set out 'to cut several sections through the ditches and ramparts, and to observe what relics might be found on the line of the old surface, beneath the rampart, and in the bottoms of the ditches, to excavate the pits . . . to cut trenches in the interior to ascertain whether any foundations of habitations could be discovered . . .' (*ibid.*, 434). To counter any incredulity that the 'relics' proved to be medieval the General insists repeatedly on the reliability of his evidence: 'In order that the evidence obtained may be strictly reliable it should, if possible, be of a character that might be accepted in a court of justice' (*ibid.*, 436).

As noted before Caesar's Camp was, with Mount Caburn, the first site for which Relic Tables were prepared and published though our faith in them as scientific aids may be somewhat lessened by the comment on the pottery sherds in the 'Remarks' column that 'there were numerous small fragments, less than 1 inch [2.5 cm] across, not counted' (*ibid.*, 438). The General's work at Caesar's Camp has been claimed as the first scientific excavation of a medieval site in Britain (Bennett 1988, 17).

BRITTANY, OCTOBER–NOVEMBER 1878 AND MARCH–APRIL 1879

The excavation at Caesar's Camp and the second brief season at Mount Caburn in the summer of 1878 brought to an end Fox's fieldwork on the south coastal downs. In the following autumn and spring he visited Brittany where he carried out surveys of megalithic and earthwork monuments. Thompson has rather whimsically called these 'practice' trips, suggesting that Fox went to Brittany simply to prepare himself for the role of Inspector of Ancient Monuments which he was to take up in 1883 (1960; 1977, 61). However, Lubbock's Ancient Monuments Bill, which he had been trying to push through Parliament for the best part of ten years, did not reach the House of Lords until 1879 and even then it was clear that the Bill could not survive the impending dissolution of Parliament. Lubbock does not seem to have raised the question of who should fill the role of Inspector of Ancient Monuments until the Bill was finally passed. On 25 October 1882 he wrote to the General to ask who he thought would be the best man for the job: 'You know the Monuments as well as anyone but I presume you would not think of it' (Pitt Rivers Papers AM1). If Lubbock was genuine in phrasing himself thus, and this was in a private letter, it weakens Thompson's case for seeing the Brittany trips as practice for the Inspectorate, though it remains possible, of course, that this was in the back of Fox's mind.

Fox's interest in Brittany seems more likely to have stemmed from the 1868 International Congress at Norwich where the Rev. W. C. Lukis had drawn attention to the destruction of the Brittany megaliths. A committee, on which both Fox and Lubbock served, had been set up to deal with this problem (International Congress 1869, 417). It is more than likely that Fox's travels to Brittany were a result of this commitment rather than a back door method of practising field survey techniques. Thompson was perhaps misled by the accident that the General's Brittany notebooks were at some time filed with his official Inspectorate notebooks and are now perpetually united with them (PRO WORK 39/1 and 2).

Fox seems to have travelled to Brittany alone. He spent about a month there on either occasion in the course of which he surveyed about twenty-three megalithic monuments. Many of these surveys consisted of a perspective sketch and measured sketch plan. In addition he made notes and sketches of church architecture, Roman remains and various objects of archaeological and ethno-archaeological interest. Most of the megaliths were recorded on the first visit. The second visit was dominated by these miscellaneous items (Thompson 1960, 104–5).

DENMARK, SUMMER 1879

In the summer of 1879 Fox travelled to Scandinavia with George Rolleston. While in Schleswig they visited the Dannewerke, a major multi-period linear earthwork crossing the Danish peninsula: 'Borrowing a spade from a neighbouring cottage we dug into this rampart at a place where a natural breach had already been partly made' (Pitt Rivers 1881a, 460). They discovered timber lacing within the rampart, a construction technique which they then noticed elsewhere along the line of the earthwork, presumably in other places where erosion had exposed the timbers. The only publication of this exercise was a single paragraph in the Mount Caburn report which gave no locational information and was not illustrated. No dating evidence was recorded.

DANE'S DYKE, OCTOBER 1879

Since he had worked in the Wolds with Greenwell in 1867 Fox had intended to return to the area to excavate the Dane's Dyke on Flamborough Head, but the idea had never found much favour with his 'archaeological friends, most of whom thought, and with much reason, that the chance of finding anything . . .

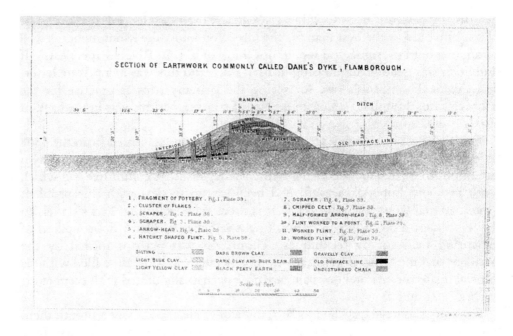

22 Section of Dane's Dyke

was too remote to warrant the undertaking' (Pitt Rivers 1882a, 463). However, with increasing experience of excavating earthworks Fox decided that there was a good chance of finding some dating evidence for the Dyke. He was sure that the Dane's Dyke represented the bridgehead of an invading force coming ashore at Flamborough, a view which Greenwell had already put forward on his behalf (1877, 123–4), and that the other dykes on the Wolds represented stages in the westward advance of this invading force, or in its subsequent retreat, but the date of this invasion was an open question (Pitt Rivers 1882a, 455–62).

The excavation was finally begun in October 1879, Fox choosing a location close to the point where a stream passes through the Dyke on the grounds that 'as this was a spot from which water supply had been obtained by the defenders, they would probably have congregated on the rampart and dropped their utensils about in this place' (*ibid.*, 463). Fox describes in some detail the excavation method he adopted:

> The cutting was made by a succession of trenches 20 feet [6.1 m] in length and 8 to 10 feet [2.4–3.0 m] wide, side by side, commencing the first trench near the foot of the interior slope, and throwing the earth towards the inside of the rampart; the second trench was dug above and parallel to it, throwing the earth into the first trench, and so on; By this means a section 20 feet wide through the rampart was obtained. The objects found were noted hour by hour as the work went on and the position of anything of importance was at once taken with a spirit level. (*ibid.*, 463–4)

A baulk 1 ft (0.3 m) wide was left between each trench. Four trenches were completely dug at which point Fox considered that he had obtained 'sufficient evidence'. A fifth trench was subsequently opened in the rampart crest but taken down only about 1.6 m. Fox explained that: 'By cutting a rampart in this way I have found that a cleaner section can be taken, and the position of the objects marked with greater accuracy than by cutting a continuous section through' (*ibid.*, 464). Why this should be so is not made clear but the published section drawing (*ibid.*, opp. 468) is the most detailed that Fox had produced up until this time.

Fox's optimism concerning the abundance of finds proved to be justified. A number of flint flakes, implements, axes and one sherd were found in the body of the rampart and a scraper and an arrowhead on the old ground surface. Then in the fifth trench a knapping floor was discovered at the top of the rampart:

> About 4 o'clock on the 23rd. October, three of the men digging into the rampart at about 2 feet [0.6 m] beneath the crest, viz., Robson, Gilbank and Jordan-Bilton, drew my attention to the fact that all the flakes they were finding lay horizontally in the earth. I immediately went to the spot and shortly picked out 10 flakes with my own hands all lying perfectly horizontally in the earth . . . they were evidently in the position in which they had fallen . . . as they were thrown down by the people who made them . . . an extension of the trench was made along the dyke to the south, I myself observing the position of every flint flake as it lay in the earth; 57 more flakes were here found, every one of which lay horizontally in the ground . . . but on extending the cutting beyond the crest towards the outside of the rampart no more flakes were found. This I attribute to the fact of there having been a stockade on the top of the rampart, and the defenders naturally moved about and performed their ordinary avocations behind and not in front of it. (*ibid.*, 466)

There is no mention of the possibility of finding any physical remains of this 'stockade'.

Fox now had no doubt of the date of the Dane's Dyke. It 'is not later than the bronze period; it is, in fact, of the same age as the tumuli of the Yorkshire Wolds' (*ibid.*, 467). He reiterated his belief that the other dykes on the Wolds must be of the same period.

An appendix to the report listed the physical measurements and description of eighty-nine inhabitants of Flamborough village, which was supposed to have been virtually cut off from the rest of Yorkshire until recent times. Fox, who noted that he took all the measurements himself, discerned 'little or no trace of the fair-haired element, which is generally observable in this part of Yorkshire' (*ibid.*, 470) but came to no other explicit conclusions. Nor does he tell us how the operation was organised. The measurement of troops under his own command (Fox 1877a) was, no doubt, easy to arrange but the measurement of an independent community of fishermen and fishwomen, agricultural labourers and tradesmen must have caused more problems.

NILE VALLEY, EGYPT, MARCH 1881

A Thomas Cook's Tour, perhaps a celebration of his recently acquired wealth, was the occasion for one of the General's most important and controversial discoveries.

The origin of worked flint and chert found in abundance on the surface in the Nile valley had been causing some discussion in anthropological circles in recent years. Some scholars believed that they represented tools used by the Egyptians of dynastic and classical times in the digging and decoration of tombs and embalming of corpses, while others, including Sir John Lubbock, thought that they represented a much earlier, Palaeolithic, phase of activity. Pitt Rivers, as Fox had by now become, with his considerable experience of river gravel deposits, decided to investigate the matter. All previous discoveries had been of surface material and thus lacked an archaeological context. Pitt Rivers knew that the only way of proving the Palaeolithic origin of the flints, the hypothesis which he preferred, was to find them *in situ*, stratified within the riverine deposits. However, he was concerned to be fair to both sides in the debate and by experiment he demonstrated that flint and chert could indeed be used for carving hieroglyphs in either sandstone or limestone (Pitt Rivers 1881c, 383–4).

On 4 March he began his investigations in a series of tombs cut into the side of a wadi at Koorneh near Thebes. Almost immediately he found struck flakes of chert embedded in the gravel into which the tombs, themselves not later than Eighteenth Dynasty in date, were cut. Knowing that this discovery was to be controversial Pitt Rivers was careful to find flakes embedded in the gravel in such a way that they could not have been accidentally struck by the tomb diggers and to bring a reliable witness to the scene. This witness, the geologist J. F. Campbell, described the event:

> Yesterday will probably make a paper for the learned Societies, on flints, &c, so I may as well write my private paper to you for comparison, without consultation with General Pitt Rivers . . . There is no sort of question about the antiquity of temples and tombs in which inscriptions tell the story: 1500 BC. The shape of the street of tombs was much the same as it is now. The delta of this waddy had been built and cemented, and a late direction had been given by it to running water, which caused the water to undercut the hard gravel and make cliffs, before the tomb [builders], however, drove their galleries into the gravel. 'If you, with your knowledge and authority, can find anything of human work in that hard gravel,' said I to P. Rivers, 'you will find something beyond calculation older than these Egyptian temples and tombs.' He went back, and he found worked flints in the hard gravel.
>
> Yesterday we went together. We sought in the walls of hewn tombs for ends of flints. When our authority pronounced favourably of the appearance of an end, James (my servant) and I hammered and worked about it, till it was got out. Many were rejected, many were selected, one had been cut off in hewing the tomb. It came out a finished 'flake', with the bulb of percussion far inside in the hard gravel. I am witness to the find and its place. It is a work of human art according to a good judge.

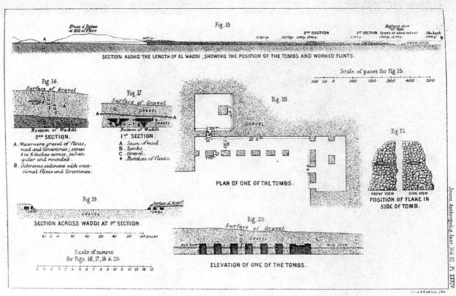

PLANS AND SECTIONS AT EL WADDI, SHOWING THE POSITION OF THE IMPLEMENTS.

23 Plan, elevation and sections of the tombs at El Waddi, Nile Valley

It belongs to the geological delta formation, and beyond question it is older beyond calculation than the tomb which was cut into the gravel, and cut through the end of this particular flint flake. We got more, and they are being marked for the famous collection at South Kensington.

This is my story of yesterday's work, which may yet live in history as a date from which to calculate the antiquity of man. (*ibid.*, 396–7)

This was undoubtedly a discovery of major import. The controversy which arose after the publication of Pitt Rivers' paper was based entirely around the question of whether the flakes he had found were man-made at all or whether they were the result of natural breakage. Pitt Rivers had partly anticipated this problem and in his paper had insisted on his experience both with the study of river gravel deposits and with flint working:

For some years I had made a particular study of river gravels. I had discovered palaeolithic implements *in situ* in the drift gravel at Acton . . . I had also examined every section in which palaeolithic implements had been found by others in England or on the Continent. Following the example of Dr. John Evans, F.R.S. . . . I had myself constructed flint implements many years ago, and had by that means acquired a thorough knowledge of the fracture of flint, a qualification of the first necessity to any one who proposes to examine a section of gravel for this purpose . . . (*ibid.*, 389)

Despite these well established claims Sir J. W. Dawson, the Canadian geologist, gave it as his opinion that the flints Pitt Rivers and Campbell had found

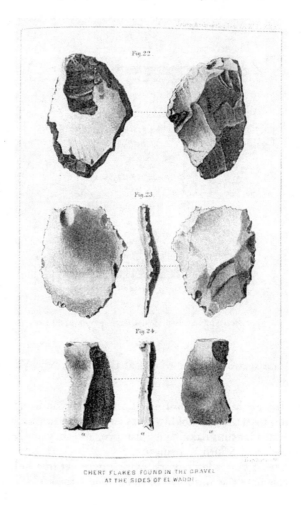

24 The flakes found in the sides of the tombs at El Waddi

were natural forms. Pitt Rivers was forced to reiterate his case in his Presidential Address to the Royal Archaeological Institute in 1897:

> The production of a single bulb on the flat side of the flint, two or more facets at the back with the hollows left by the bulbs of flakes previously struck off on them, and the small flat surface at the top, being the residuum of the flat surface of the core on which the blow was given to flake it off, all formed by blows delivered nearly at the same spot and in the same direction, could not possibly be produced otherwise than by the hand of man. This is an axiom so thoroughly established as to be familiar to the merest tyro in prehistoric investigations. (Pitt Rivers 1897, 313)

One further incident of the 1881 trip to Egypt remains to be mentioned, although Pitt Rivers himself apparently made no record of it. On 22 February Flinders Petrie had recorded in his diary:

I heard a traveller say to his dragoman, 'Wait, I want to take an angle here.' So I looked up, & after observing . . . the traveller said 'We seem to be working in the same line' & began chatting. Finding I was doing it [a survey of the Great Pyramid] on such a scale, he asked if I was fixed to read an account to any Society, as he should like me to do so to the Anthropl., for 'I am President this year, for the second time.' Still I did not recognize him till afterwards he said he was Genl. Lane Fox *alias* Pitt Rivers. I cannot yet recognize the same man that I have seen in London, but differences of dress & whiskers would account for my failure. He said, 'Do you know anything of Mr Petrie, he's done a good deal in this line', or some such phrase; so I handed out my card at which we both laughed. He became more chatty & said he was very glad I was out here doing this thoroughly, & at last went off to Sphinx &c, while I went on with survey. (Burleigh and Clutton Brock 1982)

'SOME UNSEEN HAND'

By the time that Fox inherited Lord Rivers' estates and changed his name in 1880 he had been actively involved in archaeology, more or less continuously, for eighteen years. The breadth of his experience was considerable. Not only had he worked extensively in the British Isles but also in France and Denmark and he had visited archaeological sites elsewhere in Europe. The sites he had been concerned with were widely different in date and type as well as location. Although it is difficult to be precise about the chronological range of the sites he worked on he had investigated thirteen Bronze Age and Iron Age sites, two Palaeolithic and two Neolithic sites, the Anglo-Saxon barrows at Guildford and the medieval castle at Folkestone. The comparatively small number of funerary monuments involved has already been mentioned but the fact that Fox took part in only two predominantly Roman projects is also noteworthy.

Fox had also worked with many of the leading archaeologists of the day, notably Canon William Greenwell, William Owen Stanley and the anatomist Professor George Rolleston. He also knew and took advice from men of the calibre of Albert Way, John Lubbock, John Evans and Augustus Franks. Even before he had made an impact on the archaeological world with his fieldwork, however, Fox had been exerting a powerful influence on the learned societies. He had joined the Anthropological Society in 1865 and was elected to the Council and the Publication Committee before withdrawing from the Society, with Evans, Lubbock and other progressives, in 1868 (Chapman 1989, 31–2). They were suspicious of the unscientific attitude of the leaders of the Society, such as James Hunt and the explorer Richard Burton, and of their adherence to the tenets of polygenesis. He had been General Secretary of the International Archaeological Congress in 1868 and became Honorary Secretary of the Ethnological Society of London in the same year. The Ethnological Society at this time was a meeting place for anatomists and Chapman says that this had been Fox's main reason for joining in 1861. Here he met Richard Owen, John Beddoe, George Busk and John Thurnam, all of whom he was to work with in the years to come. In 1871 Fox with Huxley, Lubbock and Evans brought about the amalgamation of the Anthropological Society and the Ethnological Society to form the Anthropological Institute and ensured a predominantly archaeological outlook for the new body (Chapman 1989, 30, 34; Lorimer 1988, 411). The General's leading role in this fusion of the Societies is indicated by Huxley's correspondence with Evans on the subject (Evans 1943, 157). The General was elected Vice-President of the Society of Antiquaries, whose director was now Augustus Franks, in 1871, Fellow of the Royal Society in 1876 and President of the Anthropological Institute in 1880.

Not only had the General mastered the contemporary techniques of field survey and excavation but he could be regarded as a pioneer of surface artefact collection and experimental archaeology. His field survey methods were sound. He had progressed from pacing and taping in the 1860s to the detailed plan and profile surveys of megalithic sites in Brittany in 1878–9. His published surveys of this period match the superbly accurate, if small scale, plans being made by Henry MacLauchlan at the same time (for example MacLauchlan 1857) and are well in advance of the general standards of the day.

The General's excavation techniques are less commendable. His recording was meticulous but his physical digging methods let him down. Though recognising the importance of stratigraphy and the interrelationship of features he failed to excavate in such a way as to be able to see them clearly. He dug in spits and not by layers, a technique which he was to retain until the end of his life. At Cissbury in 1875 he carefully preserved and recorded a vertical section illustrating the relationship between the hillfort ditch and a flint mine shaft, but two years later at Mount Caburn he had apparently forgotten the technique. It was not until Dane's Dyke in 1879 that he published another detailed section drawing.

Collection of artefacts from the surface of ploughed fields was little reported though it may have been a common activity amongst mid-nineteenth century antiquaries. That Fox took surface collection very seriously is demonstrated by his Stonehenge report and his published report on the results of artefact collection in Oxfordshire and Kent appears to be a new departure in British archaeology. Unfortunately he did not publish all his endeavours in this aspect of field archaeology. On 30 August 1869 Kate Amberley wrote in her journal, 'Augustus & I ride to Wheybury [Uleybury?]; I held his horse while he walked over the field & found some flints which proved it to be a British camp, at all events pre-Roman' (Russell and Russell 1937b, 280).

Not the least remarkable achievement of Fox's early fieldwork was the experimental work he did at Cissbury in 1875. John Evans was an accomplished flint knapper, as even 'Flint Jack' acknowledged (Evans 1943, 119), and Fox took lessons from him (Pitt Rivers 1881a, 389) but Fox was the first archaeologist to experiment with antler picks and perhaps the first anthropologist to throw a boomerang (Fox 1872b, 161).

6

The Inspector of Ancient Monuments

The protection of ancient monuments has perhaps commanded a greater amount of attention from recent scholars than any other aspect of the General's work. A number of papers and books (for example Chippindale 1983a; 1983b, 160–1; 1983c; Saunders 1981; Thompson 1960; 1963; 1977, 58–74) have covered the subject very comprehensively.

The Ancient Monuments Act of 1882 was almost entirely the product of the energetic and persistent efforts of Sir John Lubbock. It took him a full decade to bring the idea of legal protection for ancient monuments from the first drafting of a bill to the Statute Book. The Act made provision for a salaried Inspector to recommend monuments for protection, to gain the consent of the landowners involved and to oversee the passage of the sites on the Schedule to the List of Protected Monuments. Inclusion in the List meant that the owner was prevented from undertaking any works which would damage or destroy the monument and, in some cases, that the monument could be further protected by the erection of a fence or similar minimal action. The government department responsible for executing the Act was the Office of Works.

The Act was purely permissive. If a landowner refused to have a site on his property protected, and many did, that was the end of the matter. The considerable resistance to the bill on its tortuous passage through Parliament had largely been from the property owning classes who were extremely jealous of any measure which seemed to them to infringe their rights and privileges. Similar objections had been raised against the Historical Manuscripts Commission in the 1870s (Levine 1986, 119). During the debate on the Ancient Monuments bill in the House of Lords on 12 March 1880 Earl de la Warr stated that 'The bill in its present shape was an objectionable one; the third clause was especially so. A monument on any part of the land of a private owner was as much his property as if it were in his park, garden or pleasure ground. Under that clause the proprietor was dealt with not as the owner of his property, but as a mere trustee of it.' The Duke of Richmond and Gordon proposed that the bill should be referred to a select committee because it was 'just one of those measures, dealing as it did with property in so summary a way, which ought to receive such consideration' (Kains-Jackson 1880, 109–10). As a landowner himself Sir John was sympathetic to this point of view and was at pains to make it clear that no infringement was intended. When the General inherited the Rivers estate in 1880 he became the ideal choice for the post of Inspector; a leading archaeologist with an extensive knowledge of prehistoric monuments, and a proven record of activity in their protection, who would nevertheless enter into the feelings of individual landowners and command their respect. Pitt Rivers had long been associated with Lubbock in the cause of protecting ancient monuments (Thompson 1977, 58–9) but it does not necessarily follow that Lubbock had intended Pitt Rivers to be the Inspector from the start, as Thompson and others (e.g. MacIvor and Fawcett 1983, 12) have assumed. The evidence of private correspondence between the two men (Pitt Rivers Papers AM1) suggests that the choice of the General was made at the last moment. Lubbock broached the subject of the Inspectorship in October 1882, an official invitation followed in November and Pitt Rivers took up the post on 1 January 1883.

Fifty sites in England, Wales and Scotland were listed on the original Schedule. These were twelve megalithic monuments, nine hillforts, eight stone circles, seven inscribed stones, five henge monuments, five brochs, three miscellaneous sites and just one enclosed settlement site (Kains-Jackson 1880). Apart from the hillforts there is a clear and almost total lack of coincidence between this list and the types of site which the General was wont to excavate, partly reflecting the predominantly highland zone distribution of the Scheduled sites.

THE INSPECTOR IN THE OFFICE

Persuading owners to give their consent to having monuments placed on the List was to be one of the Inspector's main headaches. This was signalled at the very outset when Lubbock himself expressed doubts about giving his consent for Silbury Hill to be protected (Pitt Rivers Papers AM1a). The 'List of Ancient Monuments Scheduled under the Act and Placed under the Protection of the Act' up to 1889 (*ibid.*, AM2) begins with Plas Newydd, Anglesey, owned by Pitt Rivers' father-in-law, Lord Stanley. Under the column headed 'Owner's consent' is the terse statement, 'refused'.

By 1889 about ninety monuments had been surveyed, forty-six had received the owners' consent for listing and twenty-two had been refused. Coverage was extremely uneven. Hampshire alone had forty-four of the monuments on the list though none of these were actually protected. The reason for this was that the Act included no mechanism for recommending monuments for protection. It was left entirely to the Inspector to 'tout' for monuments, or for owners to offer them voluntarily, or for local interest groups to put suggestions to the Inspector.

Landowners were continually concerned that by giving their consent to listing they were giving up their rights and opening themselves to bureaucratic interference. While bringing Mayburgh henge and King Arthur's Round Penrith, under the protection of the Act the General noted in an internal

I have found in the course of my function as Inspector that it is only by explaining away any idea of future confiscation or meddling with proprietary rights that the Act has been attended [by] any measure of success. That marks should be put to define the area placed under the operation of the Act appears desirable but they should in my judgement be as inconspicuous as possible and above all should avoid any possible misinterpretation of transfer of ownership to the Crown. (*ibid.*, AM5)

The owner of the two henges at Penrith had, quite rightly, objected to the Office of Works digging holes in the earthworks for the erection of notice-boards and markers.

Shortly afterwards the General was writing to the owner of the Glenelg brochs to assure him that

the Act of appointing the Commsrs. of Works Guardians of the Monuments does not interfere in any way with ownership nor does it establish any right of way. They can be sold or disposed of as before only they cannot be destroyed nor is it proposed to meddle with them in any way beyond such protection as may be necessary to keep them in repair. In fact the only object of the Act is to secure them to posterity . . . (*ibid.*, AM31)

The weakness of the Act in preserving those monuments which were placed under its protection also caused increasing alarm. Pitt Rivers wanted to put railings round the monuments that he felt were particularly vulnerable but that proved too expensive. In 1885 a sum of £25, a quarter of the entire ancient monuments budget for one year, was spent on the erection of railings round Kit's Coty House, Aylesford (Saunders 1981, 53). In 1887 Pitt Rivers wrote an internal memorandum on what he saw as the fundamental failure of the Act: 'The Act gives legal powers for prosecuting delinquents. Is that to be the only advantage which the Act affords. To what extent will Government secure these monuments. The whole thing appears to me to require consideration' (Pitt Rivers Papers AM8). The almost despairing note of the General's internal memoranda contrasts strongly with the optimistic view he put forward in public. In 1883 he had assured the Royal Archaeological Institute that 'About a third of the scheduled monuments in England have been already registered, and are for ever saved from destruction, and there is every reason to believe that the greater part of the remainder will also be shortly included' (Pitt Rivers 1884a, 78), although earlier in the same year he had confided to his colleagues in the Office of Works his belief that a large number of monuments '. . . have already been destroyed through the operations of Agriculture and other causes and the improved appliances for rapid and deep tillage render it likely that the destruction unless stopped will continue in an increasing ratio in years to come . . .' and concluded that the Act '. . . will only go a short way towards preserving all the relics of pre-historic ages that are likely to be valuable to Archaeologists in time to come' (Pitt Rivers Papers AM57). These two statements are not, of course, strictly contradictory in that the former relates only to scheduled monuments and the latter to the total population of archaeological sites, but the difference of emphasis is striking. Also of interest to the modern archaeologist is the identification of the increasing power of cultivation machinery as the principal agent of archaeological destruction at this early date.

Pitt Rivers was not alone in feeling that the Act was too weak in certain fundamental respects. In March 1889 D. Christison wrote to Thackeray Turner, Secretary of the Society for the Protection of Ancient Buildings:

> I cannot refrain from expressing, privately, the painful feeling which I have experienced . . . of the futility . . . of any effort to save Ancient Monuments from destruction, as long as we are backed by an Act so inefficient for their protection as the one now in force . . . the opinion of Scottish Archaeologists who have paid attention to the subject is that, so far as Scotland is concerned, the Act for the Protection of Ancient Monuments is little better than a dead letter. (*ibid.*, AM38)

Turner passed Christison's comments on to Pitt Rivers who replied in his encouraging and optimistic public manner. Christison was not entirely convinced, however, as his reply to the General indicates:

> I laid your letter before the Council of our Society [The Society of Antiquaries of Scotland] and I am instructed to express their gratification on learning that the Act has been attended with a larger amount of success than they had supposed. At the same time their opinion of the insufficiency of the Act is but little modified in the first place because the number of monuments brought under Protection still falls far short of what seems to them to be desirable . . . The measure of success attained has been almost entirely due to your personal and voluntary action in undertaking the duty . . . of asking the Proprietors of Monuments to place them under the Act. This success therefore says much for your zeal, but very little for the initiative power in the Act itself. (*ibid.*)

The Press was also concerned by the weakness of the Act and was more critical of the General. On 9 September 1888 *The Globe* reported that the Ancient Monuments Act 'was by its nature tentative and "permissive" enough to suit the Liberty and Property Defence League, of which General Pitt Rivers, whose duty is to carry out the Act, is himself a member.' *The Globe* argued that the Act should be strengthened even if more public money had to be spent.

The Act ran into other problems, though none so persistent as the ownership hurdle or the fundamental legal weakness of the Act itself. The Commissioners of Works were very reluctant to give their protection to sites which were not specifically mentioned in the original Schedule even if the owner offered them. Thus when Kit's Coty House was accepted into guardianship Little Kit's Coty House was excluded although the owner wished both sites to be placed under the Act (Saunders 1981, 52). This problem could be overcome if a case could be made for seeing two sites as one monument. The Duke of Rutland was very willing to have Arbor Low protected but the question arose as to whether the nearby barrow called Gib Hill could be included. This legal point was settled by Pitt Rivers' 'archaeological opinion' that the henge and the barrow were connected: 'There are grounds for supposing the two works were originally associated and theories have been based on their relative position to one another' (Pitt Rivers Papers AM4). This was enough for the department's solicitor to rule that the two could be considered as one monument.

A more personal problem for Pitt Rivers arose over the case of Bewcastle cross. In 1890 Canon Greenwell sought permission from the Cumberland and Westmorland Antiquarian and Archaeological Society to make a cast of the cross. Knowing the Canon's reputation Richard Ferguson had advised that permission should be given (Ferguson 1893). However, the work was entrusted to a 'tradesman from Corbridge' who, according to Ferguson, did considerable damage to the cross:

> He did not erect a scaffold: the cross is 14 ft. [4.3 m] high: but leant ladders against it, and chipped pieces off the cross with the ladders. He made no attempt to clean the cross properly, but covered it with size, which with the moss and lichen has made a nasty paste over the Cross. His moulds would not come away easily from the Cross, and he prized them off with a chisel, and in so doing pulled away flakes of stone from the foliage . . . The appearance of the cross is now ghastly in the extreme, of a yellow, raw and hideous hue. Time may mend that, but not the injuries to the stone . . . (Pitt Rivers Papers AM7)

The Inspector of Ancient Monuments took the matter up personally with Canon Greenwell who strongly denied that the damage was anything other than 'trifling' (ibid.). There was nothing Pitt Rivers, or anyone else, could do. The damage, whether 'trifling' or not, had been done.

There was some encouragement for the hard-pressed Inspector however. A few individuals, like Sir Herbert Maxwell, were actively and voluntarily helping him to bring monuments under the Act. In April 1890 Sir George Treherne sent Pitt Rivers a completed form authorising the inclusion of an ogham stone at Eglwys Cymmum in the schedule. In a covering letter he noted that he had 'filled in the Rector for the time being as the owner altho' I venture to think that the Clergy are the last people to be trusted with precious antiquities . . .' (ibid. AM40).

In 1890 the General gave up the salary attached to his post but continued as Inspector in an honorary capacity. This important change came about because Pitt Rivers believed that the job was becoming a sinecure. The Office of Works had neither the money nor the machinery to take any more monuments into its care and they had desired the General to stop 'touting' for monuments. Pitt Rivers' despair about the usefulness of the Act reached new depths.

On 20 December 1895 he wrote to George Payne, who had hoped to be appointed Assistant Inspector, explaining the situation that existed after the turning point of 1890:

> Since then there has been little or nothing to do. There have been no applications to put the Act in force, as I expected would be the case. There have occasionally, perhaps once a year, been applications, but I have generally arranged to have the monuments protected privately without cost to the Govt. . . . I hope this will shew you that there is no possible opening for an assistant Inspector . . . I myself concur in thinking that the owners of monuments as a rule, are the best people to have charge of them & that our Govt. will not do it as well as the owner will. The interest in old monuments has increased of late. Public opinion is more in favour of them than it was. More so than a Govt, (any Government) which will attend to

25 General Pitt Rivers; oil portrait by Frank Holl ARA. The General is holding a sketchbook of the type used on the Inspectorate journeys and the Cranborne Chase excavations

27 W. S. Tomkin: he was the General's companion for the majority of the Inspectorate journeys

26 Model of Pentre Ifan chambered tomb; wood and plaster. This is one of three surviving models of the scheduled monuments visited by the General and his assistants

nothing out of which political capital cannot be made. Neither Govt. nor parliament care a button for ancient monuments but the majority of the owners take an interest in their *own* monuments as family possessions . . . I have had trouble enough, & little thanks over the business I can assure you. (Barley and Barry 1971, 220)

By the time of Pitt Rivers' death in 1900 only forty-three sites had passed into Government care (Thompson 1963, 225) and the Act was, in effect, in abeyance.

THE INSPECTOR IN THE FIELD

The work of the Inspector was not confined to office work at Rushmore or in London. It was central to Pitt Rivers' and indeed Lubbock's strategy for protecting ancient monuments that they should be accurately surveyed and recorded and the General saw it as the Inspector's duty to undertake the survey work in person. He was certainly well qualified for this part of the task. He had been surveying archaeological sites for twenty years by the time he became Inspector and was already personally acquainted with at least some of the sites on the Schedule. In 1869 he and Kate Amberley had crawled on their stomachs into Hetty Pegler's Tump, the chambered tomb at Uley (Russell and Russell 1937b, 280–1) which had recently been excavated by John Thurnam.

Thompson has described in graphic detail the journeys which the General made with his assistants to survey monuments on the List (1960; 1977, 65–73). They travelled by train, the Inspector first class and the assistant or assistants third class. Pitt Rivers was not reimbursed for his expenses. As he wrote somewhat bitterly to George Payne 'they pay no travelling expenses. They made such a fuss over the first account I sent in that I desisted & after that did all my travelling at my own expense' (Barley and Barry 1971, 220). Surveying equipment was necessarily carried as well as personal luggage, though photographic equipment was taken only on the two final journeys in 1889 and 1890. Hired carriages carried them between railway stations, hotels and the monuments. On the rare occasions when the assistants were in the field without the General whisky appears as an extra item on the hotel bills (Pitt Rivers Papers AM83).

The location of monuments on the original Schedule dictated the routes taken. They covered central southern England comprehensively but also the midlands, Wales, north-west England and Scotland, including the Orkneys. The predominance of the highland zone no doubt reflects the state of preservation of sites in those areas, though south-west England was omitted, probably because the Duchy of Cornwall was excluded from the provisions of the Act. Eastern England is the largest unrepresented area and the south-east only warranted a single brief visit.

Much field time was inevitably spent visiting landowners and tenants. These personal contacts were as fraught with difficulty as the correspondence which the General conducted. One of the assistants wrote the words 'queer character' beside the name of a Scottish landowner in his notebook (PRO WORK 39/13).

The monuments were recorded by plan, elevation, a sketch and written description. Thompson has reproduced a list of the equipment carried by the General and his assistants on the 1889 journey (1977, 68–9) which allows a degree of reconstruction of his field methods. The sites were surveyed graphically so there was no need to carry delicate instruments or cumbersome equipment. Horizontal angles were measured with a prismatic compass and distances with tapes. On excavations the General used an engineer's level and tripod for vertical measurements but for these journeys a pocket level, infinitely easier to carry, was considered sufficient. A clinometer was also taken for measuring slope angles. The surveys were drawn up in notebooks, probably in the field, or possibly in the hotel in the evening, using scale rules and a protractor. Having ensured that the surveying equipment was easily portable the General saddled his team with a camera lucida with table and seat as well as photographic apparatus on this journey. The list of equipment taken in 1884 (PRO WORK 39/15) is shorter and certainly does not include these bulky objects. None of the records were published but the notebooks and related papers form a considerable body of evidence on the condition and appearance of these monuments at the time of the General's visits (Thompson 1960). Unfortunately none of the photographs taken on the latest journeys seem to have survived.

The General undertook one excavation in his official capacity as Inspector. There had been considerable controversy over the origin of the Pen Pits near Penselwood in Somerset. One faction believed this group of amorphous surface undulations to be 'an ancient British metropolis' while the other, led by the Rev. H. H. Winwood, claimed they were merely quarries. The excavation was undertaken to resolve the controversy and ascertain whether any part of the site should be scheduled. The report (Pitt Rivers 1884b) was addressed directly to Shaw Lefevre, the First Commissioner of Works. Pitt Rivers concluded that the pits were indeed quarries for the procurement of quernstones and the site was not to be scheduled.

For all practical purposes the Act of 1882 died with the General. By the time that Government responsibility for ancient monuments was revived by the Ancient Monuments and Historic Buildings Act of 1913 the three Royal Commissions on Historical Monuments, for England, Scotland and Wales, had been created by royal warrant. The remit of the Royal Commissions, being to make inventories of all ancient monuments and historic buildings, effectively removed the responsibility for surveying and recording from future Inspectors.

7

Excavations in Cranborne Chase

CRANBORNE CHASE

> I inherited the Rivers estates in the year 1880, in accordance with the will of my
> great uncle, the second Lord Rivers, and by descent from my grandmother, who
> was his sister, and daughter of the first lord. The will was excessively binding,
> and provided amongst other things that I was to assume the name and arms of
> Pitt Rivers within a year of my inheriting the property . . . Having retired from
> active service on account of ill health, and being incapable of strong physical
> exercise, I determined to devote the remaining portion of my life chiefly to an
> examination of the antiquities on my own property. Of these there were a
> considerable number . . . most of which were untouched and had been well
> preserved . . . I had an ample harvest before me, and with the particular tastes that
> I had cultivated, it almost seemed to me as if some unseen hand had trained me up
> to be the possessor of such a property, which up to within a short time of my
> inheriting it, I had but little reason to expect. (Pitt Rivers 1887a, xi–xiii)

Cranborne Chase, on the borders of Dorset, Wiltshire and Hampshire, was a
medieval hunting preserve, a tract of chalk downland dedicated to the favourite
sport of kings and nobles. The deer were sacrosanct. The inhabitants of the
Chase were not only forbidden to harm the deer directly but were also prevented from undertaking any activity which might damage the 'vert', the vegetation on and in which the deer lived. Until the disenfranchisement of the Chase
in 1830 (Hawkins 1981, 57, 82–5) this strict control of agricultural pursuits led
to a preservation of archaeological sites of earlier periods unequalled in lowland
southern England. In 1880 the Rushmore Estate, 3,500 hectares in the heart of
the Chase, was indeed the perfect inheritance for an archaeologist.

The bounds of the Chase are difficult to define precisely. The Outer Bounds
included a vast area stretching from Salisbury to Blandford Forum and from
Shaftesbury to Ringwood. The Inner Bounds ran from Compton Abbas on the
west to Woodyates on the east along the Ox Drove and then south to Sixpenny
Handley. The southern edge ran from Handley through Gussage St Andrew
and Stubhampton to a point somewhere south of Iwerne and thence due north
to Compton Abbas (ibid., 175–80). Rushmore House, in Tollard Royal parish,
lies at the centre of this block of land. Along the line of the Ox Drove the chalk
forms a steep north-facing scarp looking out over the Ebble and Nadder valleys
and Salisbury Plain. From the highest point on the crest of this scarp, Win

Green (277 m above sea level), the land slopes gently away to the south and east. A number of dry valleys run down towards the river valleys of the Allen and the Crane, which in turn flow into the Stour and the Avon respectively. Over most of the region the chalk lies immediately below the soil but on the higher ground there are extensive patches of clay-with-flints and in the dry valleys deposits of gravel.

WORKING METHODS

By his own account Pitt Rivers lost no time in setting his excavations in motion and his first action was to recruit 'such a staff of assistants as would enable me to complete the examination of the antiquities on the property within a reasonable time' (1887a, xiii). Assistants were also essential for the fieldwork connected with his duties as Inspector of Ancient Monuments (*ibid.*, xviii). He was very clear about the skills his assistants would need. Of paramount importance was draughtsmanship. For other aspects of the work they could be trained in service: 'Surveying I was able to teach them myself, having always been fond of field sketching as a soldier' (*ibid.*). At first the General seems to have had some problem in finding suitable candidates but shortly he settled on three men, Frederick James, W. S. Tomkin and F. W. Reader. James, who had been recommended by Charles Roach Smith, was the head assistant and was to stay with the General for ten years. He supervised the excavations and took 'a chief part' in surveying and in the supervision of the other assistants, acting also as the General's secretary. Tomkin did most of the publication drawings and travelled with the General on the Inspectorate journeys. Reader also worked as draughtsman, made models for the museum and arranged the museum exhibits at Farnham. The division of labour was not clear cut, however, as all three attended the excavations and travelled on the Inspectorate journeys from time to time.

The General soon showed that he was an exacting taskmaster. Tomkin had to redraw both skulls and coins for the first Cranborne Chase volume because the General was not satisfied with the accuracy of his first drafts (*ibid.*, xix). In this first volume he said of his assistants, or clerks as he usually referred to them, 'These gentlemen have been assiduous in their duties, taking much interest in their work, and have acquitted themselves to my entire satisfaction' (*ibid.*, xviii), praise indeed from the General. He also acknowledged the labourers, some of whom 'aquired much skill in digging and detecting the relics . . . so as to enable them to be regarded as skilled workmen, upon which no small share of the success of an investigation of this kind depends' (*ibid.*, xix). As the General sometimes only visited the excavations three times a day unless sent for (*ibid.*, xviii) the responsibility of both assistants and workmen was great.

Frederick James went to Maidstone Museum as curator in 1891. Tomkin stayed with the General for eight years and Reader for four, the latter being asked to leave without the two-months notice to which he thought he was

28 Frederick V. James

29 Claude Gray

30 Charles Flower

31 G. Waldo Johnson

entitled (Pitt Rivers Papers L607). The reason for his dismissal remains obscure. The Gray brothers arrived in 1888 and Charles Flower in 1890. Harold St George Gray took over Frederick James' position as the General's secretary and stayed until the General's death. His elder brother Claude left in 1892, apparently after a quarrel with Pitt Rivers, and emigrated to Canada. Flower too stayed for only four years. Herbert Toms, a local man from Winfrith Newburgh, arrived in 1893 and stayed with the General for three years before taking up a post as museum assistant at Brighton. When Toms left he was replaced by G. Waldo Johnson who remained with the General until the end and is a prominent figure in the photographs of the Iwerne excavations.

Toms was to return to Rushmore after the General's death to re-survey the area around South Lodge and Barrow Pleck, with particular reference to the lynchets which Pitt Rivers had not surveyed (Toms 1925). This episode raises questions about the relationship between the General and his assistants. Toms almost certainly knew of the existence of these lynchets in the 1890s so either he did not draw the General's attention to them, or he did so and was ignored.

The assistants were part of the General's household: 'Living in my house they must necessarily be men of good character as well as energy' (Pitt Rivers 1897, 338). Arrival at Rushmore must have been a daunting experience for a new assistant, confronted as he was not only by an exacting and frequently bad-tempered employer, but his employer's mean and shrewish wife and arrogant children. Agnes' remarks about the clerks give an indication of the family's attitude to these fellow inhabitants of Rushmore: '. . . a whole heap of clerks came yesterday. Three – and the money the Man gives them and the food they eat, if only we could have it we should be quite rich. Oh it is a wicked waste of money and they do no good. Drawing old stones and bones and skulls etc.' (Hawkins 1981, 141). This remark illustrates the family's reaction to the General's scientific work. Mrs Pitt Rivers was quite indifferent to anthropology and archaeology. The sons were mildly interested and Douglas even made some positive contributions to his father's researches but the daughters, especially Alice and Agnes, were openly hostile. In 1870 J. H. Parker had commented forcibly on the lively and intelligent interest taken in antiquarian studies by young ladies of the highest social rank (Daniel 1967, 141). This was a fashion which the General's daughters did not follow, in contrast to the young Misses Baden-Powell who sought the General's archaeological advice in the 1890s (Pitt Rivers Papers L401, L415).

The social status of the clerks is unclear. Herbert Toms was the son of a gardener and in 1902 was to marry Mrs Pitt Rivers' French lady's-maid, Christina Huon (Holleyman and Merrifield 1987, 13, 28) but presumably the clerks ranked above the household servants. Thompson calculates that their wages were higher than those of a servant and that they could be considered well paid when their free board and lodging was taken into account (1977, 94), though not all of them would have agreed. Tomkin was forced to leave the General's service because he could not afford to marry on the 'pittance' he was paid (Tomkin Papers). Francis Reader, a gentle, unassuming man, found Pitt

Rivers hectoring, inconsiderate and a hard taskmaster but nevertheless had a high opinion of his precision and attention to detail in recording (Clive Rouse, personal communication).

The workforce was drawn from the labourers on the General's own estates, necessitating occasional absences for seasonal agricultural activities (Bradley 1973, 48). They worked a six day week, the usual agricultural regime, for which they received, in 1893, 2s. 6d. per day.

Pitt Rivers continued to be largely indifferent to local archaeology societies but he remained active in several national ones. Though he had been an 'adviser' to the Essex Field Club for a short time and was President of the Wiltshire Archaeological Society for three years he was a member of only six county societies. He never sought to involve local societies in his own excavations or to take an active role in their work.

RECORDING STANDARDS

A peculiarity of the excavations in Cranborne Chase is the uneven quality of the published section drawings in the four volumes. It has often been said that the General gradually improved his techniques over the years (for example Piggott 1959, 44–5) but careful study of the volumes does not bear this out. The drawings in the first two volumes are of a uniform standard. In the third volume there is a marked improvement, Bokerley Dyke and Wansdyke being illustrated by a series of section drawings at a larger scale which could hardly have been bettered at any subsequent date (for example Pitt Rivers 1892, pl. CCXVI). However, in the fourth volume the standard of drawing has regressed in some ways to a point inferior to the standard achieved in the first two volumes, with artefacts apparently floating in space in the 'average sections' (for example, Pitt Rivers 1898, pl. 237).

One possible explanation for this fluctuation is the changing team of assistants responsible for the day to day running of the excavations and for all the publication drawing. If this is the case then Claude Gray must be responsible for the superb quality of the recording of the sites published in volume three. James, Tomkin and possibly Reader were all involved in these excavations and Tomkin is expressly credited with 'many of the plates' in the third volume (Pitt Rivers 1892, xv) but the quality of the work far outstrips anything they had achieved before. Harold Gray does not seem to have been employed extensively at Wansdyke. Charles Flower did not arrive until these excavations were nearly over, though he must have been involved in preparing the material for publication, and although he was present for the first of the volume four excavations he had left long before they were published. If the quality of the published drawings reflects the quality of the site recording we can only conclude that Claude Gray, who alone was present for both excavation and post-excavation work for volume three and for no other aspect of the excavations in Cranborne Chase, should have the credit for the superb work in the third volume. It is ironic that he is one of the least regarded of the General's assistants, being totally overshadowed by his younger brother, and that he seems never to have worked in archaeology again.

Only the General's failing health after his serious illness in 1892 can explain his failure to ensure that the fine standards achieved in the third volume were maintained in the fourth. Detailed section drawings were still made. Bradley has reproduced two sections of parts of the Wor Barrow mound (1973, pls. VI and VII) and there is a brief reference in a site diary to Herbert Toms making stratigraphic section drawings of the Wor Barrow ditch (Gray Notebooks). As the latter drawings have not survived there is no way of knowing how detailed they were but Bradley suggests that Toms' site records at South Lodge contained more detail than the published report (1989, 31).

RUSHMORE BARROWS, 1880–1884

The excavations in Cranborne Chase began on 9 August 1880 when a round barrow next to the South Drive, Rushmore, was opened in the presence of the General, Professor George Rolleston and the Rev. H. H. Winwood, a geologist. Within the mound they discovered a cremation accompanied by some fragments of bronze. The mound also contained flint implements and pot sherds. Shortly after the opening Rolleston died and Pitt Rivers, naming this barrow after his friend, planted a beech tree on its rebuilt mound in his memory (Pitt Rivers 1888a, 1).

Over the next four years the General dug twenty-one barrows in Rushmore Park. His methods followed a regular pattern. Where there were surface indications of a ditch this was excavated fully, except where growing trees were left standing, but if there were no traces of a ditch the General did not look for one. The largest mounds were dug by driving a trench into the centre from one side, generally the south or south-east. Lower mounds were excavated by opening a rectangular trench covering the centre and one side, again generally towards the south. These trenches could be extended in pursuit of particular features. The smallest mounds were totally removed.

Pitt Rivers' concentration on the central and southern parts of the mounds was the result of previous experience: 'It may be thought perhaps that this barrow [No. 10, Scrubbity Coppice] was not sufficiently excavated . . . but the large barrows generally are very unproductive, and the centre and southern part as well as the ditch was sufficiently explored' (*ibid.*, 32). He felt confident enough to base a limited excavation strategy on his growing experience that finds clustered in these areas, a subjective approach and a not unreasonable one. The re-excavation of Barrow 18 in 1981 was based on a sampling strategy which, while somewhat more sophisticated and based on different assumptions, was broadly comparable (Barrett *et al.* 1983, 203).

The level of recording of the Rushmore Barrows is not beyond reproach, however. While the record of finds and findspots is meticulous the General's weakness over stratigraphy is very evident in these excavations. Different layers within mounds or ditches are rarely mentioned or depicted in the publi-

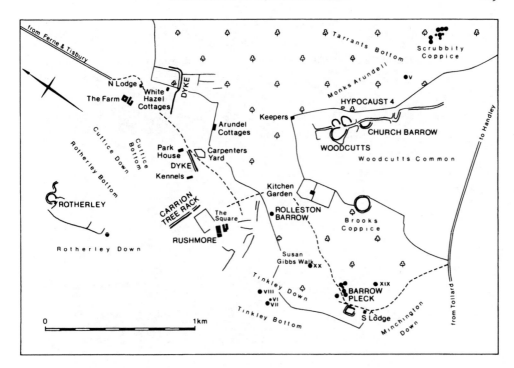

Map 3 Rushmore Park

cation drawings, though one surviving field drawing (Pitt Rivers Papers R8) shows slightly more detail. Frequently the whole excavated area of mound and ditch is shown as an undifferentiated mass of 'brown mould'. Cogbill has drawn attention to this weakness in regard to the barrows (1982, 79). At the other extreme are section drawings showing details not mentioned in the text and which are, indeed, impossible to accept. An instance of this is the case of Barrow 20, the Beaker burial in Susan Gibbs' Walk, which is shown (Pitt Rivers 1888a, pl. LXXV) with the grave apparently cut through the chalk rubble of the mound and the topsoil.

Pitt Rivers 'restored' the barrows after excavation. The mounds were rebuilt and where a ditch was excavated the ditch silts were added to the mound before returfing. In the case of Barrow Pleck, however, situated close to the South Lodge and the most accessible of the excavated groups, a different approach was adopted. The General described how the barrows were 'cemented over to preserve them, and to show the relative positions of the primary and secondary interments' (ibid., 29). Re-excavation at Barrow Pleck in 1981–3 revealed the details of this bizarre proceeding and much else about the General's barrow excavations.

The re-excavation of Barrows 2, 3 and 18 was undertaken as part of a major project on the prehistory of Cranborne Chase (Barrett et al. forthcoming). During re-excavation it was noted that the General's workmen had failed to identify the edge of the ditch of Barrow 3 and had left part of the filling intact,

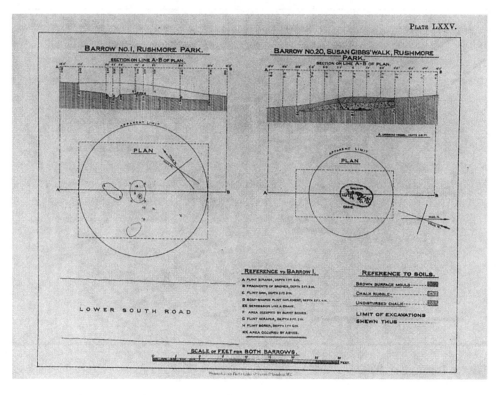

32 Plans and sections of Barrows 1 and 20

33 Finds from Barrow 20, Susan Gibbs' Walk, Rushmore Park. Boxes were made by the General's estate carpenters to preserve the limb bones of the skeletons he excavated

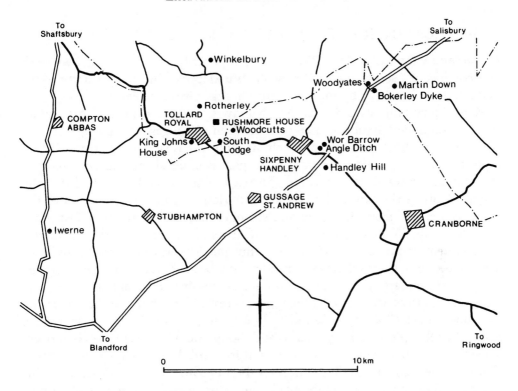

Map 4 Cranborne Chase, the area within the inner bounds

including a cremation and a deliberate packing of flint nodules which the General had not recorded. Barrow 2 was found to have a ditch which Pitt Rivers had not discovered. The ditch of Barrow 18 also contained a deliberate packing of flint which is not recorded in the General's report. In both Barrows 3 and 18 the General seems to have dug more of the mounds than his published plans show (Barrett *et al.* 1983, 195–6). In the case of Barrow 18 this may reflect a certain frustration at finding no evidence for funerary activity. The General placed a replica late-Roman urn in the rebuilt mound of this barrow, containing his medalet, two coins, some contemporary china sherds and a piece of paper whose message was unfortunately indecipherable by 1981. Both Barrows 2 and 3 had been left open and cement rafts, with depressions marking the positions of cremations and a stakehole, had been laid on the floors of the trenches (*ibid.*, 197, pl. xxiv) as Pitt Rivers himself described. The mound of Barrow 2 had been moved on restoration so as to make the primary cremation central. This unique attempt to display excavation results *in situ* must be seen not only in terms of the Ancient Monuments Act's aim to preserve 'typical' sites for future generations (*ibid.*, 196) but also in the light of the General's own overriding concern for public education. The Barrow Pleck cemetery was more accessible to the public than any of the other Rushmore barrows.

WINKELBURY, OCTOBER 1881–FEBRUARY 1882

In the mild winter of 1881–2 Pitt Rivers temporarily abandoned his own park and conducted a series of excavations on Winkelbury Hill, the property of his neighbour and relative by marriage Sir Thomas Grove of Ferne House.

Winkelbury Hill has a Bronze Age barrow group, an Iron Age fort and an Anglo-Saxon inhumation cemetery. The General began by cutting sections through the hillfort ramparts. Winkelbury hillfort has two peculiarities. It is in a poor defensive position and its ground plan is unusual, having wide gaps in the ramparts towards the southern approach. The General remarked that the 'dividing off of the lower and consequently less commanding portion of the camp as a citadel from the upper and stronger half, seems to imply that other considerations in addition to those of defence, influenced the particular arrangement of this camp' (1888a, 235) but put forward no suggestions as to what these 'other considerations' might have been. Having checked that the gaps in the ramparts were genuine and not the result of differential survival, he explained them as necessary for the rapid ingress of large flocks or herds in time of sudden attack (*ibid.*, 234). Winkelbury has subsequently been described as an unfinished fort (Feachem 1971, 32–3) and though neither explanation is entirely satisfactory no better idea has yet been put forward. It is perhaps worth noting that the outer rampart to the south resembles in some respects, though not all, the cross-ridge dykes that are found elsewhere on the surrounding chalk downs and it may, therefore, have an origin independent of the fort. The General also excavated a long hollow inside the fort extending from the entrance, which he saw as the 'main street' of the settlement, and a number of pits both in the interior and outside the main south rampart. In addition he excavated a larger circular pit on the hillside below the eastern rampart which he described, somewhat tentatively, as a 'pit dwelling' but which is simply a small chalkpit. Finds were not numerous but they were well recorded and preserved. From the Relic Tables (Pitt Rivers 1888a, 269–80) and museum collection Hawkes deduced that an early Iron Age settlement was represented by the pits while the ramparts had been added only shortly before the Roman invasion, commenting that though the General was unable to be certain of the date of the fort himself, 'by his magnificently detailed account of his work, and his preservation of material at Farnham Museum, he has now enabled a closer dating to be fixed' (Hawkes and Dunning 1932, 428).

The excavation of the barrows followed. These proved to be of the Bronze Age but two of them had secondary interments with grave goods which Pitt Rivers recognised as being of Anglo-Saxon date. Unfortunately, as in the case of the Rushmore barrows, the section drawings do not corroborate the written description. Barrow 1 not only had an Anglo-Saxon burial in a coffin inserted in it but had subsequently been disturbed by grave robbers. However, the published drawing (Pitt Rivers 1888a, pl. CLXIX) shows neither of these later cuts because the line of the section is to one side of the features with only the bottom of the grave projected onto it.

An event connected with the excavation of Barrow 3 is of interest. Pitt Rivers noted that the contents of the barrow had been destroyed, probably 'during the insertion of a dead yew tree, locally called a "scrag". I removed the tree during the excavations, and I afterwards learnt that the people of the neighbourhood attached some interest to it, and it has since been replaced by Sir Thomas Grove' (*ibid.*, 258). The Rev. W. Goodchild, rector of Berwick St John, subsequently recalled that

> the cottagers . . . objected very strongly to the opening of the barrows and Anglo-Saxon graves, said that they did not hold with the disturbing of dead men's bones and when General Pitt Rivers' workmen uprooted the 'Scrag' before exploring Barrow III, in which it was planted, much indignation was expressed. The local excitement was only allayed when a new dead yew tree was fetched up from Ashcombe and planted with much ceremony in the tumulus. (Anon. 1930, 75)

The purpose of the 'scrag' was said to be to ensnare witches and thus to protect the inhabitants of Berwick St John from their malignant influence while the absence of the 'scrag' would cause sterility in both humans and livestock. However, 'Tom Blandford, one of the old Ferne workmen . . . has a perfectly precise story, from tradition in the village, that the tumulus no. III . . . was just the site of a great bonfire raised in 1820 to celebrate the 60th. year of George III's reign and the "Scrag" was merely the last log brought up to keep the fire going' (*ibid.*). Doubtless the General had this episode, amongst others, in mind when he remarked to members of the Royal Archaeological Institute that 'a morbid reverence for the calcareous portions of miscellaneous dead bodies is not only superstitious in itself, but it greatly impedes the advancement of knowledge' (Pitt Rivers 1884a, 65).

The discovery of the Anglo-Saxon secondary burials led to a thorough examination of the surrounding area which revealed a number of 'long narrow depressions in the turf all lying, more or less, east and west' (Pitt Rivers 1888a, 259). Thirty were excavated. All contained extended inhumations with a few grave goods, sufficient to establish the Anglo-Saxon dating without doubt. The General compared the orientations of the graves and concluded that, with few exceptions, all could have been laid out according to sunrise at different times of the year, though this would mean that all but two were buried during the summer, 'not the season of the year most conducive to mortality in this climate' (*ibid.*, 261). Pitt Rivers was the first archaeologist to consider this problem which has been much discussed since but never understood (Kendall 1982).

CARRANTY RACK, PARK HOUSE, SHIFTWAY COPPICE AND THE SUNK FENCE, RUSHMORE PARK, NOVEMBER 1881–NOVEMBER 1882

These small excavations occupied the General for only a few days. In November 1881 he dug a section across a linear earthwork near Rushmore House without finding any convincing dating evidence. The earthwork was known as the Carranty Rack or Carrion Tree Rack and in his report Pitt Rivers devoted more space to a discussion of the possible origins of this name than to the archaeology itself (1887a, 2–4, 243).

Two months later one of the workmen, who had been digging at Winkelbury, noticed a slight depression while planting trees near Park House. This proved to be a pit containing a human skull and sherds of Romano-British pottery. Three more pits were found, all containing Romano-British artefacts. The General believed that these pits represented part of a settlement adjacent to the Carranty Rack (*ibid.*) but he did not extend the excavation, perhaps because the proximity of several buildings would have made it inconvenient but perhaps also because he was fully occupied with the later stages of his Winkelbury excavations.

In November 1882 the General cut two more sections across a northern extension of the Carranty Rack in Shiftway Coppice and discovered Romano-British pottery in the ditch silts but nothing dateable within or under the bank. This was especially disappointing in that he had sited his cuttings carefully in relation to an area of disturbed ground suggestive of occupation (*ibid.*, 241).

Nothing is recorded about the work at the Sunk Fence except that, while digging the fence and a pond beside it, a drain was found containing Romano-British pottery. A fibula and some other artefacts were also recovered (*ibid.*, 5, 245–8) but no mention of the Sunk Fence is made in the Relic Tables.

WOODCUTTS, SEPTEMBER 1884–DECEMBER 1885

The earthworks on Woodcutts Common had been partly excavated by the Rev. J. Austen, vicar of Tollard Royal, in 1863 (Austen 1867, 168–70). Having undertaken little excavation in the previous year Pitt Rivers commenced a total excavation of Woodcutts in September 1884. This was by far the largest excavation he had ever undertaken but he did it with his usual workforce of about ten labourers and it took eight months over two seasons:

> After having excavated both main ditch and rampart all round, we commenced trenching the interior space, placing the men in line at working distance apart, digging down everywhere through the surface mould until the chalk beneath was reached, and noticing carefully any irregularity in the latter. Where the mould went deeper it was dug out, and in this way pits, hearths, ditches, and irregularities of all kinds were cleared out and exposed. As a rule, we worked in this trenching from the western side of the north-west quarter eastward, but without adhering rigidly to this system, taking care, however, that the whole was thoroughly explored. (Pitt Rivers 1887a, 10)

This description does not entirely agree with the dates given in the Relic Tables, which suggest that surface trenching began at the same time as excavation of the large well and pits while the excavation of the main rampart and ditch did not begin until the end of October but no doubt it is a good descrip-

tion of the digging methods employed here and subsequently at Rotherley and
the Bronze Age enclosures. The first season at Woodcutts lasted until April
1885 by which time both wells and most of the pits and ditches had been dug.
The second season began in October after the General's return from Scotland
and was taken up by the completion of the ditches and pits and the excavation
of the 'hypocausts' and 'Church Barrow'.

Pitt Rivers employed professional well-sinkers to dig out the wells (ibid.,
9–10). From this work he concluded that, 'water in Roman times was obtained
in the village 33 feet [10 m] higher than it is now obtained in Rushmore' (ibid.,
27) and postulated from this higher water table that the rainfall must have been
greater during the Roman period.

The pits were the smallest features discovered. Pitt Rivers found no structural evidence and formed no opinions about the precise type or location of
buildings on the site. Austen had suggested that the westernmost of two
rectangular depressions was a building platform but Pitt Rivers dismissed this
for lack of positive evidence. Hawkes, who reinterpreted the site in the 1940s,
thought that the main dwelling for his phases 1 and 2 was in the centre of the
phase 1 enclosure, an area clear of pits. The discovery of a hearth and bronze-
mounted casket he found particularly suggestive, thinking that the latter
looked like 'a hoard abandoned inside a dwelling in decay in the later third
century' (Hawkes et al. 1947, 46) but he did not consider the other evidence. It
is worth resurrecting the idea of the two depressions as the platforms for
rectangular timber-built houses of some quality and substantial size, up to
24×12 m, especially as the bulk of the building materials and architectural
ironwork was found in this area. In Hawkes' terms we should see the depression in the Central Quarter as the main house of phase 2, probably on the same
site as the main phase 1 house, with the depression in the North West Quarter
as its replacement in phase 3. A recent reassessment of the site (Corney,
forthcoming) has shown that Hawkes' late Iron Age phase 1 site is a 'banjo'
enclosure, the northern entrance being a later modification. The importance of
both Woodcutts and Rotherley in the Iron Age is reinforced by the imports,
including amphorae and Terra Rubra, found by the General but not recognised
either by him or by Hawkes (Mark Corney, personal communication).

Pitt Rivers was of course aware that the site had gone through a number of
changes in its long life but he was unable to work out the details in the sense
that Hawkes, fifty years later, could: 'The little banks . . . showed evidence of
having been altered, and . . . in some places, banks had been raised over spots
where ditches had previously existed' and some pits 'had a plan in the form of
two or three circles cutting into each other, suggesting side chambers or
cupboards, yet suggesting also the possibility of one pit having been cut and
filled up again before the others were made' (Pitt Rivers 1888b, 192–3).

He was aware, however, that the pits were an early element in the life of the
site because there were neither coins nor nails in the pit fillings and because 'a
much larger quantity of good things, and things of decidedly Roman construction, have been found on the surface than in the pits . . .' (ibid., 193–4). At the

time of his excavations at Mount Caburn Pitt Rivers had discussed the idea that large chalk-cut pits were for grain storage but he did not consider this interpretation at Woodcutts, Rotherley or Woodyates. His belief now was that the pits were purely for refuse disposal (1887a, 60).

An unresolved problem at Woodcutts is the existence of two low earth mounds. Pitt Rivers excavated both of them and found very little except for an urned cremation under the edge of the one in the North West Quarter. He came to no conclusions about the mounds and neither did Hawkes, though he placed them in his second phase, based on the few sherds found within them and the fact that 'the General's stratification shows that [the north west mound] is earlier than the bank of the Phase III "Main Ditch" ' (Hawkes *et al.* 1947, 46). This, however, is a mistake. The section drawing suggests that the mound is stratified under nothing except the General's reconstructed main rampart. It is likely that the mounds are a post-Roman feature and that the presence of the cremation was a coincidence.

One enigma remains: Pitt Rivers described 'Church Barrow' as an amphitheatre (1887a, 23) and Hawkes accepted this interpretation. Clearly it is later than the road ditches which it overlies but they in turn seem to respect an earlier feature which has not been found. No alternative explanation of this part of the site has yet been offered.

ROTHERLEY, OCTOBER 1886–APRIL 1887

The earthworks on Rotherley Down had apparently not been noticed before Pitt Rivers saw them in 1885 and they were so slight that he would have ignored them had he not also seen sherds of Romano-British pottery and samian in some mole hills (Pitt Rivers 1888a, 52).

The excavations, supervised by Francis Reader, followed the same pattern as the Woodcutts excavations but only occupied one winter season. Rotherley differs from Woodcutts in several respects, notably in altitude and topographical location but also in the fact that while Woodcutts lies on a deposit of clay-with-flints Rotherley lies on the chalk. Features are much more easily recognised on chalk and Pitt Rivers found several large postholes at Rotherley, mostly in four-post arrangements. Pitt Rivers suggested that these represented granaries 'such as are still to be seen in the villages about here, standing on four supports' (*ibid.*, 55), an interpretation which is still the most widely accepted (Gent 1983) though Piggott has pointed out that the group of postholes towards the west side of the Main Circle might have been the central supports of a large roundhouse (Hawkes *et al.* 1947, 38–9).

Pitt Rivers also found a series of intercutting circular hollows which he thought were sunken huts (1888a, 53–4) but which Hawkes, with the experience of Little Woodbury to draw on, recognised as 'working hollows' (1947, 37).

Rotherley turned out to be poorer than Woodcutts in both the quantity and quality of artefacts. Moreover the average stature of the inhabitants of

Rotherley was lower than at Woodcutts, a point that interested the General greatly and which he discussed at length (1888a, 58–9, 61–6). His sample of skeletons from all his excavations in Cranborne Chase to date was only twenty-eight, consisting of three Bronze Age and twenty-five Romano-British, to which he added Thurnam's twenty-five Neolithic and twenty-seven Bronze Age skeletons from Wiltshire barrows. This small sample covering such a long time span could not sustain the weight of interpretation which he placed upon it. The Rotherley report was also the first in which the General made a lengthy analysis of the sizes of the animal bones recovered:

> An almost new branch of enquiry has been added to this volume by the careful measurement of all the bones of domesticated animals, of which a large number have been found in the Romano-British villages: 15 animals have been killed for comparison as test animals after external measurement, and by this means the size of all animals whose bones have been found in the villages has been ascertained. (*ibid.*, xvi, 209–25)

The section drawings of Rotherley are similar to those of the earlier excavations and demonstrate the same faults (e.g. *ibid.*, pl. XCV and CXXVII).

The General noted the high proportion of scrapers to waste flakes at Rotherley contrasting with the situation at Woodcutts because, he thought, the local flint at Rotherley is of poor quality and finished tools had been imported to the site. However, he was still unsure as to whether the presence of flint tools on Romano-British sites was evidence of their use in the Roman period or not (*ibid.*, 186–7).

Pitt Rivers found structures at both Woodcutts and Rotherley which he called 'hypocausts'. He was unsure of their purpose but tentatively suggested that they were 'very probably . . . intended for warming a room' (1887a, 17). These structures have been almost universally interpreted as corn driers, as Hawkes noted (Hawkes *et al.* 1947, 37), or as malting kilns (Morris 1979, 7).

BOKERLEY DYKE AND WOODYATES, 1888–90

Given the General's concern with linear earthworks it was almost inevitable that he would investigate Bokerley Dyke, a massive earthwork on the north-eastern edge of Cranborne Chase.

He began his report on Bokerley Dyke with a discussion of the development of defensive works from hillforts, which were places of refuge for the local population, to linear works designed for the defence of a region. Although these linear works would be 'difficult, or impossible, to defend at all points' this was the system adopted by the Romans on their frontiers. In this 'higher state of civilization' individual settlements did not need their own defences. Bokerley Dyke was therefore a defensive work erected by 'superior people' against 'inferior people, in a lower condition of life', though the General was forced to concede that 'It may not accord entirely with modern ideas of a military position . . .' (Pitt Rivers 1892, 7–8, 61). He needed to excavate the

Dyke in order to demonstrate the date of its construction. However, there was no known settlement on the line of the Dyke and therefore little likelihood of finding dateable artefacts until, in 1888, a farmer removing soil from the Dyke found a number of Roman coins.

Pitt Rivers immediately sought the landowner's permission to excavate and in May drove his first section through the Dyke. The finds from this section showed that the Dyke was not constructed before the late third century AD. The second section, cut the following month, produced a coin of Honorius from the body of the rampart and confirmed the late Roman or early post-Roman dating of the earthwork.

Trenching along the counterscarp of the ditch revealed a number of pits and gullies near the point where the Dyke crossed the Roman road, Ackling Dyke, at Woodyates. The settlement thus revealed was excavated between November 1889 and May 1890. Pitt Rivers identified this settlement as the Vindocladia of the Antonine Itinerary (*ibid.*, 20) which Colt Hoare had previously placed on Gussage Hill, four miles to the south-west. Vindocladia is now thought to be the settlement adjacent to Badbury Rings (Rivet and Smith 1979, 500).

The excavations of both the Dyke and the settlement were meticulously recorded and beautifully illustrated by large scale plans and section drawings. The section drawings of the two phase ditch of Bokerley Dyke confirm the General's own conclusion that the outer ditch pre-dated the rear ditch (Pitt Rivers 1892, pl. CLXIII) though he was unable to read the section in this way himself, underlining his own belief that the excavator should record every detail even if he himself could not understand them fully. The main plans were contoured as those at Woodcutts and Rotherley had been, the vertical heights measured 'with great care with a spirit level – not in the ordinary way of marking contours by the angles of the slopes' (*ibid.*, 62).

The General described his method of excavating the trenches through the Dyke. They were 'cut in steps, and each step was clean cut, and swept, before the next was commenced' (*ibid.*, 77). This seems to echo the description of his method of digging the Dane's Dyke where he had dug a series of trenches eight or ten feet (2.4–3.0 m) wide along the line of the rampart but clearly no baulks were left at Bokerley as they had been in Dane's Dyke. It seems probable, given the existence of longitudinal sections at the various pickets, which were placed at five foot (1.5 m) intervals, that the sections were dug in five-foot-wide trenches and in vertical spits, probably of two feet (0.6 m).

Chronological relationships of features smaller than the Dyke itself were still a problem for the General. Indeed in excavating the remains of the settlement at Woodyates he seems not to have considered the possibility of chronological depth. The 'Cross Dyke' crossed several rectangular structures, 'from which it may be conjectured that they were buildings of no great importance, perhaps workshops' (*ibid.*, 66).

The excavations at Bokerley and Woodyates were not entirely a happy experience for the General. Not only did he lose the services of Frederick James and W. S. Tomkin but he was distrustful of his workforce, which consisted of between ten and nineteen men 'who happened to be out of employ, and who consequently could not be expected to prove themselves amongst the most efficient of their class' (*ibid.*, 23–4). He even attributed the small number of coins found in the first section to their dishonesty: 'The workmen at that time were a newly collected set of loafers from the neighbourhood, and though very closely watched, it is possible that all the coins may not have come into my hands at first: afterwards, when it had been found that coins were too abundant to be of any intrinsic value, there was no temptation to conceal them' (*ibid.*, 72–3).

The coins found in Bokerley Dyke and Woodyates showed that Woodyates was occupied later than either Woodcutts or Rotherley. The chronological range of the coins was illustrated by two frequency graphs and the coins themselves were the subject of two photographic plates, the first that Pitt Rivers ever used. A frequency graph was also used to illustrate the chronological range of a hoard of silver Roman coins which had been found near Sixpenny Handley in 1877. These coins were drawn by Tomkin for publication, on which the General commented that, 'Probably an experienced numismatist will hardly consider these ordinary coins worth the trouble that has been spent upon them . . . [but] they will not be without use in assisting future identifications. In most numismatic works that are used for reference, rare coins only are illustrated, and the numerous varieties of ordinary coins are not given' (*ibid.*, 280).

The human remains from Woodyates were studied by Dr J. G. Garson. He concluded that, '. . . the Woodyates specimens belonged to a more mixed race than the inhabitants of Rotherley, whilst the Woodcutts people were intermediate in this respect . . . the people in the neighbourhood of Woodyates did not live isolated from the Roman population, as the Rotherley people evidently did, more or less, but mixed and inter-bred with them' (*ibid.*, 230). His belief that he was seeing a mix of Romans with a pre-Celtic dolichocephalic British population was based on only eighteen skeletons found at Woodyates.

The list of visitors to the excavations at Bokerley Dyke and Woodyates includes J. Romilly Allen, George Fox, who was one of the Society of Antiquaries' excavation directors at Silchester, H. J. Moule of the Dorset County Museum, George Payne, John Mansell-Pleydell, T. Wake Smart, the Dorset antiquarian, and the Rev. J. H. Ward, a numismatist.

Further excavations have been undertaken at Bokerley Junction since the General's lifetime, in 1942–3 and 1958. The 1958 excavations, while suggesting a slightly revised chronological sequence for the development of the earthwork, confirmed the observations made by Pitt Rivers and Hawkes and their late Roman dating for the Dyke (Rahtz 1961).

WANSDYKE, APRIL 1889, JUNE–AUGUST 1890 AND MAY 1891

In June 1888 Pitt Rivers received a letter from the Rev. A. C. Smith urging him to undertake excavations in Wansdyke in north Wiltshire. He accepted the challenge and began the work in April of the following year. The second season was interrupted by a serious illness and the work was not completed until 1891. During the excavations the General stayed at the Bear, Devizes, and his assistants lodged at Calstone. Site visitors included the local antiquarians B. H. Cunnington and W. Heward Bell, who was present nearly all the time.

The General calculated that Wansdyke, a massive earthen bank and ditch, was sixty miles long: 'This is the length of the wall of Hadrian between Newcastle and Carlisle, which work Wansdyke greatly resembles in the general principles of its construction' (Pitt Rivers 1892, 25–6). The General had seen Hadrian's Wall, though only in the poorly preserved eastern sector. Other comments of his about the similarity of Wansdyke and Hadrian's Wall possibly indicate a degree of confusion between the Wall and the Vallum. The General also likened the four hillforts on the line of Wansdyke to the forts on Hadrian's Wall (*ibid.*, 26, 245).

By his excavations Pitt Rivers proved conclusively that Wansdyke was either of Roman or post-Roman date and he favoured the idea that it was a British defence against the Saxons, constructed around AD 520, though he was prepared to accept the possibility of a dating as early as the time of Aulus Plautus or as late as a West Saxon defence against the Mercians (*ibid.*, 28–30).

Like those in Bokerley Dyke the sections across Wansdyke were 'cut in steps of 2 feet (0.6 m), and each step was swept before beginning another one. A diagram of the section, to scale, was kept on the ground during the excavations, and the position of every object was fixed with a spirit level, and marked on the diagram immediately it was discovered. This method was employed in all the sections, and it ensures perfect accuracy' (*ibid.*, 252).

A seam of turf in the bank suggested the possibility that it was a two-phase construction with a substantial chronological gap between the phases. This theory was tested by a longitudinal section which showed that the turf layer was discontinuous and consisted of dumped material rather than living turf (*ibid.*, 253).

There is a distinctly defensive note about the General's comments on these excavations and little doubt exists that someone had been criticising his methods and conclusions:

> I have dug 24 sections through the ramparts of Camps and Dykes in different localities . . . and am tolerably familiar with the appearance of the seams of earth and rubble found in them . . . I have seldom or never failed to find something in a rampart capable of throwing light on the date of its construction. My experience is, I believe, almost unique in this particular branch of investigation, and if archaeologists could be persuaded of its importance as a test of time, it would, I think, be more frequently resorted to. (*ibid.*, 254)

The best dating evidence for Wansdyke in Section 1 consisted of an iron knife and a nail at the bottom of the bank. The discovery of these objects is described with almost obsessive detail:

> The finding of these two objects is well authenticated. My assistant, Mr. James,

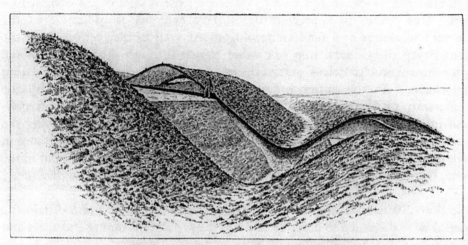

GENERAL VIEW OF SECTION I, WANSDYKE,
TAKEN FROM THE COUNTERSCARP, LOOKING WEST.

34 Perspective drawing of Section 1, Wansdyke, showing layers within the rampart and ditch. These layers were depicted in great detail in the formal section drawings

> was watching the digging at the time, and he noticed the discolouration of the white chalk rubble, caused by the rust from the iron objects, before they were picked up. The knife and the nail were then picked up by the workman and handed to him. Mr. C. Gray was also on the spot at the time, and witnessed the discovery. I myself saw the find within a few minutes of the discovery, and investigated the circumstances on the spot with great care. All who were present, were made to stand in the positions they occupied at the time of the discovery, and each one described the appearance of the soil and of the objects, at the moment they were first noticed . . . There can be no doubt whatever that these objects lay upon the surface of the ground, before the rampart was thrown over them. (*ibid.*, 254–5)

He also found fragments of samian pottery under the counterscarp bank. The identification was checked by John Evans and Augustus Franks so that 'No unprejudiced person can for a moment doubt their identification . . .' (*ibid.*, 255).

Section 3 was a longitudinal section of the counterscarp bank at Brown's Barn showing the rampart and ditch of the Brown's Barn enclosure sealed beneath it. The published section drawing is extremely clear but the General was again so concerned to name his witnesses to its veracity that his account is almost incoherent: 'Several persons were present who saw the lines in the section, including amongst others, Mr. Heward Bell, Mr. B. H. Cunnington, of Devizes, and others' (*ibid.*, 258).

Sir Richard Colt Hoare had already deduced from field observation that the

Brown's Barn entrenchment pre-dated Wansdyke but Pitt Rivers was inclined to dismiss this evidence and to rely instead on the results of his own spade-work. This failure to appreciate the surface evidence is indicative of the General's weakness as a field archaeologist. As well as the section along the counterscarp the General dug one other trench through the rampart of the entrenchment and 'trenched' part of the interior. Finds were few and the dating inconclusive. As the entrenchment was apparently only overlain by the counterscarp of Wansdyke, Pitt Rivers was not entirely sure that the entrench-ment might not be contemporary with the main rampart of Wansdyke, the counterscarp being a later addition: 'it is a position of such great importance in its bearing on the age of the great Dyke . . . if other sections are to be cut in the Dyke, I can, at present, suggest no better place for the purpose than this' (*ibid.*, 261).

Section 2 was a cutting across Wansdyke near Brown's Barn. Again the General was concerned to describe in detail the process of finding and analysing his dating evidence:

> Each piece [of pottery] was at once washed quite clean with a scrubbing brush, to enable its quality to be identified, and it was then put in a pill-box with the depth beneath the surface of the rampart written on it. One piece of Samian was picked out of the old surface line in my presence by a workman, who had come to the diggings on that day for the first time, and who was ignorant of the different kinds of pottery found in the section. He would therefore have been unable, even if he desired it, by any species of legerdemain, to have introduced a piece of Samian into the rampart . . . The very greatest vigilance and accuracy is necessary in recording the finds in these sections. An experienced excavator must not merely conduct his investigations, so as to furnish the materials for fair criticism, which he will cordially welcome, but he must also be prepared to meet hyper-criticism, and that not always in the interest of truth. (*ibid.*, 263)

The description of individual objects drawn in the plates also frequently includes a description of the circumstances of its discovery, even to the name of the workman who found it.

The General's career-long interest in linear earthworks did not end with Wansdyke. He planned to excavate a section across Offa's Dyke. Permission for this project was gained through the offices of Willy Fox Pitt, who wrote to his father just after Christmas 1894 from Powis Castle, 'Powis says he would be delighted to give you permission to dig up Offa's Dyke as long as you leave it outwardly as you found it – this I told him was your custom. He & Violet hope that when you come you will put up with them here' (Pitt Rivers Papers L1134). Only illness and pressure of other work prevented the General from taking up this invitation.

KING JOHN'S HOUSE, TOLLARD ROYAL, 1889

King John's House near Tollard Royal church was by tradition a medieval hunting lodge frequented by King John, but in the late nineteenth century there was nothing in its outward appearance to suggest that it was really any earlier than the sixteenth century. In 1889 the House fell vacant and Pitt Rivers seized the opportunity 'to examine the walls, and see if anything could be found to confirm the tradition of its great antiquity' (Pitt Rivers 1890, 8). Stripping the stucco and plaster from the walls soon revealed medieval features. The General had a very clear restoration policy:

> . . . the work of both [medieval and Tudor] periods should be preserved, only removing that of the later period, where it completely hid the earlier work; but that the quite modern additions, some of which had been done by Lord Rivers not more than 40 or 50 years ago, and which were of very inferior workmanship . . . should be entirely removed. (ibid., 9)

Paint was stripped from panelling, modern grates were removed from fire-places, rotten beams and floorboards were replaced and medieval windows were uncovered. Every room and every architectural feature was numbered:

> The door No. 12 had evidently opened outwards, and this led me to conjecture that there must have been a tower at this angle of the building. On peeling the walls outside the alternate bonding stones of the tower were seen . . . and this caused me to excavate the ground beneath, which resulted in the discovery of the foundations of the tower. (ibid., 11)

A memorandum in one of Tomkin's notebooks (PRO WORK 39/10) suggests that the General considered rebuilding this tower but he abandoned the scheme and, having repointed the foundations of the tower, he turned his attention to the roof of the House and examined the loft:

> having had the rafters removed, I crept into it to examine the top of the wall, when to my surprise and delight, I found the tops of two pointed arches, just showing above the floor of the loft, and exactly above the two windows, Nos. XV and XVI. The latter of these . . . was at that time quite blocked up . . . but No. XV had been turned into a rectangular Elizabethan window . . . Only a few minutes after this discovery sufficed to remove all the Tudor work from this window, and it was then found that there were stone seats in the wall on each side, of the form well known to be of the thirteenth century . . . This discovery showed me that my search had been rewarded, and that we had now found work nearly approaching if not actually dating down to the time of King John. (Pitt Rivers 1890, 12)

The General was as rigorous in recording his restoration work here as he was in recording his archaeological excavations: 'Careful models have . . . been made of both windows, showing their exact condition at the time they were found, and the position of each stone and brick is given by means of which architects and antiquaries will be able to see clearly what has been done, and what authority exists for the slight restorations that have been made' (ibid., 13). The General's thorough recording of architectural details at King John's House has recently been held up as an example for investigators of historic buildings (Smith 1985, 7–10, figs. 1–3).

In addition to the tower at the south-west corner, the General excavated

35 King John's House, elevations

36 King John's House, interior view

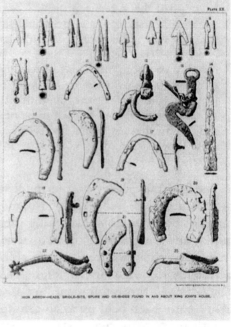

37 King John's House, medieval pottery

38 King John's House, medieval ironwork

extensively along the west side of the House where he found the foundations of outbuildings, including one with an oven and fireplace. This excavation resulted in the recovery of a number of medieval and early post-medieval 'relics' including pottery, clay pipes, knives, forks and spoons, spurs, horse and ox shoes, purses, arrowheads, locks and keys, nails, buckles, brooches, animal bones and coins. Pitt Rivers wanted to use these finds as the beginning of a data base of medieval antiquities:

> It has not hitherto been customary . . . to give drawings of objects found during the repairs of medieval buildings . . . It is true that medieval relics have not the same importance as those of prehistoric times, in which they generally afford the only reliable evidence of time . . . Nevertheless, there are conditions in which they afford the only evidence available even in medieval times, and a more thorough knowledge of them than we possess would be desirable . . . In fact the subject has not been much studied, and it is with the hope of promoting this branch of enquiry that I have had so many little objects figured, that have been found in this House, to some of which I am unable to assign any date. (ibid., 13–14)

This is a remarkable advance on his earlier statement that,

> From the relics of this [medieval] period little is to be learnt . . . the interest which attaches to such objects is more sentimental than useful. The main outlines of the picture have already been built up in our minds through the agency of more reliable and direct evidence, and they do no more than supply some of the lights and shadows. (Pitt Rivers 1884a, 59)

The combined evidence of the medieval windows and archways which certain 'competent architects' pronounced to be of the early thirteenth century and some of the pottery, which the General thought was of a similar date, was substantiated by two coins of Henry III. Pitt Rivers concluded that all this went 'a good way' towards confirming the tradition of the House's early origins and its occupation by King John during his hunting expeditions. This argument was further strengthened by a long list of thirteenth-century castles and houses with parallel architectural features including Acton Burnell and Stokesay in Shropshire whither the General's son Douglas was despatched to draw plans, elevations and sketches (Pitt Rivers Papers L2436). Claude Gray drew some fine sketches of windows in Lochleven and Kinnaird Castles while on the Inspectorate journey that summer (PRO WORK 39/3).

Fantastically, Pitt Rivers concluded his reasoned scientific report on his activities at King John's House with a headlong political attack on the Ground Game law recently introduced by the Liberal government. Starting with the contention, itself false, that the Chase and King John's House within it had witnessed 'six or seven centuries of continually increasing freedom and respect for the rights of private property' he claimed that,

> it has again witnessed a relapse in our idea of liberty. It has seen existing contracts broken into and tyrannical measures again introduced – not this time in the interests of kings or nobles, or agriculturalists, or of the people, but of demagogues and political agitators. It has seen the ground game – the private property

of the landowners – arbitrarily confiscated and given to others in exchange, as it was vainly hoped by these robbers, for parliamentary votes for themselves. (Pitt Rivers 1890, 25)

The Ground Game Act of 1880 was intended to allow tenant farmers to protect their crops against injury from hares and rabbits without having to arrange a contract with the landlord, though the taking or killing of these animals was still to be under tight state control. Interference with 'freedom of contract' was one of the principle objections to the bill put forward by conservative land-owners who made the convenient but false assumption that there was an equality of bargaining power between themselves and their tenants (Porter 1986). Pitt Rivers did not believe the Act to be significant in itself and admitted that he was not personally interested in ground game but he thought such reforms 'potent for evil as a precedent for further confiscation and robbery' (Pitt Rivers 1890, 25).

After this outburst the General resumed his measured scientific tones to explain what was now being done at King John's House. The House was refurnished, mostly with seventeenth-century pieces, and became a 'sup-plementary Museum' with a 'small collection of original pictures, illustrating the history of Painting' and, in the basement, a reading room for the villagers (*ibid.*).

Pitt Rivers' work at King John's House is remarkable for the detailed archi-tectural recording, the carefully thought out restoration policy for the fabric of the building itself and for the deliberate attempt to use the episode for the purpose of putting the study of medieval antiquities on a sounder basis.

SOUTH LODGE CAMP, APRIL–JULY 1893

Pitt Rivers was seriously ill in 1892 and did not begin to excavate again until the Spring of 1893. He now turned to the entrenchment on the west side of the carriage road at Barrow Pleck which he had noted and surveyed nearly ten years earlier. The thick nut-wood was cut down and grubbed out leaving only a few more substantial trees, and the entrenchment was resurveyed in more detail and contoured. Six sections were then cut across the ditch and rampart. The fourth of these, on the east side, uncovered a large complete barrel urn, now known as the South Lodge Urn. This was the first evidence that the South Lodge entrenchment was a Bronze Age enclosure. Total excavation followed. A large part of the interior was dug in trenches about 3 m wide, only the area supporting living trees remaining unexcavated. A number of features were discovered in the interior, including one posthole, a trough, some 'soft places in the chalk' and a slight mound containing 201 sherds of pottery. A large number of sherds was also found in the body of the rampart from which the General concluded that the location had been occupied before the construction of the enclosure (Pitt Rivers 1898, 12).

South Lodge is the first Pitt Rivers excavation for which we have a published photographic record. There are photographs of the excavated ditch, including

39 Excavation of the ditch of South Lodge Camp. Charles Flower and Herbert Toms (with black armband) are on the left

one of the South Lodge Urn *in situ*. Some of the details are of interest. In one plate (*ibid.*, pl. 236, fig. 2) the General is watching the excavations from a deckchair at the side of the trench, in another (*ibid.*, fig. 1) he is standing with a rather detached air near his carriage on the box of which sits a liveried coach-man. The assistants' bicycles lean against a tree and the site hut. This is a mobile shepherd's hut, of well-known Dorset type, which is preserved and stands outside the Pitt Rivers Museum in Oxford. One assistant, H. S. Toms, stands by the level while another, probably Charles Flower, sits at a table outside the hut. A large white board lying on the spoilheap next to the level is presumably the field plan on which the position of every sherd and relic was noted (*ibid.*, 7). The workmen are using no tools smaller than pickaxes and shovels.

In other respects South Lodge is not so well recorded. Although detailed plans showing the position of every sherd have fortunately survived in the archive (Pitt Rivers Papers R23 and un-numbered plan) they were never published. More seriously, South Lodge is the first site at which detailed stratigraphic section drawings were abandoned in favour of the 'average sec-tion', a generalised profile of rampart and ditch with all the finds projected on

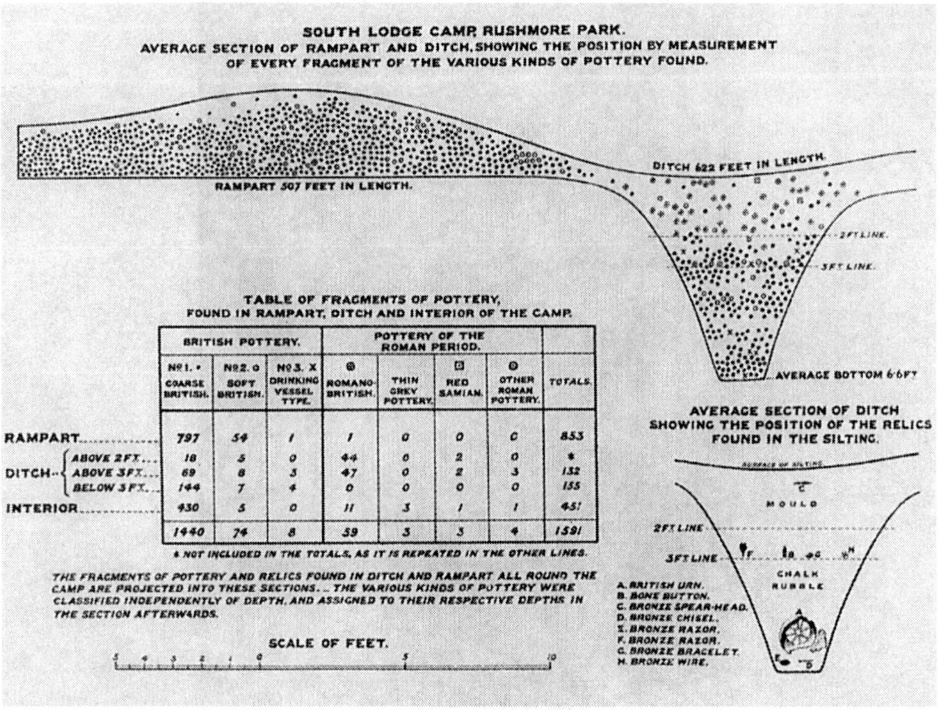
SOUTH LODGE CAMP, RUSHMORE PARK.
AVERAGE SECTION OF RAMPART AND DITCH, SHOWING THE POSITION BY MEASUREMENT OF EVERY FRAGMENT OF THE VARIOUS KINDS OF POTTERY FOUND.
RAMPART 507 FEET IN LENGTH.
DITCH 622 FEET IN LENGTH.
2FT LINE.
3FT LINE.
AVERAGE BOTTOM 6·6FT
TABLE OF FRAGMENTS OF POTTERY, FOUND IN RAMPART, DITCH AND INTERIOR OF THE CAMP.

	BRITISH POTTERY.			POTTERY OF THE ROMAN PERIOD.				
	Nº1. • COARSE BRITISH.	Nº2. o SOFT BRITISH.	Nº3. X DRINKING VESSEL TYPE.	ROMANO-BRITISH.	THIN GREY POTTERY.	RED SAMIAN.	OTHER ROMAN POTTERY.	TOTALS.
RAMPART	797	54	1	1	0	0	C	853
DITCH ABOVE 2FT.	18	5	0	44	0	2	0	*
DITCH ABOVE 3FT.	69	8	3	47	0	2	3	132
DITCH BELOW 3FT.	144	7	4	0	0	0	0	155
INTERIOR	430	5	0	11	3	1	1	451
	1440	74	8	59	3	3	4	1591

* NOT INCLUDED IN THE TOTALS, AS IT IS REPEATED IN THE OTHER LINES.
THE FRAGMENTS OF POTTERY AND RELICS FOUND IN DITCH AND RAMPART ALL ROUND THE CAMP ARE PROJECTED INTO THESE SECTIONS. _ THE VARIOUS KINDS OF POTTERY WERE CLASSIFIED INDEPENDENTLY OF DEPTH, AND ASSIGNED TO THEIR RESPECTIVE DEPTHS IN THE SECTION AFTERWARDS.
SCALE OF FEET.
5 4 3 2 1 0 5 10
AVERAGE SECTION OF DITCH SHOWING THE POSITION OF THE RELICS FOUND IN THE SILTING.
MOULD
2FT LINE
3FT LINE
CHALK RUBBLE
A. BRITISH URN.
B. BONE BUTTON.
C. BRONZE SPEAR-HEAD.
D. BRONZE CHISEL.
E. BRONZE RAZOR.
F. BRONZE RAZOR.
G. BRONZE BRACELET.
H. BRONZE WIRE.

40 'Average section' of the bank and ditch, South Lodge

to it and no real indication of the different layers within the fill. This is a clear retreat from the standards of Bokerley Dyke and Wansdyke.

South Lodge is currently perhaps the best known of Pitt Rivers' sites due to the re-excavation of 1977–81 (Barrett *et al.* forthcoming). This re-excavation has refined many of the details of this site recovered by the General. In particular, his solitary posthole is now known to be one of thirteen forming the larger of two roundhouses in the enclosure and the slight mound of dark earth and sherds was probably an abandonment deposit connected with the same structure. The trough, which lay adjacent to a burnt flint mound excavated in 1980–1, might now be interpreted as a cooking trough while the 'soft places in the chalk' are probably storage pits. The General was correct in his belief that occupation predated the enclosure. Herbert Toms demonstrated that the enclosure overlay the field system (1925), a point that was confirmed by re-excavations and a series of postholes near the entrance of the enclosure are arguably part of a pre-enclosure structure (Barrett *et al.* 1983, 198–202).

While he was working at South Lodge Pitt Rivers undertook two small excavations outside the enclosure. One of these, on 30 June, was a trench through the lynchet on Barrow Pleck (Pitt Rivers 1888a, pl. LXXX), part of the field system underlying the enclosure, in which he found flint flakes and a scraper. This excavation was recorded in a Relic Table but mentioned nowhere else. On the previous four days he had been excavating an enigmatic pit on the hillslope to the west of the enclosure. This contained some human skeletal material, a flint axe and some pottery sherds, most of which were Romano-British or medieval. Pitt Rivers was unable to explain this pit and it remains something of a problem, though it can now be seen to cut a double lynchet trackway associated with the Bronze Age field system (Barrett *et al.* 1981, fig. 10). Possibly it is a Roman or medieval chalk pit which has disturbed a prehistoric burial. The General remarked that he had investigated many depressions of similar type which 'have either been pit-dwellings or dug for chalk for agricultural purposes, and some have contained flint scrapers' (Pitt Rivers 1898, 43).

HANDLEY HILL ENTRENCHMENT, AUGUST 1893

Between August 1893 and April 1895 the General mounted a series of excavations along the eastern boundary of his property on Handley Hill and Handley Down where it marched with the property of Lord Shaftesbury. This work was done in three distinct campaigns, the first running from August to November 1893, the second from March to June 1894 and the third over the winter of 1894–5.

The Handley Hill entrenchment was similar to South Lodge but about half the size and of much slighter relief. Pitt Rivers decided to excavate it because of 'the number of similar square-shaped earthworks that are to be found on the surface of the Downs in this county and Wiltshire' (1898, 47), a striking example of his adherence to Huxley's principle that that which is important is that which is persistent. The whole entrenchment was contoured and excavated. The excavation began at 7.30 a.m., the usual start of a working day, on Thursday 10 August with seven men, all of whom had dug at South Lodge. They were supervised by Charles Flower, Herbert Toms and Harold Gray (Gray Notebooks). A coin of Trajan found on the 'old surface line' beneath the rampart would have dated the site firmly to the Roman period or later, except that Pitt Rivers considered that it might have worked its way down through the very slight rampart. Nevertheless he felt that the entrenchment was probably of Roman date, though there were ample signs of prehistoric activity on the site. This interpretation was reinforced by the discovery of sherds of pottery which the General believed to be Romano-British, though he noted their similarity to sherds from Maddington, Wiltshire which were possibly medieval. This illustrates the crucial importance of Pitt Rivers' system of labelling each individual sherd and preserving them in the museum at Farnham, because over forty years later Stuart Piggott was able to relocate them and confirm that they were indeed of the twelfth century AD. Despite its superficial similarity to South Lodge and other Bronze Age enclosures, Handley Hill is one of a group of medieval enclosures on the Wessex chalkland (Piggott 1936) including those surveyed by Toms in later years (Bradley 1989).

A number of pits outside the enclosure were excavated. The largest of these produced human and animal bone and some pottery. This pit was excavated by a labourer called Rigg using a pickaxe with which he broke the human skull (Gray Notebooks). Like the large pit near South Lodge this was possibly a chalk pit which had disturbed earlier deposits, though it may have been a neolithic feature. The other pits contained prehistoric and Romano-British finds. None of the smaller features appeared on any published plan.

The labourers at Handley Hill Entrenchment were paid £1. 2s. 6d each for the ten days work. In addition 16 shillings were expended on beer (*ibid.*).

BARROWS 23 AND 24, AUGUST–SEPTEMBER 1893

Two slight round barrow mounds lying close to the crossroads, now the Handley roundabout, were excavated as soon as the Handley Hill Entrench- ment was finished. Neither of these barrows showed any sign of a ditch on the surface but both were found to have ditches on excavation. This led Pitt Rivers to pen some comments at the expense of his mentor Canon Greenwell, who he suspected of failing to find ditches round his Yorkshire barrows: 'I have no doubt that in many cases they have not been noticed, owing to the ditches being, in some cases, at a little distance from the foot of the barrow' (Pitt Rivers 1898, 144). This is a little disingenuous of the General, given that he had not looked for barrow ditches in his excavations in Rushmore Park in the 1880s and had certainly missed at least one (Barrett *et al.* 1983, 196).

Barrow 23 was found to cover a number of cremations, two of them in collared urns, and an inhumation accompanied by a bronze awl. The bronze awl was important to the General in dating the barrow to the Bronze Age though he was aware of the possibility that this was a secondary interment. He does not seem to have been very sure about the dating of the collared urns though he had recovered similar vessels at Scrubbity Coppice.

Barrow 24, which was only about half the size of Barrow 23, was to be one of the General's most important excavations. The mound was found to cover three large holes in the chalk, none of which yielded any finds. Pitt Rivers' remark that 'These graves may have been opened, but no trace of such opening could be seen in the superficial mould' (1898, 147) shows at least that he was looking for such features, a point which one could not learn from perusal of the totally uninformative section drawings (*ibid.*, pl. 295).

It was the features outside the barrow ditch, however, which were of major importance. First he found a rectangular pit, then a series of no less than fifty- two secondary cremations in an urnfield stretching around the west, south and east sides of the mound. None of these features were visible on the surface and the General claimed that they would not have been found, 'had it not been for the practice I have established of trenching, down to the undisturbed chalk, the entire surface of the ground contained within the area of the contoured plan of the Barrow' (*ibid.*, 148). This statement begs the question of when and why the General established this practice. Certainly he had not done anything of the kind in his earlier barrow excavations in Rushmore Park and Barrows 23 and

41 Model of Barrow 24, Handley Hill, showing the flat cremation cemetery; mahogany

24 were the first barrows he had excavated since then. Barrow 23, being much larger than 24, almost fills the area of its contoured plan (*ibid.*, pl. 295), so barrow 24 must have been the first for which a really substantial external area was trenched, in which case the discovery of the urnfield was a lucky chance. If this is the case it has been disguised by the General's decision to publish Barrows 23 and 24 after Barrows 26 and 27 in the report although they were excavated a full eight months earlier.

Nevertheless the discovery of the urnfield at Barrow 24, the first flat cremation cemetery discovered in Britain, is a significant landmark in British archaeology and the thoroughness of the General's curation of the finds has paid handsome dividends: '. . . several urns were found but in excavating them they came to pieces except one which was got out nearly entire & sent to Rushmore in the carriage . . .' (Gray Notebooks). Despite the obvious technical difficulties of excavating these features all the cremated bone from the various deposits was carefully bagged and stored at Farnham and this material has now yielded a range of radiocarbon dates (Barrett *et al.* 1981, 232).

WOR BARROW, SEPTEMBER–OCTOBER 1893 AND MARCH–MAY 1894

Having finished the investigation of Barrows 23 and 24 the General moved his scene of operations northwards from Handley Hill to Handley Down to deal with the complex of sites around Wor Barrow and the as yet undiscovered Angle Ditch.

Wheeler has described the Wor Barrow as 'the first long barrow scientifically excavated' but he criticised the excavation nevertheless (1954, 120–1). He thought there should have been a longitudinal section through the mound and a number of section drawings of the ditch rather than the General's diagrammatic 'average sections'. It would be hard to disagree with this assessment. In fact the site diary shows that detailed section drawings of the ditches were prepared: 'Toms made a section across the ditch on the line AB showing the seams in the chalk rubble' (Gray Notebooks). However these were not published and have since been lost.

From the plan (Pitt Rivers 1898, pl. 249) it is clear that the ditch of Wor Barrow has not only been recut on at least one occasion but that it has had a number of later graves cut into it. Section drawings of the quality of those prepared for the Wansdyke report might have provided information of immense value to later researchers on these matters. There is one published stratigraphic section drawing of the mound and both ditches (*ibid.*, 65) but it is on too small a scale to be really useful and certain vital details are clearly missing.

Pitt Rivers excavated the massive ditch of Wor Barrow in the autumn of 1893, leaving the mound until the following spring. Finds of all periods from the Neolithic to the Medieval were found in the ditch and recorded apparently by depth from the surface although the General himself pinpointed the major weakness of this system: 'The surface of the silting during the Bronze Age must have been concave as it is now, and objects deposited on the side of the Ditch must have rested higher up than objects deposited in the middle' (*ibid.*, 63).

The General admitted that he could not recognise Neolithic pottery, but there were some fragments in the ditch which corresponded with sherds which were to be discovered with the primary burials in the mound. These sherds, like all the other finds, were 'carefully preserved for future comparisons' (*ibid.*, 64). Amongst the human skeletons found in the ditch silts were those of a man and child together. By the ribs of the man was a leaf-shaped flint arrowhead which Pitt Rivers thought might have been the cause of death. Despite this evidence he preferred to employ skull shape for dating these burials, arguing that from the 'hyperdolichocephalic form of the head . . . I have assumed that this was a secondary interment of the Stone Age' (*ibid.*, 63).

The General began the excavation of the mound by driving a massive trench into it from the southern end. Finds were apparently still to be measured by depth from the surface, though in the event they were relatively few. The site photographs show the engineer's level set up and a staff is in evidence at all stages of the excavation so perhaps finds were measured fro.n an overall datum. The report is ambiguous on this point. The excavation of the mound was interrupted by poor weather. On 23 April the site diary recorded, 'All the men present except Barret. Rather wet, but not enough to prevent the men digging. The rain came on in the dinner hour & it looked like setting in for the remainder of the day, and Cooke, Elliott and G. Fry went home. However, it cleared up about three o'clock & the men continued digging until 5 o'clock' (Gray Notebooks).

42 Excavation of the ditch of Wor Barrow; Herbert Toms stands on the right. This photograph, which the General did not publish, shows the ditch fills and also demonstrates the spit digging method

43 Excavation of the ditch of Wor Barrow, general view. Pitt Rivers is standing on the mound with his cousin, Lady Magheramorne

They encountered a series of secondary interments high in the mound. Several of these had been decapitated. They were accompanied by Roman coins and sherds but again the General referred primarily to skull form in assigning these burials to the Roman period. Beneath the chalk rubble of the mound the General found traces of a rectangular timber enclosure, 'a wooden version of the stone chambers so often found enclosing the interments in long barrows in other districts . . .' (Pitt Rivers 1898, 65). Within the enclosure was a low circular turf mound containing the primary burials, three articulated and three unarticulated adult males. There was a posthole at either end of the deposit and a foundation of flint nodules on the west side of the turf mound. These latter details have often been overlooked in later reassessments of this site because they do not appear in any published plans or sections or in the site model.

The site model gives a false impression of the neatness of the excavation which is belied by the published photographs of the digging in progress (*ibid.*, pls. 254, 255, 256). The trench is far from 'clean' in the modern excavator's phrase, while in fig. 2 of pl. 252 two lenses of dark material are visible in the section, neither of which is mentioned in the text. There are further discrepancies between the photographs and the other records. The large sarsen stone 'marking apparently the angle of the Entrance to the Enclosure' (*ibid.*, 80), which is depicted on the site plan and on the site model as if it is lying on the original ground surface, is shown by the photograph (*ibid.*, pl. 255, fig. 1) to be about 1 m higher up in the body of the long barrow mound. It is doubtful whether it has any structural relevance to the timber enclosure.

One further matter of interest arises from the photographs of Wor Barrow. A general shot of the barrow during the excavation of the ditch was taken 'from a scaffold erected for the purpose' (*ibid.*, 74), perhaps the first photographic tower in British archaeology.

While agreeing with Wheeler's strictures on the lack of a stratigraphic record it has to be said once again that recent reassessment of Wor Barrow and its neighbouring monuments, Barrows 26 and 27, has been based on Pitt Rivers' careful curation of the finds and exquisitely detailed site models (Bradley *et al.* 1984, 98–9). A fragment of antler firmly labelled 'Found at the bottom of the Ditch, 13 Foot' has now given a radiocarbon date (Barrett *et al.* forthcoming) and human bone from the barrow has been used in bone chemistry analyses (Antoine *et al.* 1988).

At Wor Barrow the General abandoned his usual practice of restoring earthworks to what he considered to be their former shape. He had other plans for this site. The excavated materials were 'wheeled to the outside, where they have been since formed into an amphitheatre with terraces, with a view to using the old surface line of the barrow as an arena for games or other amusements, and exhibitions' (Pitt Rivers 1898, 74). This earthwork has now been scheduled in its own right.

ANGLE DITCH AND SURFACE TRENCHING, HANDLEY DOWN, OCTOBER–NOVEMBER 1893 AND MAY–NOVEMBER 1894

While excavating the ditch of Wor Barrow the General had been examining the ground to the south but finding no earthworks; 'The pick was then used to hammer on the surface, and by this means, the Angle Ditch was discovered. The sound produced by hammering on an excavated part is much deeper than on an undisturbed surface . . .' (Pitt Rivers 1898, 59). Why the General examined this apparently unpromising piece of downland in the first place is not explained, nor is the adoption of the exploratory technique now known as 'bosing' which he did not record using elsewhere. Possibly the General is disguising the fact that the Angle Ditch had been recognised as an earthwork by his assistant, Herbert Toms, but not by himself (Bradley 1989, 34).

The Angle Ditch, as its name implies, was an L-shaped length of ditch, much like the one excavated at South Lodge in section and containing similar deposits. The General's workmen recovered a grain rubber, a palstave, bronze implements and part of an urn with other Bronze Age sherds. The ubiquitous Romano-British sherds were again confined to the upper levels of the fill. Pitt Rivers described the Angle Ditch as 'draining or protecting the north-east angle of an inhabited area' (Pitt Rivers 1898, 60). He immediately began to trench the surface within the angle, where he found only a shallow drain. This, according to the General, 'appeared to have been on the ground before the cutting of the Angle Ditch, as it drained across it' (ibid.), though it seems more likely to be a later feature dug across the backfilled Angle Ditch, given the amount of Romano-British pottery found in it.

Several more areas were trenched in the following spring and autumn. This resulted in the discovery of much more pottery of both Bronze Age and Romano-British types, a Beaker burial and the complete skeleton of an ox. The Beaker burial lay between the Angle Ditch and Wor Barrow. Its presence was indicated by a vegetation mark and Pitt Rivers states that this led to its excavation (ibid., 114) though the plan (ibid., pl 248) shows it within one of the trenched areas. The ox burial however was outside the area marked as trenched on the site plan and its discovery is unexplained. The site diary shows that the Beaker burial was indeed found prior to surface trenching. On 2 November 1893, 'J. Fry . . . pitched upon a pit & discovered a drinking vessel, which suggested the probability of finding a skeleton, care was taken after this and in the afternoon the skull was discovered. Then the skeleton was covered up and left in consequence of the rain' (Gray Notebooks).

The whole area was under cultivation in the Roman period and perhaps in the preceding Iron Age, which accounts for the disappearance of the Angle Ditch as an earthwork and for the quantity of Romano-British pottery. This pottery probably represents a manuring scatter rather than the habitation which Pitt Rivers envisaged and the shallow drain cutting the Angle Ditch is probably an element of this field system.

Angle Ditch was recorded by two 'average sections', one for pottery and one for 'relics', 'in accordance with the practice I have pursued in recording the excavation of other ditches of the same nature' (Pitt Rivers 1898, 102). Again Pitt Rivers drew attention to the completeness of the chronological sequence presented by the sherds of pottery and regretted that 'few, if any, explorers have experience of this nature, and are obliged to form their opinions solely by the position of the more generally known relics' (*ibid.*, 103).

Tool marks had been found near the bottom of the Ditch and these fitted 'fairly well' the blade of the broken palstave which had been found lying on the bottom. The General showed a very proper circumspection in connecting these two discoveries: 'it appears to me not at all impossible, that this very celt may have been employed to dig out the narrow bottom of the Ditch . . . and being broken in consequence of the flaws in the metal, which are apparent, may have been left and lost in the rubble which accumulated over it' (*ibid.*, 104).

BARROWS 26 AND 27, MAY–JUNE 1894

These round barrows lie at either end of Wor Barrow and have to be considered in association with that monument (Bradley *et al.* 1984, 98–9). Pitt Rivers dug them immediately after completing the excavation of the mound of Wor Barrow.

Barrow 26 covered two burials, one of which was accompanied by a shale belt slider. This began to disintegrate within a day of its discovery but the General, with great foresight, had already had detailed drawings and a wooden replica made (Pitt Rivers 1898, 140). Barrow 27, which had previously been opened by Colt Hoare, also contained a primary burial, as well as a Roman secondary cut into the ditch. It was the ditches of these two barrows which held the General's attention, and he devoted two pages of the report to a discussion of round barrow ditches (*ibid.*, 137–8). He identified three distinct types; irregular ditches, regular continuous ditches and regular ditches with a causeway. He considered barrows without ditches but again concluded that ditches might have been overlooked: 'I would recommend that a barrow should be dug all over. That has been my custom recently, and in fact I have usually trenched all round for a yard or two beyond the barrow on all sides' (*ibid.*, 138). This is a lesser claim than he made in connection with Barrows 23 and 24 (*ibid.*, 148).

Barrow 27 had an irregular ditch consisting of many different elements probably representing several distinct chronological phases (Bradley *et al.* 1984, 99). Barrow 26 had a regular ditch with causeway, according to the text, but was described as 'very irregular' in the Relic Table. This contradiction is more apparent than real because the word 'regular' was applied to the plan of the ditch and the word 'irregular' to its profile. Barrow 27 was illustrated (Pitt Rivers 1898, pl. 293) and the General wrote that 'plans of the dug-out ditches of the barrows should, when possible, accompany the record of them' (*ibid.*, 138). This statement renders even more inexcusable his failure to publish a plan of the ditch of Barrow 26. The only record we have of this feature is his bald statement that it was 'regular' and a very small scale model. The model seems to show that the ditch, though regular, had a double recut, substantially modifying its form but apparently respecting the original causeway (Bradley *et al.* 1984, 99 fig. 7.5). A similar double recut on a continuous ring ditch has been found recently at Down Farm less than 3 km to the south (Bowden and Lewis forthcoming). The double recut explains the phrase 'very irregular' used in the Relic Table.

Once again it must be emphasised that the General's failure at recording structural and stratigraphic elements of these barrows is balanced by the curation of well provenanced finds which has allowed later generations to reconstruct the sequence and relationship between Wor Barrow and these two significant late Neolithic round barrows (Bradley *et al.* 1984, 98–9).

BARROWS 28 AND 29, APRIL 1895

The General's final excavations in this area were of two further round barrows on the south side of Handley Hill. Both contained urned cremations and Barrow 29 had secondary interments, assumed to be Romano-British, in the ditch. The published records of these excavations suffer from the same inadequacies as the others in the fourth volume.

Pitt Rivers' excavations on Handley Hill and Handley Down were constrained by his property boundary. He had now excavated every ancient monument he could find on his own side of the fence. Beyond it to the east were the tempting barrow cemeteries on Oakley Down, Bottlebush Down and Wyke Down and the 'supposed British Trackway' (the Dorset Cursus) but this was Shaftesbury property. The General had usually managed to obtain permission to excavate on his neighbours' land but the Earl of Shaftesbury was a man of strong principles. He 'did not share Pitt Rivers's enthusiasm for disturbing ancient burial places. He believed that the desecration of graves was deplorable' (Cooper n.d., unpublished). It was probably Lord Shaftesbury who offered Pitt Rivers permission to excavate only 'on condition that I would not disturb the human bones or rebury them immediately. Of course I refused to avail myself of permission so hampered with unscientific conditions. This excessive reverence for bones of hoary and unknown antiquity is a great hindrance to Anthropological science' (Pitt Rivers 1898, 19).

NURSERY GARDENS, RUSHMORE, FEBRUARY 1894

A length of ditch and some adjoining pits were found in laying out the new Nursery Gardens adjacent to the Kitchen Garden at Rushmore. The finds from these features included Romano-British sherds, two uninscribed British coins and two coins of Claudius. The animal bones found included 'a nearly entire horse' (Pitt Rivers 1898, 241).

These discoveries were made close to the circular enclosure in Brooks Coppice, a site which the General barely mentions despite its position in the heart of his property (see Pitt Rivers 1887a, 5).

MARTIN DOWN, NOVEMBER 1895–MARCH 1896

The enclosure on Martin Down is of the same type as South Lodge but about twice as large. It occupies a relatively flat area above a slight combe on the east but is overlooked by higher ground on the other sides. In the 1890s a winter spring rose in the combe 550 m from the enclosure but 'in all such cases, it is reasonable to suppose that it ran out higher up in ancient times' (Pitt Rivers 1898, 185). The General thought this spring explained the positioning of the enclosure which he believed to have been primarily a corral. The wide gaps in the earthworks 'perhaps . . . made for the ingress and egress of cattle' (*ibid.*) seemed to support this interpretation.

With the permission of the landowner, Eyre Coote, and 'the sanction of the copyholders of the Down' Pitt Rivers excavated the Martin Down enclosure over the winter of 1895–6. The excavation employed between twelve and sixteen men for four months. The report says that the whole surface was trenched but a thick growth of gorse over parts of the area meant that in fact nearly half was not excavated. The site was supervised by Herbert Toms, and Pitt Rivers visited every day to inspect the finds made in his absence. Bronze Age and Romano-British pottery was found and a few bronzes but the relative scarcity of finds confirmed the General in his belief that the site was a cattle enclosure rather than a dwelling place, though he argued that the small amount of burnt flint and animal bone found and the presence of pits indicated some human habitation. Now that re-excavation of South Lodge has recovered evidence of occupied buildings there is little reason to doubt that Martin Down and other similar enclosures were occupied. A pit outside the enclosure yielded Romano-British finds, including a key, with some flint flakes: 'This affords additional confirmation of the fact noticed in the digging of the Ditch, that flint flakes in this Camp are especially characteristic of Romano-British deposits. This circumstance is remarkable and unexpected . . .' (*ibid.*, 189).

The ditch of Martin Down enclosure was recorded by six schematic section drawings showing the findspots of six individual 'relics' and an 'average section' showing the position of the different 'qualities' of pottery. The 'average section' (*ibid.*, pl. 310) shows some definite clustering of sherds in the ditch which Pitt Rivers does not mention in the text. Three pits were also shown as profiles.

Photographs of the excavation show Herbert Toms standing by the level, a dozen workmen and a boy, as well as a tent, a site hut and a two-wheeled horse-drawn vehicle. The tools include the inevitable picks and shovels and three or four wheelbarrows.

While the excavation was in progress some labourers levelling the rampart of a small linear ditch nearby for a horse gallop found a Roman coin. The

44 The digging team at Iwerne. G. Waldo Johnson is on the left

45 Excavations at Iwerne, painted wall plaster in the north-west corner of the villa

General's attention was called to this discovery. 'I then caused 300 feet [91.5 m] of both Ditch and Rampart to be excavated' (*ibid.*, 190). Romano-British pottery was found near the top of the ditch silts and Bronze Age pot beneath it. Though the labourers claimed that they had found the coin well down in the rampart the General was inclined to dismiss their evidence and assign a Bronze Age date to the ditch, which is part of an extensive system running across Martin Down and into Vernditch Chase to the west. Recent excavations have shown that other elements of this linear ditch system date to the later Iron Age (Evans and Vaughan 1985).

A small round barrow about 100 m to the west of the Martin Down enclosure escapes notice in Pitt Rivers' account.

The General's customary practice of restoring the earthworks he had excavated was modified in the case of the Martin Down enclosure. The ditch of South Lodge had been restored to its original depth but Martin Down now exists as a very slight earthwork. Presumably Eyre Coote and the copyholders of the Down did not relish the idea of a steep-sided two-metre-deep ditch in the middle of their sheep walk.

IWERNE, SEPTEMBER–DECEMBER 1897

A promising site at Park House Farm, Iwerne Courtney, below the western scarp of Cranborne Chase had been brought to Pitt Rivers' attention by the Rev. Sir Talbot Baker in 1891, and the General apparently dug a trial trench there in 1895. This was so successful that he returned in 1897 to undertake what was to be his last excavation. He was very ill and could visit the site only about four times a week, driving the eight miles from Rushmore in a landau and pair, though this was, according to Gray, 'the finest autumn in my recollection' (Hawkes *et al.* 1947, 50). Gray was in charge of the site with the assistance of G. Waldo Johnson. They employed as many as twenty-nine men and three boys. The latter washed the finds, which were then boxed and labelled and taken by waggon to Rushmore, where they were stored in a shed by the stables except for the small finds which were taken straight to the Museum.

Pitt Rivers intended to continue the excavation in 1898 but his health deteriorated so much over the winter that he never returned and never published the site. The pottery which had been stored at Rushmore was thrown out, though not until after the General's death, for Gray saw it when he went down to Tollard for the funeral. The site plan and finds register were also lost or destroyed.

Nevertheless, using the site model and the few finds fortuitously preserved at Farnham, Christopher Hawkes and Stuart Piggott were able to reassess the site exactly fifty years after the excavation. They isolated three phases of occupation and wrote a brief report based on a plan derived from the site model. 'In this we both feel a modest confidence', wrote Hawkes (*ibid.*).

8

Public education

Above all he was an educator. (J. Pitt Rivers 1983 unpublished)

Public education was the ultimate purpose of all the General's efforts in archaeology, just as it was the ultimate purpose of all his anthropological work. The motivation was his belief in political and social evolutionary progress:

> For good or for evil . . . we have thought proper to place power in the hands of the masses. The masses are ignorant, and knowledge is swamped by ignorance. The knowledge they lack is the knowledge of history. This lays them open to the designs of demagogues and agitators, who strive to make them break with the past, and seek the remedies for existing evils, or the means of future progress, in drastic changes that have not the sanction of experience . . . The law that Nature makes no jumps, can be taught by the history of mechanical contrivances, in such a way as at least to make men cautious how they listen to scatter-brained revolutionary suggestions. (Pitt Rivers 1891, 115–16)

The study of anthropology and archaeology, like the study of English literature (Eagleton 1983, 24–6), was to be a force for the maintenance of Victorian social order.

The General had been interested in education and educational systems from an early stage in his career (Russell and Russell 1937a, 121) and he was not impressed by existing museums as educational tools. The museums formed by learned societies 'succeed in collecting a stray Chinese umbrella or two, and a stuffed monkey, or a few bronze implements in a case' (Fox 1872b, 172) while the collections of the British Museum were too large, too diverse and too poorly displayed to be anything other than 'bewildering' to the average visitor (Pitt Rivers 1891, 115). His reasons for making his anthropological collections public, both in London and later in Oxford, were purely educational. No sooner was he established in Cranborne Chase than he began to create a complex of educational opportunities for the people of the Chase and the surrounding towns. This complex was centred on the Museum at Farnham, which was established in the early 1880s and the 'supplementary Museum' or art gallery at King John's House opened in 1891. In the same year Pitt Rivers explained his philosophy in a lecture to the Society of Arts:

> I hold that the great desideratum of our day is an educational museum, in which the visitors may instruct themselves . . . The knowledge of the facts of evolution,

46 Farnham Museum

and of the processes of gradual development, is the one great knowledge that we
have to inculcate . . . and this knowledge can be taught by museums, provided
they are arranged in such a manner that those who run may read. The working
classes have but little time for study. (*ibid.*, 115–16)

Pitt Rivers saw a clear distinction between 'research' museums and 'educational' museums. In the latter 'originals are not necessary. Casts, reproductions
and models are preferable . . . Museums of casts do not compete with research
museums, in which the originals should be stored' (*ibid.*, 116). His collections,
both at Farnham and at Oxford, included many plaster casts of artefacts, such
as the West Buckland hoard of bronzes (Taylor 1982), allowing him to display
complete sequences. The social and political implications of the educational
museum were constantly stressed. The agricultural collection at Farnham
included 'a series of crates carried by country women of different countries on
the shoulder, and collected expressly to show the women of my district how
little they resemble the beasts of burden they might have been if they had been
bred elsewhere' (Pitt Rivers 1891, 119). Ultimately the creation of educational
museums might ensure social stability:

> If no more good came of it than to create other interests, which were to draw
> men's minds away from politics, the greatest of all curses in a country district,
> good would be done . . . museums might be made the means of inculcating
> sounder views on social questions. (*ibid.*, 120)

'Politics' in this case meant, of course, 'radical politics'.

The building which the General chose to house his new Museum had been a
farmhouse converted for use as a Gypsy School in the 1850s. The School had
failed and in 1880 it stood vacant. The building was plain and therefore fulfilled
the General's requirements for an educational museum: 'Architectural features,

47 Model of a Silesian plough from the Agricultural Collection at Farnham
Museum

handsome halls and corridors are impediments; at any rate they are points of
secondary importance.' (*ibid.*, 117.) The building was large enough for the
General's immediate purposes, but soon he was adding new wings and eventually the Museum comprised nine rooms as well as an external reconstruction of
a Norse mill. The collections were extraordinarily wide-ranging. The first
room contained the 'Peasant Series', illustrative of rural life in Europe, and the
second room Breton carvings and other French artefacts. Room 3 was devoted
to household utensils of different periods and Room 4 contained pottery and
locks and keys from all over the world. The archaeological collections, from
Cranborne Chase and elsewhere, including models of ancient monuments,
occupied Rooms 5 and 6, alongside further ceramics, glass and enamels. The
seventh Room contained the Celtic cross models as well as examples of carving, sculpture and earthenware. This room also contained a 'series of the
drawings of savages, and one for comparison, showing the best performances
of untaught children and adults from the neighbourhood' (le Schonix 1894,
168). Some of these drawings have been preserved (Pitt Rivers Papers M39a).
Room 8 was specially built to house the agricultural collection and Room 9,
added in the 1890s, contained series of ethnographic objects, largely from the
Pacific, and eventually the Benin bronzes.

   Every object was labelled and descriptive accounts were liberally provided.
In the General's time the cases were divided by 'thin red satin tapes placed
across the shelves from the top, whilst the larger divisions are marked by
broader bands of red satin with the word 'Division' embroidered on them' (le
Schonix 1894, 167).

   The most unusual aspect of the General's museum display was the series of
site models:

   The use of carefully made models of excavations are of the utmost importance in museums . . . My models are of well seasoned mahogany and are carved from the contoured plans. Carpenters should be trained to the work; my estate carpenters are so used to it, that I have only to put a contoured plan before them on a proper scale, and they will cut it out with the utmost precision, but of course I supervise the construction of the models very closely. (Pitt Rivers 1897, 333)

Gray described the process of making the models in more detail (1929b). In fact there were two types of models. Most were of the carved mahogany type described by the General but a few were built up of plaster on a base board with brass rods let in to indicate the ground level as a guide for the modelmaker. This was an unsuccessful experiment, however, and the General went back to the solid wood method. Salisbury Museum have over fifty of the General's topographical models of which only seven, all dating from the period 1888–90, are of the plaster type. Surface detail was painted on the models with annotations recording finds. In the larger scale models finds were indicated by pins, the heads set at the precise level of the findspot. In many cases a pair of models records a site before and after excavation. As well as the models of excavated sites there are topographical models of some sites visited on the Inspectorate journeys and about twenty models of Celtic crosses.

The General was a zealous collector to the end of his life (Gray 1905, xxxi). Gray recalled that he had,

with my old chief had much experience in buying in the London sale-rooms and elsewhere. By arrangement, on some occasions, the General, myself and a friendly dealer were apparently bidding against one another and opposing, at times, Sir Wollaston Franks and Sir Hercules Read, who were buying for the British Museum, and Canon Greenwell; these, I can assure you, were exciting times. (Gray Papers)

The *Wiltshire Archaeological Magazine* recorded the occasion on which the General bought the Bulford Mould:

For this most interesting object a spirited contest took place between the British Museum and Gen. Pitt-Rivers, and in the end it fell to the latter bidder for £30. Gen. Pitt-Rivers also secured for £8 the smaller of the two fine torques of bronze and three bronze finger rings from Lake, the larger torque going for £7. 10s. to Mr. Graves. (Anon. 1896)

'Mr. Graves', however, turned out to be none other than St George Gray acting for the General (Moore and Rowlands 1972, 62).

King John's House by Tollard Royal church was refurbished in 1889 and laid out as an art gallery. The collection on display included works by Giovanni Bellini, Lucas Cranach, P. Brueghel the elder, Tintoretto, Durck Stoop, Peter Tyssens and George Morland, hung as far as possible in chronological order and augmented by examples of embroidery and needlework (le Schonix 1894, 170). The finds from the excavations were also displayed in the House with modern reproductions of medieval pots.

Even before the Museum opened Pitt Rivers had started to lay out the Larmer Tree Grounds at Tollard Royal. The Larmer Tree was an ancient wych

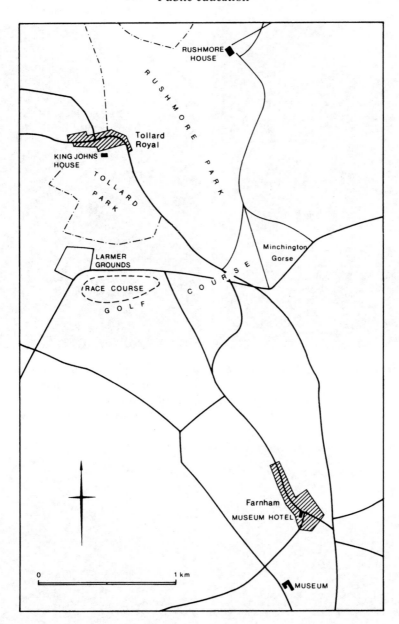

Map 5 Farnham Museum and the Larmer Grounds

elm on the Dorset-Wiltshire border, traditionally the meeting place of the hunt since King John's time. When the General came to the Chase the tree was in its dotage and he replaced it with an oak. At first the pleasure grounds at the Larmer may have been intended mainly for the enjoyment of the family and guests though the General was later to claim (1888 unpublished) that he had always intended the Larmer Grounds to be a meeting place for the inhabitants of the neighbouring villages. Thompson suggests that the idea came from the Black Fen pleasure grounds at Bramham Park, which the General had known

48 The art gallery, King John's House

49 The Temple was the first building to be constructed at the Larmer Grounds; the General's name above the door is partly obscured by foliage in this view

50 The Hounds Quarter, one of the picnic bowers in the Larmer Grounds

51 'The Hunter of Early Days' by Sir Joseph Edgar Boehm, in the Larmer Grounds. Boehm was an associate of the later Pre-Raphaelites. He also undertook commissions for Mrs Pitt Rivers' brother-in-law, George Howard, Earl of Carlisle (Vickers 1989, 73–4)

52 A performance at the Singing Theatre in the Larmer Grounds, Whit Monday,
22 May 1899. In the left foreground are Sir John Lubbock (with megaphone), the
General and two unidentified ladies

53 Indian Room, Yaks Quarter, Larmer Grounds

as a boy (1977, 12). The General himself hinted that the inspiration had been
the pleasure grounds he had seen while travelling on the Continent, where
people could meet and relax on Sundays (1888 unpublished). He stated quite
clearly his belief that loneliness and isolation were a major cause of insanity and
that the creation of the Larmer Grounds as a meeting point for the inhabitants
of the scattered villages and farms in the area was an attempt to counter this
evil. He invited anyone who had not yet visited the Larmer Grounds to do so

and promised 'that they will find it preferable to any lunatic asylum' (*ibid.*). Whatever the original inspiration for the Larmer Grounds, however, their central role is seen in Pitt Rivers' remark that museums 'must be supplemented by other inducements to make them attractive' (1891, 119–20).

The Larmer Grounds were open every day although 'The gates are locked by order of General Rivers in the evening until about 11 o'clock on the following day, for the preservation of rights' (Pitt Rivers 1899, 5). The main day of activity at the Larmer Grounds was Sunday. When some religious groups objected to this use of the Sabbath the General very reasonably pointed out that there was really no other day of the week when agricultural labourers could be expected to meet for recreation and entertainment. He received support from some of the local clergy in this matter. The Rev. Mr Woods of Alvediston wrote,

> I know from experience as a Parish clergyman that most of the sensual sins and sexual irregularities are committed at that time which is usually spent in strolls or lolling at Corners or Crosses. When I heard that you had inaugurated this recreation for the people I thought it was a wise step and the evidence of a healthy mind so contrary to puritan negation. (Pitt Rivers Papers M29g)

As the years passed the scope of the Larmer Grounds increased enormously. Many buildings were erected, some of them designed by the General himself in the *ferme ornée* tradition. There were picnic bowers, dining halls, statues, a temple, an open-air theatre and a bandstand. 'Indian Houses', designed by the General and built by the estate carpenters, were erected in 1897. They were decorated with carvings brought from the Earls Court Exhibition of the same year and a huge and very fine Moultan Ware fireplace purchased from the 'Indian Art Gallery' of Proctor & Co., one of the multitude of dealers the General had business with (Gray Papers; Pitt Rivers Papers B423–5). A racecourse was laid out on a piece of land adjoining the Larmer Grounds and then a golf course which stretched from the Grounds across Minchington Down to the South Lodge of Rushmore Park.

The General formed his own band which performed at the Larmer Grounds, free of charge, on Sunday afternoons in the summer between 3 and 5 o'clock. The bandsmen were dressed in the style of eighteenth-century Chase Keepers in the Pitt Rivers livery colours of blue and yellow. Membership of the band was no sinecure. The General required the musicians to give up worktime for rehearsal for which he paid them only half wages. 'If a man attends 10 times by this arrangement he will lose 5 shillings pay for the whole time which is a very small amount considering that the instruments have been provided for them at a cost of 150£' (Pitt Rivers Papers M29b). Five shillings may have been a small sum for a landowner who could afford to spend £150 on musical instruments and over £100 on uniforms but it was nearly half a week's wages for an agricultural labourer. However, a bandsman could make up to £2 in a season of Sunday afternoons. The band was not entirely successful. There were episodes of drunkenness and indiscipline (*ibid.*, M29d) and eventually it was disbanded.

54 The General's Band. The bandmaster, Albert Lawes, is sitting in the centre of
the front row. His elaborate uniform cost more than twice as much as a
bandsman's. The figure on the extreme left is possibly George Staples who, on
being reprimanded by Mr Lawes for inattention at Handley Fete in 1887, 'was very
Insolent, so much so, that I informed him I should report his conduct to you, he
stated, I could do as I pleased, but he should give up the Drum' (Pitt Rivers Papers
M29d)

In later years there were three major events at the Larmer Grounds in
addition to the Sunday openings. These were on Whit Monday, August Bank
Holiday and the first Wednesday in September. The latter was the greatest day
in the Larmer calendar with sports, entertainments, illuminations employing
12,000 Vauxhall lights and travelling shows. It was the evening dance at the
September meeting in 1895 that Thomas Hardy recalled in his poem 'Concerning Agnes'.

Visitor figures for the Larmer Grounds were very high, with 44,417 being
recorded in 1899, and many of these came from some distance. Racks for 100
bicycles were provided for the use of visitors and the General noted that fifty or
sixty machines would frequently be seen at the Larmer Grounds on a Sunday:

> Bicycling is an institution that must not be overlooked in any project for the
> improvement of the masses. The enormous distances bicyclists can go by road
> . . . has rendered the population of country districts locomotive to an extent that
> has never been known before. (Pitt Rivers 1891, 120)

The General's support for bicycling as a recreation for 'the masses' is remarkable in the light of the respectable outcry against 'The Cyclist Terror' in the
1890s (Pearson 1983, 66–9) though that phenomenon perhaps appeared only
later in the decade. The bicycle was widely seen as a potent force for social
change at this time and few conservatives had such positive feelings about it as
Pitt Rivers. A bicycle club was established at the King John Hotel in Tollard
Royal and bicycle races formed a major part of the Larmer Grounds sports.

Pitt Rivers even went so far as to build the Museum Hotel in Farnham village
for the convenience of visitors from further afield. Refreshments could be
obtained here, at the Larmer Grounds themselves or at King John's House

55 The Museum Hotel, Farnham

where 'any amount of bread and butter, tea and buns can be obtained at slight cost' (Pitt Rivers 1891, 120).

The menagerie in Rushmore Park, the primary purpose of which was zoological experimentation in cross-breeding and the acclimatisation of foreign species, was not generally open to the public but could be seen on application. Ted Coombs recollected that the General 'had a zoo – yaks and zebras and so on. Always experimenting, he was. He crossed yaks with cows and worked them as oxen, for a curiosity. I near as nothing got killed by one – it went mad' (Hawkins 1948 unpublished). Some of the hybrids were not unsuccessful. The Yak-Jersey and Yak-Highland oxen, 'although somewhat treacherous animals, were used in carts for hauling hay, etc. They were very strong' (Gray Papers). The llamas on the other hand had to be confined in paddocks 'on account of their causing much annoyance to the sheep by chasing them' (*ibid.*).

From the later eighteenth century it had been part of a landowner's occupation to breed livestock, a fact of which the General, with his Lane Fox background, was well aware. In the course of the nineteenth century an alternative to the familiar British domestic breeds had become increasingly available in the form of exotic animals from the Empire, and several noblemen and gentlemen turned to the acclimatisation and breeding of these beasts and their hybridisation by crossing with domestic breeds (Ritvo 1987, 53, 234–5). Although there was a commercial element to these experiments, such as the General's use of his hybrids as draught animals, this aspect of the enterprise was rarely successful. The appeal of such experiments was rather that they allowed the private menagerie owners, by confining and controlling wild animals in their parks, to 'celebrate their own splendid pre-eminence among their fellow humans and their dominion over nature' (*ibid.*, 242).

The cost to the General of providing public education for the people of Cranborne Chase was enormous, both in time and money. How successful was he? The General himself had no doubt that he had succeeded magnifi-

56 Bull Yak in Rushmore Park: many of the General's exotic animals were obtained from the leading London dealer Charles Jamrach, who also traded in antiquities and objects of ethnographic interest (Ritvo 1987, 225, 244–5; Pitt Rivers Papers B371)

cently: '. . . at any rate my Provincial Museum may be claimed to be a success, judging by the constantly increasing numbers that are found to visit it, and that in a district which, at first sight, appeared very unpromising' (Pitt Rivers 1891, 120). The Museum visitor figures bear this out. Their numbers rose from 5,706 in 1888 to 12,611 in 1899 (Thompson 1977, 79–80). Although these figures show that less than a third of the numbers visiting the Larmer Grounds were being enticed into the Museum they are impressive statistics. However, the success of an exercise in public education cannot be measured by a simple assessment of the number of people taking part. The effect on those people is the only measure of success.

Those who had worked on the General's projects should have been affected most. Certainly the local under-gardener's son, Herbert Toms, became a more than competent archaeologist, but he was exceptional. Some of the labourers who worked on the excavations took an interest in their work, particularly in the discovery of skeletons on which they worked overtime (Gray Notebooks). Others, however, totally misunderstood the General's purpose. One man who had taken part in the excavations later recalled that the General 'had bin always lookin vur King John's treasure' (M. Pitt-Rivers 1977, 24).

For many of the local people attending the Larmer entertainments the serious purpose behind the fun must have been an irrelevance. For others it was an opportunity to curry favour with the General, as Frank Adams recalled: 'Now if you should happen to pick up a half dozen coins which is quite an easy thing to do after these excavations . . . proudly take them to Larmer on a Sunday afternoon; if you see him by himself strolling across the lawn and show him these coins, it would please him immensely that would. He thought you had an interest in archaeology . . .' (Constanduros 1953 unpublished). For most, however, the wealth of serious information being offered was merely confusing, a fact amply demonstrated by Ted Coombs, one of the bandsmen, who told Desmond Hawkins, 'I played clarinet. We had big felt hats and swallowtail coats, breeches and gaiters – period of King John, they said' (Hawkins 1948 unpublished).

The history of Farnham Museum in the twentieth century has not been all that the General might have wished. Controversy broke out immediately after his death over the question whether the Museum belonged to the family or to a charitable trust. This argument was resolved in favour of the family and the Museum ran smoothly for the next thirty years though at one point St George Gray found that 'a temporary lady curator . . . was giving away MSS., notebooks and drawings (without authority)' (Gray 1948 unpublished). By 1925, however, the fabric of the Museum building needed extensive repairs. The General's grandson, Captain George Pitt Rivers, later to become notorious for his fascist sympathies, undertook these repairs and relabelled and rearranged the collections over the following seven years. In 1927 he came to an agreement with the Inland Revenue that death duties would not be levied as long as the collection was not sold. To mark the refurbishment a new Museum handbook was issued (Dudley Buxton 1929). The expense of the repairs had been enormous, however, and in 1932 Captain Pitt Rivers began to seek means of recouping his losses. An advisory committee was set up to discuss alternatives. The committee included Tancred Borenius, Mortimer Wheeler, Sir Henry Miers, O. G. S. Crawford, Miles Burkitt, Cyril Fox and Colonel Drew. Captain Pitt Rivers advanced a series of wildly impractical schemes for a 'Museum of museums' with university funding, on which Wheeler commented laconically, 'such a museum might take shape in about 200 years'. However, Wheeler was eventually able to write to Frank Stevens of Salisbury Museum that, 'At the end of an interminable meeting, Pitt Rivers was at last persuaded to separate the Cranborne Chase stuff from the rest, and he is now prepared (or was yesterday) to hand the stuff over . . . to the new Institute of Archaeology . . . or to you at Salisbury.' Two months later, in April 1933, it was reported that Captain Pitt Rivers was preparing to sell the entire collection to Bournemouth Corporation. He was dissuaded from this course of action and he announced his intention to sell off some items in order to maintain the rest of the collection at Farnham (Salisbury Museum Pitt Rivers Boxfiles, Farnham Museum File).

These organisational problems and its increasingly 'dusty, dull' appearance (Cunliffe 1984 unpublished) did not prevent Farnham Museum from continuing to be a source of delight to the public and of inspiration to archaeologists and artists (for example Simpson 1990) right up to its final closure.

Farnham Museum remained open to the public almost continuously until Captain Pitt Rivers' death in 1966. After his death it appeared that he had sold the Museum to a Trust Company, thus breaking the 1927 agreement, and stories about the disposal of parts of the collection abounded (Salisbury

57 General Pitt Rivers, oil portrait by Fred Beaumont, 1897

Museum Pitt Rivers Boxfiles). In 1973 another committee was convened to acquire the collection or otherwise prevent its breakup. In 1975 it was announced that the archaeological material would go to the Salisbury and South Wiltshire Museum by arrangement with the Treasury under the Finance Act of 1973. Much of the ethnographic material, as well as a few archaeological pieces, had already been sold by the Trust Company and ex-Farnham Museum objects continued to appear in the London sale rooms. The removal of the archaeological collection from Farnham to Salisbury has been described in detail by Saunders (1976). The Pitt Rivers Gallery at Salisbury Museum was opened in November 1983.

9

The father of scientific archaeology

Pitt Rivers' contribution to archaeology is well established but has often been a matter for somewhat bland assumptions based on prevailing archaeological concerns. For many years he was seen principally as an innovator in field techniques, recording and publication, and this view has persisted. Levine, for instance, sees him as little more than a clever technician (1986, 170, 176) but, as Bradley has stressed (1983, 1), he was also a theorist. In order to see his role in the development of British archaeology in a broader perspective it is necessary to demolish some of the pedestals that have been constructed for him and to reconsider some of the more neglected aspects of his work. It is also necessary to see his work in the context of the very real achievements of some of his contemporaries.

Though he was an innovator himself many of Pitt Rivers' successes derived from the ideas of his colleagues and much of his greatness lay in his ability to adopt and amplify these ideas. His insistence on the detailed recording of excavations is partly a result of the teaching of his acknowledged mentor Canon William Greenwell:

> It is impossible to reprobate too strongly that ignorant and greedy spirit of mere curiosity-hunting . . . the urn, the dagger and the arrowhead possess a very trifling interest and give us comparatively little information, unless we know the circumstances of their deposit, and the objects with which they were associated. (Greenwell 1865, 241).

However, Pitt Rivers far outstripped his teacher in this respect. Greenwell persisted in publishing the results of his investigations without benefit of plan and section drawings (for example Greenwell 1890). Other antiquarians, such as Roach Smith, insisted on the importance of provenance for objects in their collections (Evans 1943, 129) but the idea of context in excavation was new. The labelling of individual sherds of pottery, a crucial aspect of the General's later excavations, had been advocated over half a century before by the Rev. Thomas Leman (Simpson 1975, 12), though Pitt Rivers was the first to apply it in practice.

In explanation of the significance of his work at Woodcutts and Rotherley the General stated that,

> Whilst others have been occupied with the examination of the towns and military

works of the Roman Age ... my attention ... has been given chiefly to an agricultural district of the same period ... From the richer and more populous localities objects of greater intrinsic value and more advanced art might be expected, but from the poorer agricultural regions not less valuable evidence of the social condition of the settled mass of the population of the country may be obtained. (1898, 12)

This apparently novel statement is in fact almost an echo of the words of the Oxfordshire antiquary Stephen Stone about his excavations on the Thames gravels as early as 1857:

From the variety and extent of these discoveries it may fairly be concluded that Standlake offers a wide if not rich field for the investigation of the antiquary. He may indeed fail to find relics of that costly description which have been found in some other districts; but if a collection of facts tending to elucidate an interesting but obscure subject be to him, as it ought to be, of greater importance than a mere collection of curiosities, however valuable they may be ... he may perchance reap a rich harvest here. (1857, 99)

Moreover the justly famous Pitt Rivers models may be traced back to Stone's scale models of his excavations at Standlake (Hingley and Miles 1984, 52). The General examined these models, possibly when they were exhibited at the Society of Antiquaries in 1857 or maybe later in the Ashmolean Museum (Pitt Rivers 1887a, 20). He had also been exposed frequently to the military use of topographical models (Thompson 1977, 14, 28). The General's earliest models date to the early 1870s.

More importantly, Pitt Rivers did not invent the archaeological stratigraphic section as Thompson has claimed (1977, 117). The General's first approach to a section drawing was at London Wall in 1867, followed by the perspective sketch of a section at Cissbury (1875b, pl. XVI) and some unpublished watercolour sections of the Thames gravel terraces (Pitt Rivers Papers R5). His first real section drawing in the modern sense was at Dane's Dyke (1882a pl. XXXVIII). The London Wall section drawings were more or less contemporary with the Rev. J. Joyce's more detailed watercolour sections of his excavations at Silchester, which the General probably saw when they were exhibited at the Society of Antiquaries in 1867 (Boon 1974, 24–6). Furthermore they were more than a decade later than the fine section drawings executed in India by that unsung archaeological hero Captain Meadows Taylor (Wheeler 1954, 22–4). In any case the analogy between geological and archaeological stratigraphy had been clear to Albert Way and his followers for many years and this was one of the factors which had led to the rift between Way and Wright (Levine 1986, 95). It remains true nevertheless that Pitt Rivers and his assistants brought the art of section drawing to a higher standard than had been achieved before in their work on Bokerley Dyke and Wansdyke.

As we have seen, the General's excavation techniques, the mainstay of his reputation in recent years, left much to be desired. The worst aspect was his habit of digging in spits and his consequent failure to understand fully the stratigraphy of his sites or to assign artefacts to their stratigraphic context. This was exacerbated by the physical digging methods of his labourers. The deposits were literally shovelled out as in other nineteenth-century excavations. This had ramifications not only for the General's appreciation of stratigraphy but also for his rate of artefact recovery. Re-excavation at South Lodge Camp has shown that his workmen missed many flint artefacts, while Frank Adams' statement that coins were always to be found on spoilheaps after the General's excavations of Roman sites (Constanduros 1953 unpublished) is significant. This point is reinforced by Pitt Rivers' own admission that a pen-annular brooch was washed out of the earthworks at Woodcutts ten years after his excavations there (1898, 85).

The General also fell short of his own ideals of publication. In his presidential address to the Royal Archaeological Institute at Dorchester in 1897 the General explained his methods of excavation and recording, stating some truths which seem to be rediscovered by every generation of archaeologists, for instance that 'The record of an excavation takes about five times as long as the actual digging' (1897, 336). The General spoke of his Relic Tables as if they were an impartial and non-selective record of facts recovered. He also claimed that there had been no selection of objects for illustration in the fourth volume of *Excavations in Cranborne Chase* but was immediately forced to qualify this statement: 'everything has been drawn, down to the most minute fragment of pottery that had a pattern on it' (*ibid.*) The evolution of chevron-decorated pottery was very much on the General's mind. The illustrated material from South Lodge only accounts for about twenty per cent of the diagnostic pottery recovered (Barrett *et al.* 1981, 204). More significantly the lack of plans for sites such as Handley Barrow 26 and the missing details on so many section drawings are extremely frustrating for archaeologists trying to reassess the General's sites. His sister-in-law's remark that 'I never knew anyone put his ideas & principles so little into practice as Augustus' (Russell and Russell 1937a, 121) springs to mind. However it is true that few other nineteenth-century excavation reports equalled the General's and none surpassed them. The published plans and sections of the great Yorkshire barrow excavator Mortimer (1905; see also Kinnes *et al.* 1983, 105–7) are no better and no worse than those in the first two volumes of *Excavations in Cranborne Chase*. Furthermore, the level of supervision of Pitt Rivers' excavations was extremely high by nineteenth-century standards:

> No excavation was allowed to proceed unless one at least of the assistants was present to supervise the workmen; to record everything, whether of momentary interest or not; to mark every relic discovered on plans and sections kept for the purpose. The General was generally at the diggings when important discoveries were taking place, sometimes for the whole day. Occasionally he has been known to be in the field at 7 a.m. to see the workmen arrive. (Gray Papers)

The General had some shortcomings as a field archaeologist to match his shortcomings as an excavator. He produced many accurate surveys of field monuments but he was not such an acute observer of earthworks as his assistant Herbert Toms (Bradley 1989) and his dismissal of conventional hachured survey in favour of contour survey (Pitt Rivers 1892, 62) is indicative of his inability to analyse relationships between earthworks from surface evidence. The later nineteenth century saw a number of highly skilled field archaeologists working in Britain whose published work in some instances clearly surpassed that of the General. Henry MacLauchlan's 'hill sketches' (Charlton and Day 1984) and C. W. Dymond's survey of the Penrith henges (1891) are superb pieces of work, as is J. T. W. Bell's diligent survey of the aqueduct at Great Chesters on Hadrian's Wall (Bruce 1853, 225–8). Recent resurvey has confirmed the accuracy of Bell's original work (Mackay forthcoming). It is unfortunate that Pitt Rivers did not publish the field surveys he made in his official capacity as Inspector of Ancient Monuments. In this connection it is worth noting that while the General's recording of the fabric of the upstanding building, King John's House, was thorough and accurate, his illustrations are not outstanding when compared with contemporary work in this field (Smith 1985, 7).

If the General's excavation techniques, though in advance of his day, were seriously flawed and if his field techniques were no better than those of his best contemporaries, the true basis of his reputation as the father of scientific archaeology must be sought elsewhere. One might suggest that it was the General's great wealth which allowed him to become pre-eminent in late nineteenth-century archaeological endeavour. Certainly without that wealth he could not have achieved so much, but a similar argument might be applied to Darwin (Gould 1978, 31). His wealth was undoubtedly a significant factor but alone it cannot explain his achievement. Several aspects of the General's archaeological work can be regarded in a more positive light.

In the first place curation is more important than publication. All reassessments of the General's work have relied on his museum collections more than on the data contained within his published works and it is a tribute to his care in preserving objects of all classes that so many radical reinterpretations of his sites have been possible and that modern scientific techniques have been employed to this end.

Secondly, there are specific details such as the General's advanced interpretations of many of the features he discovered in excavation. Gerhard Bersu has generally been credited with the idea that the pits found on Iron Age settlements were intended for grain storage (Shackley 1976, 10) but the General had put forward this interpretation in his report on Mount Caburn (Pitt Rivers 1881a, 449). Similarly Gent (1983, 247) gives Bersu the credit for interpreting four-posters as raised granaries but it was Pitt Rivers who first published this idea in his Rotherley report (1888a, 55). These interpretations of food storage features were backed up by specialist reports. Samples of charcoal and carbonised grain from the Cranborne Chase excavations were submitted to various specialists for analysis just as human bones were submitted to anatomists. This had been done before, by William Cunnington for instance (Simpson 1975, 11), but never on a systematic basis.

A third and more important point is Pitt Rivers' use of experimental techniques to aid analysis and interpretation. He had been experimenting with prehistoric implements of flint, bone and antler since the 1860s. In Cranborne Chase he made two major sets of experimental observations. The first of these involved the measurement of animal bones found on his excavations, a momentous innovation in itself. 'Test animals' of various breeds of domesticated mammals, having been measured, were slaughtered and their limb bones kept for comparison with the excavated bones: 'Every entire animal bone found in all the excavations has been measured and the depth recorded . . . the size can always be ascertained with accuracy, and this I have done by means of test animals of modern breeds killed for the purpose of comparison' (Pitt Rivers 1897, 327). However there were no dogs amongst the test animals: 'the measurements of dogs have been obtained from time to time as opportunity offered . . .' (1888a, 225). The second set of experimental observations was concerned with the silting of ditches. The General made a series of measurements of the side ditches of Wor Barrow after he had excavated them and reported on the rapidity with which rubble and silts accumulated in the ditch bottoms and the nature of the deposits at different stages in the process (Pitt Rivers 1898, 25). These experimental techniques were not emulated by the General's contemporaries or his immediate successors, and further advances in the study of faunal remains and the weathering of earthworks were not to be made until the second half of the twentieth century.

This experimental work shows that Pitt Rivers did not lack original and innovative ideas. Unfortunately they did not always come to fruition. In considering the importance of ceramic studies for the advancement of archaeological knowledge he wrote that,

> The grains of stone, quartz, sand, flint, shell and other substances . . . in pottery . . . may be traced to their original beds and will probably afford, when properly studied, a clue to the district in which the vessels were fabricated and when kilns are discovered the distribution of their products will be the means of tracing the trade routes that were frequented at the time. (1892, x)

He was right on both counts but it took archaeology longer to achieve such advances than the General might have wished.

While bewailing the inexperienced labourers he was forced to employ at Bokerley Dyke the General speculated on the possibility of maintaining a corps of archaeological workers, a sort of privately owned Central Excavation Unit:

> No more useful organisation could be established for archaeological purposes, than that of a permanent Corps of efficient workmen . . . It appears to me not impossible that, as the number of practical archaeologists increases, such an organisation might be introduced by passing from one to another, workmen who have been engaged in diggings of this nature . . . Such an organisation would increase the expense of the explorations, but it would amply repay the additional expenditure. Draughtsmen and surveyors might also be included in the Corps. (*ibid.*, 24)

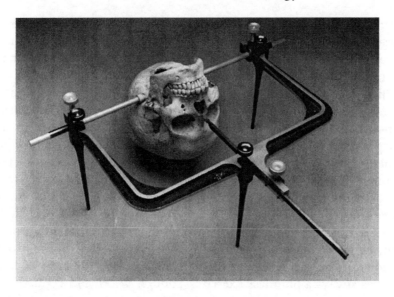

58 The General's Craniometer:

> I have contrived an instrument for taking the profiles with perfect accuracy.
> The skull is fixed by means of a blunt point into the ear openings on either
> side . . . The scale . . . enables the distance on a vertical plane between the
> centre of the meatus auditorius and any point on the profile of the skull and
> lower jaw, to be read off with great precision. (Pitt Rivers 1898, 118)

The number of wealthy private archaeologists was never sufficient for such a
development to take place, of course, and eventually the State took the
responsibility for setting up such organisations, which is precisely what Pitt
Rivers had hoped to avoid. While admitting that 'it speaks highly for the
intellectual status of the German people' that their government spent public
funds on archaeology, this was not the English way:

> It is perhaps more in harmony with the recognised custom of our country, to
> leave such works for private enterprise. As long as we retain the freedom of our
> institutions, which God preserve, private life must remain a power for good in
> England. (ibid., xiv–xv)

Although the Corps was never a reality Pitt Rivers' assistants were probably
the first people in England to be employed on a full-time, salaried basis purely
for archaeological work.

One aspect of Pitt Rivers' work which seems eccentric to modern archaeologists is his emphasis on physical anthropology, particularly in regard to craniometry. In the four volumes of *Excavations in Cranborne Chase*, which contain a
total of 317 plates, there are no fewer than thirty-three plates devoted to
drawings and photographs of skeletons and forty-three plates of drawings and
photographs of skulls. In addition there are three plates with drawings of
'living heads' measured with the General's craniometer. There are also eight

tables recording skeleton stature and skull shape. The Rotherley obelisk further emphasises the General's preoccupation with physical anthropology. Two and a half faces of the four-sided obelisk are dedicated to details of skull shape and skeletal stature. Other discoveries on the site are barely mentioned. In a discipline which has paid little attention to physical anthropology since the General's day all this looks like wasted effort, particularly as his conclusions are so questionable. However when we look at this body of work in its contemporary context it looks less strange. In the later nineteenth century physical anthropology was a mainstream scientific activity and craniometry, the measurement of skull shape, was a very popular method of trying to isolate races. Arguments raged amongst European anthropologists about the relative racial inferiority or superiority of brachycephalic and dolichocephalic skull forms. Pitt Rivers believed implicitly in skull shape as a racial indicator but, to his credit, he never made any claims for racial superiority on the grounds of cranial indices. The measurement of the cranial index, the ratio of length to breadth, was always a pointless exercise. Though W. H. Flower had criticised the whole idea of craniometry in the early 1880s (Lorimer 1988, 420) it was not until 1899, the year before Pitt Rivers' death, that the American anthropologist Franz Boas demonstrated that the cranial index was a meaningless concept (Gould 1981, 98–108).

Pitt Rivers was very much a man of his time and he shared the concerns of his contemporaries. His wish that British money should be spent on British archaeology rather than being sent to Greece, Egypt and other parts of the Mediterranean (Pitt Rivers Papers P188) is an echo of similar sentiments frequently expressed by his colleagues (Levine 1986, 93). The foremost concern of later nineteenth-century British archaeologists was, naturally enough, the construction of a firmer chronology for British prehistory (*ibid.*, 95) and in this field Pitt Rivers led the way. He had probably done more than any other individual in the field and in the committee room to promote better chronological control. His excavations in Sussex, Oxfordshire, Kent, the Thames valley, Yorkshire and Cranborne Chase all added substantial steps to the relative chronology of early man in Britain and as a leading figure with Evans, Lubbock and Franks in his uncle Albert Way's Archaeological Institute he was helping to break down the old, historically based and chronologically unsound attitudes of the antiquaries.

It is extremely significant that Pitt Rivers did not associate with historians but rather with fellow archaeologists, geologists, anatomists and anthropologists. His remarks on the value of historical evidence in relation to the archaeology of pre-medieval periods are dismissive: 'whilst I am fully alive to the importance of studying all the passages in ancient writings, which have any bearing on the subject, by competent scholars, I must confess that the evidence that can be derived from them appears to be of the weakest possible description' (1892, 11). In this respect he was following the lead of Albert Way in his great clash with Thomas Wright, who represented the older antiquaries' view that archaeology was an essentially historical discipline in which the techniques of stratigraphical geology had no place (Levine 1986, 14, 95). Like Franks, Lubbock and Evans, the General had eschewed the Archaeological Association, led by Wright, in favour of the more progressive Archaeological Institute and their own creation, the Anthropological Institute. In binding archaeology firmly to geology Albert Way and his followers had laid the foundations for the more 'scientific' development of the subject. Pitt Rivers in his turn was forging the links between archaeology and anthropology:

> Whilst geology was to carry us back to periods that had not before been thought of in the history of man, anthropology was to teach us how to estimate the stature and physical peculiarities of the skeletons found in the graves, and ethnology was to enable us to appreciate the social and material condition of the aborigines of our country by a comparison of their relics with the arts of modern savages. All these branches have now become indispensible for the prehistorian. (Pitt Rivers 1887b, 265)

Thomas Bateman, Henry Christy and William Blackmore had already begun to use ethnographic objects to illustrate their archaeological collections but the General had taken up this relationship and developed it much further. Chapman believes that this was Pitt Rivers' most significant contribution to archaeology and the measure of his success within the archaeological community (1989, 28).

For the General, however, the combination of archaeology and anthropology was the means to an end. The one theme that runs through his life and unites all his work is his theory of the Evolution of Culture. The General had espoused a most dogmatic form of Darwinism with gradualism, 'the law that nature makes no jumps', as its central tenet. Huxley had warned Darwin against an insistence on gradualism at the time that *Origin of Species* was published (Gould 1980, 149) but Darwin continued to believe in infinitely slow change and the General followed him because the theory suited his political beliefs. Ironically the idea of gradualism had been invented at the time of the French Revolution by liberal scientists who wished to transfer to nature the slow development which they advocated for human society (*ibid.*, 150). Pitt Rivers' transfer of Darwinian gradualism back to human culture thus brought the argument full circle.

> If in the whole face of nature there is undoubted evidence of any especial fiat of creation having operated capriciously, or in any other manner than by gradual evolution and development, my principles are false. (Fox 1868b, 436)

Having nailed his colours to the mast of gradualist doctrine in this way the General was prejudiced, consciously or unconsciously, in favour of interpreting everything in terms of gradual change. He could do nothing else. How he explained the existence of the phonograph which was demonstrated at Rushmore in 1891 (Hawkins 1982, 81–2) is not recorded but in a lecture delivered at Salisbury Museum, probably in 1890, the General drew on the experience of his son, St George Fox Pitt, to explain away the inventiveness of individuals through which material culture could make jumps:

Take the case of Mr. Edison's inventions for example. Mr. Edison is of course a man of very remarkable inventive genius, but . . . I find that Edison is in fact the name of a great inventing company. Young men who have ideas for the improvement of any particular machine . . . are taken into partnership, or engaged upon trial, and they are glad, for the sake of his patronage, and the pecuniary advantages accruing from it, to sacrifice their personality. If the design succeeds, or is perfected in the establishment, it comes out under the name of Edison. (Pitt Rivers Papers P142d)

While this is no doubt true it does not explain away the fact that the electric lightbulb had been invented where there had been no electric lightbulb before.

In fact the central tenet of Pitt Rivers' system of cultural evolution is false. Darwin himself never believed in the analogy between cultural evolution and natural evolution and indeed there is no such analogy (Thompson 1977, 43–4). As Gould has pointed out (1980, 71) natural evolution is Darwinian, progressing by the selection of 'random' adaptations, while cultural evolution is essentially Lamarckian in the sense that it proceeds by the direct transmission of learning. Cultural evolution can therefore act almost infinitely faster than natural evolution and Pitt Rivers' dividing line between evolution and revolution is illusory.

Nevertheless, although the political ideal of Pitt Rivers' cultural evolution is false, its underlying sequential structure is not (Thompson 1977, 115–16). The final product was sequence. Whether the material culture in question was weaponry, chevron-decorated pottery or Benin bronzes, the General's ultimate triumph was to order them in their correct sequence. Whether or not Pitt Rivers invented the word 'typology' as he claimed (1891, 116) it became the accepted term for the study of sequences of all aspects of material culture. No one before Pitt Rivers had created realistic typologies and it has been suggested (Charles Thomas, personal communication) that this was the General's principle contribution to archaeology and the aspect of his work which had the greatest influence on a later generation of archaeologists, especially Christopher Hawkes, for whom typology was of supreme importance.

Whether the creation of sound typologies or the linking of archaeology with anthropology is regarded as the General's finest achievement, both have undeniably had an enormous influence on the development of archaeology. If his excavation techniques have appeared to be his only important contribution to archaeology that has been the result of a somewhat simplistic view of his life's work but it also reflects the predominant concerns of mid-twentieth century archaeologists.

PITT RIVERS AND THE TWENTIETH CENTURY

The lead that Pitt Rivers gave was not followed by the rising generation of archaeologists and it was to be at least thirty years after his death before British archaeology in general raised itself to the standards of excavation and fieldwork which he had achieved and advocated, though at least one Wiltshire archaeolo-

59 Medalet   60 Medalet, reverse
Designed for the General by Sir John Evans, who, as President of the Numismatic
Society, had a working knowledge of coin and medal design (Evans 1943, 154–5).
The General buried the medalet, with other objects, at the bottom of most of his
excavation trenches in Cranborne Chase. One was recovered from Barrow 18,
Rushmore Park, in 1981 (Barrett *et al* 1983, pl.xxv)

gist followed the General's recording techniques slavishly (Stallybrass 1906)
and Mrs Armitage was a staunch admirer of the General's work (Armitage
1912, 2). The decline in standards of archaeological fieldwork after Pitt Rivers'
death has been noted by a number of writers (for example Evans 1988, 57)
though exceptions such as Heywood Sumner, a devoted follower of the
General, must be remembered. When Pitt Rivers died on 4 May 1900 there was
a lacuna, partly because of outside factors and partly because of his own
dominant personality which had never allowed his assistants to take an
independent and commanding role in archaeological pursuits. The spirit of the
times does not seem to have been sympathetic to his aims or methods, the
period of high Victorian scientific endeavour having passed. No Inspector of
Ancient Monuments was appointed to succeed him for over a decade. Very
few, if any, private gentlemen were sufficiently enthusiastic to conduct
campaigns of excavation on their estates and the corps of archaeological workers would not emerge until more than sixty years after the General's death and
then under government, not private, direction. Scientific research into the
composition of pottery fabrics, domestic animal populations, the behaviour of
earthworks and the use of stone and antler tools was not to be undertaken again
on any substantial scale until the second half of the twentieth century.

Of the General's assistants only four continued to work in archaeology after
leaving his service. Of these the best known is of course Harold St George
Gray who conducted excavations at several sites of major importance, notably
Avebury, Maumbury Rings and the Glastonbury and Meare lake villages.
Bradley considers that the excavation techniques employed by Gray at Maum-

bury Rings, the Neolithic henge and Roman amphitheatre at Dorchester, in 1908–13 were, in some respects, superior to the General's but, because Gray failed to publish, they did not have the influence on British archaeology that they might have done (Bradley 1975, 6; Barker 1977, 14). Other commentators have not been so kind to Gray. It might be thought that Gray would have brought the General's techniques and principles to his collaborative project with Arthur Bulleid at the Iron Age villages at Glastonbury and Meare. In fact Bulleid had already been working in the Somerset Levels for many years, guided by a committee including Pitt Rivers as well as Boyd Dawkins, John Evans and Robert Munro, and there is nothing to suggest that his earlier work was in any way inferior to that done after he was joined by Gray (Barrett 1987, 412). On the contrary Coles suggests that Bulleid's concern for the structural evidence was 'hampered by Gray's emphasis on the recovery of small finds' (1987, 13). It is unlikely that the General would have been impressed by Gray's obsession with 'objects for the museum cases', his abandonment of mounds which failed to produce exciting finds or his deliberate creation of a backlog which he knew he could never live to publish (*ibid.*, 6, 11, 13). His excavation techniques never progressed though he was digging in Somerset for half a century. He was criticised in the 1950s for digging Meare Village East like a cabbage patch. It is significant that the critic was Wheeler (*ibid.*, 15). As Bradley has pointed out (1975, 5–6) Gray was using exactly the same techniques he had learnt from Pitt Rivers and which Wheeler had praised elsewhere, but by this time techniques of excavation and recording had advanced and the standards of the 1890s were no longer acceptable.

Herbert Toms left Pitt Rivers to become museum assistant at Brighton in 1896 where he subsequently became curator in 1906, a post which he retained until his retirement in 1939. Toms took the educational side of his duties very seriously and also continued his career as a field archaeologist, founding the Brighton and Hove Archaeological Club which he led on 'flint hunts', small excavations and earthwork surveys (Holleyman and Merrifield 1987). He made considerable contributions to the study of 'Celtic' fields both in Sussex and in his native Dorset, resurveying the South Lodge field system which Pitt Rivers had largely overlooked (Toms 1925) and adding other details to sites previously surveyed by the General (Sumner 1913, 44–5). Despite his obvious abilities and achievements Herbert Toms has never been highly regarded within British archaeology, though his reputation is now enjoying a well deserved enhancement (Holleyman and Merrifield 1987; Bradley 1989).

Francis Reader was dismissed from the General's service in 1889. He went on to run an engraving and printing business in London but continued to be an active amateur archaeologist. He kept a watching brief on building sites near London Wall, as the General had done thirty years before, and published a long and detailed paper on the subject (Reader 1903). He made many contributions to the work of the London Survey Group, was a valued member of council of the Buckinghamshire Archaeological Society and pioneered the study of post-medieval domestic wall paintings, recording examples throughout south eastern England with meticulous draughtsmanship (Clive Rouse, personal communication).

Frederick James left Rushmore in 1891 to take up the curatorship of Maidstone Museum where he had been assistant curator prior to his employment by Pitt Rivers. As curator at Maidstone James entirely rearranged the displays and undertook a number of excavations but he was totally eclipsed by George Payne, Secretary and 'Chief Curator' of the Kent Archaeological Society. The two men were not on good terms (Pitt Rivers Papers L1213, 1433 and 1530). Harold Gray went to Maidstone in 1899 to study the collections and stayed with Frederick James. He later recalled that the other assistants at Rushmore

> Did not like J. who was rather overbearing and not very friendly. But I did not know all his failings until I got to Maidstone, when on my arrival early one evening he started off on a round of 'pubs' which did not interest me after one glass, but he continued. After he left [Maidstone Museum] in 1902 . . . he wrote asking for a loan of £5; but he asked for another fiver which he did not get and of course he never returned the first £5. I think on the second occasion he wrote from a hospital. I was very sorry for his wife. (Gray 1956 unpublished)

This letter perhaps tells us as much about Gray as about James, especially as Gray apparently signed it 'H. St George Gray (C.B.E., M.A., F.S.A., F.M.A.)'. Gray's assessment of James must be set against the fact that James retained his post under Pitt Rivers for ten years, no mean feat in itself, and was re-employed by the authorities at Maidstone, though he subsequently left in dubious circumstances. Apart from his skills as a curator and archaeologist, James was a knowledgeable art historian and a competent linguist.

The General's immediate professional heirs made little impact on the development of British archaeology, therefore, though for different reasons in each case. Gray was let down by his failure to publish and his inability to keep up to date with advancing techniques. Toms tended to publish his work in obscure places and his working class 'Archaeological Club' was overshadowed in Sussex by Eliot and Cecil Curwen with their colleagues in the middle class county society (Bradley 1989), so that the value of his work is only now being appreciated. Reader has been overlooked because of his unassuming nature and also perhaps because of his amateur status, while James disappears from the records after his superannuation from Maidstone Museum in 1902. In addition some of them probably suffered a degree of repression of their imagination and initiative by Pitt Rivers' dominating personality at a formative stage in their archaeological careers.

Pitt Rivers' mantle therefore fell on the shoulders of a few local enthusiasts such as Sumner who openly acknowledged his admiration for the General and maintained his standards (1913, 3; Cunliffe 1985, 117). Elsewhere in Britain excavation standards in the early years of the twentieth century fell to lamentable depths (Barker 1977, 14–15). The General would have been horrified by the lax state of supervision and recording on the excavations at Traprain Law during the years on either side of the First World War (Close-Brooks 1987). Cunliffe notes that the techniques employed by Bushe-Fox at Hengistbury Head in 1910–11, while an improvement on general standards, 'were still no match for Pitt Rivers' (1985, 117). Fieldwork standards also declined. Resurveys of the Penrith henges and the Great Chesters aqueduct in the first half of the twentieth century, for instance, were feeble in comparison with their nineteenth-century counterparts (RCHM(E) 1936, 252–3; Mackay forthcoming).

Meanwhile the connection between archaeology and anthropology died in the early years of the twentieth century because anthropologists, for various reasons, lost their interest in material culture in favour of language, ceremonies and social organisations (Reynolds 1984, 61–2) and because, under the influence of Durkheim and the French sociological school, British anthropologists concentrated on contemporary phenomena. Malinowski relegated studies of the past to a secondary role and Radcliffe-Brown rejected ethnology as 'conjectural history' (Kuper 1983, 8–9, 65; Mair 1972, 26, 34–5, 45). The revival of interest in material culture among anthropologists did not occur until the 1970s (Reynolds 1984, 61).

It was a new generation led by Christopher Hawkes, Stuart Piggott and Sir Mortimer Wheeler that revived Pitt Rivers' methods and ideals from the late 1930s onwards and brought back to British archaeology a concern with sound excavation techniques and well constructed typologies. Meanwhile the General's personal reputation seems to have fluctuated independently of his perceived effect on the development of archaeology. In 1933, for instance, W. E. V. Young was referring to the General as 'the great General Pitt Rivers' in his diary (Julian Thomas, personal communication) while exactly a decade later Evans could write her history of the archaeological family Evans with only one passing reference to the General (Evans 1943, 157) and list him in the index as 'Lane-Fox, St G.'

Since the late 1930s the General's reputation as an excavator has been established principally by the works of Hawkes and Piggott (Hawkes *et al.* 1947; Piggott 1959, 44–5), Wheeler (1954, 13, 25–9) and Thompson (1977) though it has sometimes been misunderstood. The misunderstanding seems to have arisen from R. G. Collingwood's remark that 'Pitt Rivers was a very great archaeologist and a supreme master of the technique of excavation; but as regards the problems to be solved by excavation he was for the most part (not quite consistently) in the pre-Baconian stage. He dug in order to see what he could find out' (1939, 125). Many nineteenth-century men of science claimed to be objective in their approach and to use purely inductive methods (Gould 1980, 53–5, 128). Pitt Rivers never explicitly claimed objectivity but he did hold it as an ultimate goal:

> Excavators, as a rule, record only those things which appear to them important at the time, but fresh problems in Archaeology and Anthropology are constantly arising . . . Every detail should, therefore, be recorded in the manner most conducive to facility of reference, and it ought to be the chief object of an excavator to reduce his own personal equation to a minimum. (1887a, xvi–xvii)

Despite this aim the General's own 'personal equation' is abundantly clear in all his writings. Far from digging to see what he could find out, as Collingwood claimed, the General dug to demonstrate his belief that human society progressed by infinitely small steps over an infinitely long time span and that the lower classes and the non-Anglo-Saxon population of the world must accept their lot. This is why he kept, in specially made boxes, only the limb bones and skulls of the human skeletons he excavated; they were the parts which yielded the particular information on stature and, he believed, race which interested him (Bradley 1983, 8). The evolution of material culture, rather than structural sequence, informed the design of his excavation reports. Similarly, many of the General's remarks on recording reflect his personal research interests rather than an objective ideal. Writing about the publication of artefacts he said, '. . . illustrations need not be elaborate, but sufficient to trace the transitions of forms' (1892, 27).

The aura of the four volumes of *Excavations in Cranborne Chase* has also helped to create the impression of Pitt Rivers as the impersonal and objective law-giver. Large, heavy and beautifully produced, the volumes are constantly referred to as an embodiment of authority and have been described in such terms as 'monumental' (Bradley 1973, 47). They are stamped with his authority as a high-ranking military officer and a Government Inspector while the bindings in his livery colours, blue and gold, refer to his high social status. Few twentieth-century British archaeological publications approach *Excavations in Cranborne Chase* in size and weight but amongst them, significantly, have been the Inventories of the Royal Commissions on Historical Monuments closely followed by the research reports of the Society of Antiquaries of London, the most venerable of archaeological institutions.

After Wheeler's adoption of Pitt Rivers as mentor the General's success was assured. Archaeologists from Fagan (1972, 141) to Barker (1977, 13–14) accorded him the leading role in the development of excavation and field techniques. Interest in archaeological theory has grown since the late 1960s and the links between archaeology and anthropology have been reforged. This has been reflected in changing perceptions of the General's contribution in recent years. Bradley, for instance, emphasised his theoretical work (1983) and Chapman has stressed the General's role in linking archaeology with anthropology (1989). No doubt if physical anthropology came back into archaeological fashion Pitt Rivers would be hailed as the founding father of this branch of the discipline as well. In the final analysis it is the wide range of the General's achievements which entitles him to be called the father of scientific archaeology.

Bibliography

Unpublished sources

Constanduros, D., 1953. *The Old General.* Transcript of BBC Home Service Broadcast.

Cooper, A. T. P., n. d. 'Cranborne Chase and General Pitt Rivers.' Typescript. Salisbury and South Wiltshire Museum, Cranborne Chase File.

Cunliffe, B. W., 1984. Transcript of interview, *Kaleidoscope*, BBC Radio 4, 22 February 1984.

Gray, H. St G., 1948. Letter to C. F. C. Hawkes, 31 January 1948. Maumbury Rings Letterfile, Dorset County Museum, Dorchester.

Gray, H. St G., 1956. Letter to R. A. Grove, 18 December 1956. Copy at Maidstone Museum.

Gray Notebooks. Field notebooks recording excavations at Handley, 1893–5, described by Bradley (1973). Dorset County Museum, Dorchester.

Gray Papers. Chiefly drafts of articles and lectures, held with Pitt Rivers Papers at Salisbury and South Wiltshire Museum.

Hawkins, D., 1948. *County Magazine – Cranborne Chase.* Transcript of BBC Home Service Broadcast.

Pitt Rivers, A. H. L. F., 1888. Speech at a meeting of the Electors at Handley, Election of County Councillor, printed as a handbill.

'Arms Books'. National Army Museum, Acc. No. 6807-343.

Pitt Rivers Papers. Listed according to M. W. Thompson, 1976, 'Catalogue of Pitt Rivers Papers in Salisbury Museum'.

Pitt Rivers, J., 1983. Speech at the opening of the Pitt Rivers Gallery, Salisbury and South Wiltshire Museum.

PRO WORK 39/1-16. Pitt Rivers' Inspectorate field notebooks. Public Record Office, Kew.

Salisbury Museum Pitt Rivers Boxfiles. Various documents relating to Pitt Rivers, not included in the Pitt Rivers Papers catalogued by Thompson.

Tomkin Papers. Letters, an account book and sketch book, held with Pitt Rivers Papers at Salisbury and South Wiltshire Museum.

Published sources

Works published by General Pitt Rivers under the name Fox and referenced as such in the text are listed here under Pitt Rivers.

Anon., 1896. 'The sale of the collection of antiquities belonging to the Rev. E. Duke, of Lake House'. *Wiltshire Archaeological and Natural History Magazine* 28, 261.

Anon., 1930. 'The witches "scrag" (tree) on Winkelbury Hill'. *Wiltshire Archaeological and Natural History Magazine* 45, 75–6.

Antoine, S. E., Dresser, P. Q., Pollard, A. M. and Whittle, A. W. R., 1988. 'Bone chemistry and dietary reconstruction in prehistoric Britain: examples from Wessex'. In Slater, E. A. and Tate, J. O., Eds. *Science and Archaeology: Proceedings of a Conference on the Application of Scientific Techniques to Archaeology, Glasgow, September 1987*. British Archaeological Reports 196, Oxford. 369–80.

Archer, J. E., 1985. ' "A fiendish outrage"? A study of animal maiming in East Anglia: 1830–1870'. *Agricultural History Review* 33, 147–57.

Armitage, E. S., 1912. *Early Norman Castles of the British Isles*. John Murray. London.

Austen, J. H., 1867. 'Notes on some vestiges of Roman occupation in Dorset'. *Archaeological Journal* 24, 161–70.

Baker, M., 1985. *Our Three Selves: a Life of Radclyffe Hall*. GMP Publishers Ltd. London.

Balfour, H., 1889. 'On the structure and affinities of the composite bow'. *Journal of the Anthropological Institute* 18, 220–46.

Barker, P., 1977. *Techniques of Archaeological Excavation*. Batsford. London.

Barley, M. and Barry, T. B., 1971. 'Two letters from the General'. *Antiquity* 45, 215–20.

Barrett, J. C., 1987. 'The Glastonbury Lake village: models and source criticism'. *Archaeological Journal* 144, 409–23.

Barrett, J. C., Bradley, R. J., Green, M. and Lewis, B., 1981. 'The Earlier Prehistoric Settlement of Cranborne Chase – the first results of current fieldwork'. *Antiquaries Journal* 61, 203–37.

Barrett, J. C., Bradley, R. J., Bowden, M. C. B. and Mead, B., 1983. 'South Lodge after Pitt Rivers'. *Antiquity* 57, 193–204.

Barrett, J. C., Bradley, R. J. and Green, M., forthcoming. *Landscape, Monuments and Society: the Prehistory of Cranborne Chase*. Cambridge University Press.

Bateman, T., 1861. *Ten Years Diggings in Celtic and Saxon Grave Hills in the Counties of Derby, Stafford and York from 1848–58*. Privately printed. London.

Bennett, P., 1988. 'Archaeology and the Channel Tunnel'. *Archaeologia Cantiana* 106, 1–24.

Boon, G. C., 1974. *Silchester: the Roman Town of Calleva*. Revised edition. David and Charles. Newton Abbot.

Bowden, M. C. B., 1984. *General Pitt Rivers: the Father of Scientific Archaeology*. Salisbury and South Wiltshire Museum. Salisbury.

Bowden, M. C. B. and Lewis, B., forthcoming. 'The excavation of a Neolithic ring ditch at Firtree Field'. In Barrett *et al.*, forthcoming.

Bowden, M. C. B. and Taylor, R. J., 1984. 'Two Bronze Axes from Hythe in the Pitt Rivers Collection at Salisbury Museum'. *Archaeologia Cantiana* 101, 349–52.

Bradley, R., 1973. 'Two notebooks of General Pitt Rivers'. *Antiquity* 47, 47–50.

1975. 'Maumbury Rings, Dorchester – the excavations of 1908–1913'. *Archaeologia* 105, 1–97.

1983. 'Archaeology, evolution and the public good: the intellectual development of General Pitt Rivers'. *Archaeological Journal* 140, 1–9.

1989. 'Herbert Toms: a pioneer of analytical field survey'. In Bowden, M. C. B., Mackay, D. A. and Topping P., Eds. *From Cornwall to Caithness: Some Aspects of British Field Archaeology – Papers presented to Norman V. Quinnell*. British Archaeological Reports 209. Oxford. 29–47.

Bradley, R., Cleal, R., Gardiner, J. P., Green, M. and Bowden, M. C. B., 1984.

'The Neolithic sequence in Cranborne Chase.' In Bradley, R. and Gardiner, J. P., Eds. *Neolithic Studies*. Reading Studies in Archaeology No. 1. British Archaeological Reports 133. Oxford. 87–105.

Bruce, J. C., 1853. *The Roman Wall*. Second edition. John Russell Smith. London.

Burleigh, R. and Clutton-Brock, J., 1982. 'Pitt Rivers and Petrie in Egypt'. *Antiquity* 56, 208–9.

Carver, M. O. H., 1989. 'Digging for ideas'. *Antiquity* 63, 666–74.

Caulfield, R., 1864. 'Presidential Report to the Cork Cuverian Society'. *The Constitution*. 20 May.

Caverhill, A., 1988. *Rushmore – Then and Now*. Privately printed.

Chapman, W. R., 1984. 'Pitt Rivers and his collection, 1874–1883: the chronicle of a gift horse'. In Cranstone, B. A. L. and Seidenberg, S. *The General's Gift: A Celebration of the Pitt Rivers Museum Centenary, 1884–1984*. Journal of the Anthropological Society of Oxford Occasional Papers No. 3, 6–25.

 1985. 'Arranging ethnology: A. H. L. F. Pitt Rivers and the typological tradition'. In Stocking, G. W., Ed. *Objects and Others: Essays on Museums and Material Culture*. University of Wisconsin Press. Madison. 15–48.

 1989. 'The organizational context in the history of archaeology: Pitt Rivers and other British archaeologists in the 1860s'. *Antiquaries Journal* 69, 23–42.

Charlton, B. and Day, J., 1984. 'Henry MacLauchlan: surveyor and field archaeologist'. In Miket, R. and Burgess, C., Eds. *Between and Beyond the Walls: Essays on the Prehistory and History of North Britain in Honour of George Jobey*. John Donald. Edinburgh. 4–37.

Chippindale, C., 1983a. 'Stonehenge, General Pitt Rivers and the first Ancient Monuments Act'. *Archaeological Review from Cambridge* 2 no. 1, 59–65.

 1983b. *Stonehenge Complete*. Thames and Hudson. London.

 1983c. 'The making of the first Ancient Monuments Act, 1882, and its administration under General Pitt Rivers.' *Journal of the British Archaeological Association* 136. 1–55.

Close-Brooks, J. 1987. 'Comment on Traprain Law'. *Scottish Archaeological Review* 4 part 2, 92–4.

Cogbill, S., 1982. 'The Bronze Age exhumed'. *Scottish Archaeological Review* 1 part 2. 78–90.

Cokayne, G. E., 1929. *Complete Peerage*. Vol. 7. Revised and enlarged by the Hon. V. Gibbs, H. A. Doubleday and Lord H. de Warden, Eds. The St Catherine Press. London.

Coles, J. M., 1987. *Meare Village East. The Excavations of A. Bulleid and H. St George Gray 1932–1956*. Somerset Levels Papers No. 13.

Collingwood, R. G., 1939. *An Autobiography*. Oxford University Press.

Corney, M. C., forthcoming. 'Later first millennium settlement morphology'. In Barrett *et al.*, forthcoming.

Crawford, O. G. S., 1953. *Archaeology in the Field*. Phoenix House. London.

Cunliffe, B. W., 1985. *Heywood Sumner's Wessex*. Roy Gasson Associates. Wimborne.

Daniel, G., 1967. *Origins and Growth of Archaeology*. Penguin Books. London.

 1975. *A Hundred and Fifty Years of Archaeology*. Duckworth. London.

Dudley Buxton, L. H., Ed., 1929. *The Pitt Rivers Museum, Farnham: General Handbook*. Farnham Museum.

Dymond, C. W., 1891. 'Mayburgh and King Arthur's Round Table'. *Transactions of the Cumberland and Westmorland Archaeological and Antiquarian Society* 11, 187–219.

Eagleton, T., 1983. *Literary Theory: An Introduction*. Basil Blackwell. Oxford.

Evans, C., 1988. 'Monuments and analogy: the interpretation of causewayed enclosures'. In Burgess, C., Topping, P., Mordant, C. and Maddison, M., Eds. *Enclosures and Defences in the Neolithic of Western Europe*. British Archaeological Reports International Series 403. Oxford. 47–73.

Evans, J., 1943. *Time and Chance. The Story of Arthur Evans and his Forebears*. Longmans Green and Co. London.

Evans, J. G. and Vaughan, M. P., 1985. 'An investigation into the Environment and Archaeology of the Wessex Linear Ditch System'. *Antiquaries Journal* 65 part 1, 11–38.

Fagan, B. M., 1972. *In the Beginning*. Little, Brown and Company. Boston.

Fagg, B., 1976. 'Introduction'. In reprint of Pitt Rivers, A. H. L. F., *Antique Works of Art from Benin*. Dover Publications. New York.

Feachem, R. W., 1971. 'Unfinished hill-forts'. In Jesson, M. and Hill, D., Eds. *The Iron Age and its Hill-Forts: Papers Presented to Sir Mortimer Wheeler*. Southampton University Archaeological Society. Southampton. 19–39.

Ferguson, R., 1893. 'Report on Injury to the Bewcastle Obelisk'. *Transactions of the Cumberland and Westmorland Archaeological and Antiquarian Society* 12, 51–6.

Fox, A. H. L., see Pitt Rivers, A. H. L. Fox.

Gardner, E. 1924. 'Bronze Age urns of Surrey'. *Surrey Archaeological Collections* 35, 1–29.

Gent, H., 1983. 'Centralised storage in later prehistoric Britain'. *Proceedings of the Prehistoric Society* 49, 243–67.

Girdwood, A., 1986. 'Archaeology, the historical movement and the idea of progress'. *Scottish Archaeological Review* 4 part 1, 35–43.

Gould, S. J., 1978. *Ever Since Darwin: Reflections in Natural History*. Pelican Books (1980). London.

    1980. *The Panda's Thumb. More Reflections in Natural History*. Pelican Books (1983). London.

    1981. *The Mismeasure of Man*. Pelican Books (1984). London.

Grant Duff, S., 1982. *The Parting of Ways*. Peter Owen Ltd. London.

Gray, H. St G., 1905. *Index to 'Excavations in Cranborne Chase' and 'King John's House, Tollard Royal'*. Privately printed. Taunton.

    1929a. 'General Pitt Rivers' In Dudley Buxton 1929, 17–23.

    1929b. 'Models of ancient sites in Farnham Museum'. In Dudley Buxton, 1929, 36–7.

Greenwell, W., 1865. 'Notices of the examination of Grave-Hills in the North Riding of Yorkshire'. *Archaeological Journal* 22, 97–117, 241–64.

    1890. 'Recent researches in barrows in Yorkshire, Wiltshire, Berkshire, etc'. *Archaeologia* 52, 1–72.

Greenwell, W. with Rolleston, G., 1877. *British Barrows: A Record of the Examination of Sepulchral Mounds in Various Parts of England*. Clarendon Press. Oxford.

Hamilton, Sir F. W., 1874. *The Origin and History of the First or Grenadier Guards*. Vol. 3. John Murray. London.

Harries-Jenkins, G., 1977. *The Army in Victorian Society*. Routledge and Kegan Paul. London.

Hawkes, C. F. C. and Dunning, G. C., 1932. 'The second Belgic invasion'. *Antiquaries Journal* 12, 411–30.

Hawkes, C. F. C. with Piggott, S. and Gray, H. St G., 1947. 'Britons, Romans and Saxons round Salisbury and in Cranborne Chase'. *Archaeological Journal* 104, 27–81.

Hawkins, D., 1981. *Cranborne Chase*. Victor Gollancz Ltd. London.
    1982. *Concerning Agnes: Thomas Hardy's 'Good Little Pupil'*. Alan Sutton. Gloucester.
Hibbert, C., 1961. *The Destruction of Lord Raglan*. Longmans. London.
Hingley, R. and Miles, D., 1984. 'Aspects of Iron Age settlement in the upper Thames Valley'. In Cunliffe, B. W. and Miles, D., *Aspects of the Iron Age in Central Southern Britain*. University of Oxford Committee for Archaeology Monograph No. 2. Oxford. 52–71.
Holleyman, G. A. and Merrifield, R., 1987. *Two Dorset Archaeologists in Sussex*. Privately printed.
Howard, J., 1982. *Darwin*. Oxford University Press.
Hughes, R., 1988. *The Fatal Shore: a History of the Transportation of Convicts to Australia 1787–1868*. Pan Books Ltd. London.
Huxley, T. H., 1863. *Evidence as to Man's Place in Nature*. University of Michigan Press (1959). Ann Arbor.
International Congress of Prehistoric Archaeology, 1869. *Transactions of the Third Session Which Opened at Norwich on the 20th August and Closed in London on the 28th August 1868*. Longmans Green and Co. London.
James, T. G. H., 1988. *Ancient Egypt: The Land and its Legacy*. Guild Publishing. London.
Kains-Jackson, C. P., 1880. *Our Ancient Monuments and the Land Around Them*. Elliot Stock. London.
Keegan, J., 1988. *The Mask of Command*. Penguin Books. London.
Kendall, G., 1982. 'A study of grave orientation in several Roman and post-Roman cemeteries from Southern Britain'. *Archaeological Journal* 139, 101–23.
Kinnes, I. A. and Longworth, I. H., 1985. *Catalogue of the Excavated Prehistoric and Romano-British Material in the Greenwell Collection*. British Museum Publications Ltd. London.
Kinnes, I. A., Schadla-Hall, T., Chadwick, P. and Dean, P., 1983. 'Duggleby Howe Reconsidered'. *Archaeological Journal* 140, 83–108.
Kuper, A., 1983. *Anthropology and Anthropologists: the Modern British School*. Revised edition. Routledge & Kegan Paul. London.
Leach, Sir E., 1982. *Social Anthropology*. Fontana Masterguides. London.
le Schonix, R., 1894. 'The museums at Farnham, Dorset, and at King John's House, Tollard Royal'. *The Antiquary* 30, 166–71.
Levine, P., 1986. *The Amateur and the Professional: Antiquarians, Historians and Archaeologists in Victorian England 1838–1886*. Cambridge University Press.
Lorimer, D., 1988. 'Theoretical racism in late Victorian anthropology, 1870–1900'. *Victorian Studies* 31, 405–30.
Lubbock, Sir J., 1865. *Pre-historic Times, as illustrated by ancient remains and the manners and customs of modern savages*. Williams and Norgate. London.
MacIvor, I. and Fawcett, R., 1983. 'Planks from the shipwreck of time: an account of Ancient Monumentry, then and now'. In Magnusson, M., Ed. *Echoes in Stone: 100 Years of Ancient Monuments in Scotland*. Ancient Monuments Division, Scottish Development Department. Edinburgh. 9–27.
Mackay, D. A., forthcoming. 'The Great Chesters Aqueduct: a new survey'. *Britannia*.
Maclauchlan, H., 1857. *The Roman Wall, and Illustrations of the Principle Vestiges of Roman Occupation in the North of England: Consisting of Plans of the Military Works, the Stations, Camps, Ancient Ways, and Other Remains of the Earlier Periods, in the Northern Counties*. Privately printed. London.

Mair, L., 1972. *An Introduction to Social Anthropology*. Second edition. Oxford University Press.

Mannings, D., 1986. 'Mrs. Peter Beckford'. In Penny, N., Ed. *Reynolds*. Royal Academy of Arts/Weidenfeld and Nicolson. London, 303–5.

Marsden, B. M., 1974. *The Early Barrow Diggers*. Shire Publications Ltd. Aylesbury.

    1978. 'Thomas Bateman 1821–61'. Introductory essay to reprint of Bateman 1861. Moorland Publishing Co. Buxton.

Mitford, N., 1938. *The Ladies of Alderley: Letters between Maria Josepha, Lady Stanley of Alderley and Henrietta Maria Stanley 1841–50*. Chapman and Hall Ltd. London.

Mitford, N., 1939. *The Stanleys of Alderley: their letters between the years 1851–65*. Hamish Hamilton. London.

Moore, C. N. and Rowlands, M., 1972. *Bronze Age Metalwork in Salisbury Museum*. Salisbury and South Wiltshire Museum, Salisbury.

Morris, P., 1979. *Agricultural buildings in Roman Britain*. British Archaeological Reports 70. Oxford.

Mortimer, J. R., 1905. *Forty Years' Researches in British and Saxon Burial Mounds of East Yorkshire*. A Brown and Sons Ltd. London.

Pearson, G., 1983. *Hooligan: A History of Respectable Fears*. Macmillan. London.

Piggott, S., 1936. 'Handley Hill, Dorset – a Neolithic bowl and the date of the Entrenchment'. *Proceedings of the Prehistoric Society* 11, 229–30.

    1959. *Approach to Archaeology*. A. and C. Black Ltd. London.

    1976. *Ruins in a Landscape: essays in antiquarianism*. Edinburgh University Press.

Pitt Rivers, A. H. L., Fox, 1858. 'On the improvement of the rifle as a weapon for general use'. *Journal of the Royal United Services Institution* 2, 453–88.

    1867a. 'Roovesmore Fort, and stones inscribed with oghams, in the parish of Aglish, Co. Cork'. *Archaeological Journal* 24, 123–39.

    1867b. 'Account of objects . . . found at a great depth in the vicinity of the old London Wall'. *Archaeological Journal* 24, 61–4.

    1867c. 'A description of certain Piles found near London Wall and Southwark, possibly the remains of Pile Buildings'. *Anthropological Review* 5, lxxi–lxxxiii.

    1867d. 'Primitive warfare, part 1'. *Journal of the Royal United Services Institution* 11, 612–45.

    1868a. 'On some flint implements found associated with Roman remains in Oxfordshire and the Isle of Thanet'. *Journal of the Ethnological Society of London* new series, 1, 1–12.

    1868b. 'Primitive warfare, part 2'. *Journal of the Royal United Services Institution*. 12, 399–439.

    1869a. 'An examination into the character and probable origin of the hill forts of Sussex'. *Archaeologia* 42, 27–52.

    1869b. 'Further remarks on the hill forts of Sussex: being an account of excavations in the forts of Cissbury and Highdown'. *Archaeologia* 42, 53–76.

    1869c. 'On the proposed exploration of Stonehenge by a committee of the British Association'. *Journal of the Ethnological Society of London* 1, 1–5.

    1869d. 'Primitive warfare, part 3'. *Journal of the Royal United Services Institution* 13, 509–39.

    1870a. 'Note on the use of the New Zealand mere'. *Journal of the Ethnological Society of London* 2, 106–9.

    1870b. 'On the opening of two cairns near Bangor, North Wales'. *Journal of the Ethnological Society of London* 2, 306–24.

1870c. 'On the threatened destruction of the British earthworks near Dorchester, Oxfordshire'. *Journal of the Ethnological Society of London* 2, 412–15.

1872a. 'On the discovery of Palaeolithic implements in association with *Elephas Primigenius* in the gravels of the Thames Valley at Acton'. *Quarterly Journal of the Geological Society of London* 28, 449–66.

1872b. 'Address to the Department of Anthropology'. *Report of the British Association for the Advancement of Science for 1872*, 157–74.

1874a. 'On the principles of classification adopted in the arrangement of his anthropological collection, now exhibited in the Bethnal Green Museum'. *Journal of the Anthropological Institute* 4, 293–308.

1874b. *Catalogue of the Anthropological Collection Lent by Colonel Lane Fox for Exhibition in the Bethnal Green Branch of the South Kensington Museum, June 1874.* 2 vols. South Kensington Museum. London.

1874c. 'On Early Modes of Navigation'. *Journal of the Anthropological Institute* 4, 399–435.

1875a. 'On the evolution of culture'. *Proceedings of the Royal Institute of Great Britain* 7, 496–514.

1875b. 'Excavations in Cissbury camp, Sussex', *Journal of the Anthropological Institute* 5, 357–90.

1876a. 'Opening of the Dyke Road, or Black Burgh Tumulus, near Brighton, in 1872'. *Journal of the Anthropological Institute* 6, 280–7.

1876b. 'Excavations in the Camp and Tumulus at Seaford, Sussex'. *Journal of the Anthropological Institute* 6, 287–99.

1877a. 'On measurements taken of the officers and men of the 2nd. Royal Surrey Militia according to the general instructions drawn up by the Anthropometric Committee of the British Association. *Journal of the Anthropological Institute* 6, 443–57.

1877b. 'On some Saxon and British Tumuli, near Guildford'. *Report of the British Association*, 116–17.

1878. 'Observations on Mr. Man's collection of Andamanese and Nicobarese objects'. *Journal of the Anthropological Institute* 7, 434–51.

1881a. 'Excavations at Mount Caburn camp, near Lewes, conducted in 1877 and 1878'. *Archaeologia* 46, 423–95.

1881b. 'Report on the excavation of the earthwork known as Ambresbury Banks, Epping Forest'. *Transactions of the Essex Field Club* 2, 55–67.

1881c. 'On the discovery of chert implements in stratified gravel in the Nile Valley near Thebes'. *Journal of the Anthropological Institute* 11, 382–400.

1882a. 'On Excavations in the earthwork called Dane's Dyke, at Flamborough, in October, 1879; and on the earthworks of the Yorkshire Wolds'. *Journal of the Anthropological Institute* 11, 455–71.

1882b. 'Anniversary Address to the Anthropological Institute as President'. *Journal of the Anthropological Institute* 11, 488–508.

1883a. 'On the Egyptian Boomerang and its Affinities'. *Journal of the Anthropological Institute* 12, 454–63.

1883b. *On the Development and Distribution of Primitive Locks and Keys; Illustrated by Specimens in the Pitt Rivers Collection.* Chatto and Windus. London.

1883c. 'Excavations at Caesar's Camp, near Folkestone, conducted in 1878'. *Archaeologia* 47, 429–65.

1884a. 'Address to the Antiquarian Section at the Annual Meeting of the Archaeological Institute, held at Lewes'. *Archaeological Journal* 41, 58–78.

1884b. *Report on Excavations in the Pen Pits, near Penselwood, Somerset.* Privately printed.

1887a. *Excavations in Cranborne Chase.* Vol. 1. Privately printed.

1887b. 'Inaugural Address to the Annual Meeting of the Archaeological Institute, held at Salisbury'. *Archaeological Journal* 44, 261–77.

1888a. *Excavations in Cranborne Chase.* Vol. 2. Privately printed.

1888b. 'On an ancient British settlement excavated near Rushmore, Salisbury'. *Journal of the Anthropological Institute* 17, 190–9.

1889. 'Remarks on the paper "On the structure and affinities of the composite bow" by Henry Balfour MA'. *Journal of the Anthropological Institute* 19, 246–50.

1890. *King John's House, Tollard Royal, Wilts.* Privately printed.

1891. 'Typological Museums'. *Journal of the Society of Arts* 40, 115–22.

1892. *Excavations in Cranborne Chase.* Vol. 3. Privately printed.

1897. 'Presidential address to the Dorchester meeting of the Archaeological Institute'. *Archaeological Journal* 54, 311–39.

1898. *Excavations in Cranborne Chase.* Vol. 4, Privately printed.

1899. *A Short Guide to the Larmer Grounds, Rushmore; King John's House; the Museum at Farnham; and Neighbourhood.* Privately printed.

1900. *Works of Art from Benin, West Africa.* Privately printed.

Pitt-Rivers, M., 1977. 'Cultural General'. *Books and Bookmen* 22 no. 9, 23–5.

Porter, J. H., 1986. 'Tenant right: Devonshire and the 1880 Ground Game Act'. *Agricultural History Review* 34, 188–97.

Rahtz, P. A., 1961. 'An excavation on Bokerly Dyke, 1958'. *Archaeological Journal* 118, 65–99.

Invitation to Archaeology. Basil Blackwell. Oxford.

Reader, F. W., 1903. 'Pile structures in the Walbrook near London Wall'. *Archaeological Journal* 60, 137–204.

Reynolds, B., 1984. 'The relevance of material culture to anthropology'. In Cranstone, B. A. L. and Seidenberg, S. *The General's Gift: A Celebration of the Pitt Rivers Museum Centenary, 1884–1984.* Journal of the Anthropological Society of Oxford Occasional Papers No. 3, 61–8.

Ritvo, H., 1987. *The Animal Estate: the English and other Creatures in the Victorian Age.* Harvard University Press. Cambridge, Massachusetts.

Rivet, A. L. F. and Smith, C., 1979. *The Place Names of Roman Britain.* Batsford. London.

Rodden, J., 1981. 'The development of the Three Age System: archaeology's first paradigm'. In G. Daniel, Ed. *Towards a History of Archaeology.* Thames and Hudson. London. 51–68.

Rolleston, G. and Fox, A. H. L., 1878. 'Report of excavation of a twin-barrow, and a single round barrow, at Sigwell (Six-Wells), Parish of Compton, Somerset'. *Journal of the Anthropological Institute* 8, 185–94.

Royal Commission on Historical Monuments, 1936. *An Inventory of the Historical Monuments in Westmorland.* His Majesty's Stationery Office. London.

Russell, B. and Russell, P., 1937a. *The Amberley Papers.* Vol. 1. Hogarth Press. London.

1937b. *The Amberley Papers.* Vol. 2. Hogarth Press. London.

Russell, W. H., 1855. *The War [in the Crimea]: From the Landing at Gallipoli to the Death of Lord Raglan.* Routledge and Co. London.

Saunders, P. R., 1976. 'What happened to the Pitt Rivers Wessex Collection?' *Museums Journal* 75, no. 4, 156–8.

1980. 'Saxon Barrows excavated by General Pitt Rivers on Merrow Down, Guildford'. *Surrey Archaeological Collections* 72, 69–75.

1981. 'General Pitt Rivers and Kit's Coty House'. *Antiquity* 55, 51–3.

Seaman, L. C. B., 1973. *Victorian England*. Methuen and Co. London.

Shackley, M. L., 1976. 'The Danebury Project: an experiment in site sediment recording'. In Davidson, D. A. and Shackley, M. L. Eds. *Geoarchaeology*. Duckworth. London. 9–21.

Simpson, D. D. A., 1975. 'Ancient Wiltshire'. Introduction to reprint of Sir R. Colt Hoare, *The Ancient History of Wiltshire*. EP Publishing/Wiltshire County Library.

Simpson, P., 1990. 'Subliminal influences'. *Ceramic Review* 121, 17–19.

Smith, C., 1984. 'William Owen Stanley of Penrhos (1802–1884): a centenary biography'. *Archaeologia Cambrensis* 133, 83–90.

Smith, L., 1985. *Investigating Old Buildings*. Batsford. London.

Speight, H., 1902. *Lower Wharfedale*. Elliot Stock. London.

Stallybrass B., 1906. 'Discoveries near Fonthill'. *Wiltshire Archaeological and Natural History Magazine* 34, 414–25.

Stanley, W. O., 1867. 'On the remains of the ancient circular habitations in Holyhead Island, called Cyttiau'r Gwyddelod, at Ty Mawr'. *Archaeological Journal* 24, 229–42.

Stocking, G. W., 1987. *Victorian Anthropology*. The Free Press (Macmillan, Inc.). New York.

Stone, L. and Stone, J. C. F., 1986. *An Open Elite? England 1540–1880*. Abridged edition. Oxford University Press.

Stone, S., 1857. 'Account of certain (supposed) British and Saxon remains'. *Proceedings of the Society of Antiquaries of London* 1st series, 4 (1856–9), 92–100.

Sumner, H., 1913. *The ancient earthworks of Cranborne Chase*. Chiswick Press. London.

Taylor, R. J., 1982. 'The hoard from West Buckland, Somerset'. *Antiquaries Journal* 62, 13–17.

Thompson, M. W., 1960. 'The First Inspector of Ancient Monuments in the field'. *Journal of the British Archaeological Association* 3rd Series, 23, 103–24.

1963. 'The origin of scheduling'. *Antiquity* 37, 224–5.

1977. *General Pitt-Rivers: Evolution and Archaeology in the Nineteenth Century*. Moonraker Press. Bradford-on-Avon.

Toms, H., 1925. 'Bronze Age, or earlier, lynchets'. *Proceedings of the Dorset Natural History and Archaeology Field Club* 46, 89–100.

Vickers, J., 1989. *Pre-Raphaelites: Painters and Patrons in the North-east*. Tyne and Wear Museums Service. Newcastle upon Tyne.

Ward, J. T., 1967. 'The saving of a Yorkshire estate: George Lane Fox and Bramham Estate'. *Yorkshire Archaeological Journal* 42, 63–71.

Wheeler, R. E. M., 1954. *Archaeology from the Earth*. Penguin Books (1956). London.

Woodham-Smith, C. 1953. *The Reason Why*. Constable. London.

INDEX

References to plates and tables are in italic.

South Kensington Museum, 49–51
South Lancashire Regiment, 22
South Lodge Camp, Rushmore, 108, 126–9, 156
Spencer, Herbert, 3, 40, 42, 47, 49
Spiennes, Belgium, 77–8
Staff College curriculum, 13, 49
stakeholes, 77, 85
Stanley, Blanche (Lady Airlie), 23–4, *30*
Stanley of Alderley, Sir Edward, second Lord, 6, 24–6, 29, *30*, 73, 96
  on Pitt Rivers, 18–19, 23
Stanley, Fabia, Lady, 31, 33
Stanley, Henrietta Maria, Lady, 23–6, 28, *30*
Stanley, Sir Henry (third Lord Stanley of Alderley), 26, *30*, 31
Stanley, John Constantine, 23, 28, *30*
  on Pitt Rivers, 18, 20, 26
Stanley, Maria Josepha, Lady, 23–6, 29
Stanley, William Owen, 47, 73, 77, 93
Stokesay Castle, 125
Stone, Steven, 59, 155
Stonehenge, 75–6
Sturt, the Hon Humphrey, 42–3
Sumner, Heywood, 163, 165
Susan Gibbs Walk Barrow, Rushmore, 109, *110*

Thames valley, 73–5
Thanet, Isle of, 72
Thomsen, C. J., the Three Age System, 57–8
Thurnam, John, 44, 58, 93, 101, 117
Tomkin, W. S., *100*, 104, 107, 118
Toms, Herbert, 151, 157
  assistant to Pitt Rivers, 106, 108, 127, 129, *133*, 135, 138
  later career, 128, 164, 165
traction engine, *38*
Traprain Law, 165
Treherne, Sir George, 99

Trent Incident, the, 20
Tylor, Edward Burnett, 3, 12, 45, 47, 52, 73
  racial attitude, 56
Tyndall, Plumpton, 78
typology, 55, 70–1, 162

Uleybury, 94

'Vindocladia', 118

Wake Smart, T., 119
Walker, Romaine, 37–8
Wansdyke, 107, 119–22
Ward, the Rev J. H., 42, 119
Warne, Charles, 58
water levels, 65, 115, 138
Way, Albert, 47, 58, 66, 73, 93, 155, 160–1
Webb, Philip, 37, 38
Wellington, Duke of, 15, 17
Wheeler, Sir Mortimer, 1, 152, 166–7
Whitechapel Foundation School, 11, 74
Whitmore Common, Surrey, 83–4
Willett, Ernest H., 78
Wiltshire Archaeological Society, 107
Winkelbury Hill, Wilts., 112–13
Winwood, the Rev H. H., 102, 108
Witches' 'Scrag', 113
Wolseley, Field Marshal Lord, 39
Woodcutts, 114–16, 117, 156
Woods, the Rev Mr, 148
Woodyates, 118–19
Wor Barrow, 108, 131–4, 136, 158
'working hollows', 116
Wright, Thomas, 58, 155, 160–1

Yorkshire Wolds, 66–7
Young, W. E. V., 166
'Yusuf Bey', *see* Lane Fox, Charles

Lightning Source UK Ltd.
Milton Keynes UK
UKOW03f0007090115

244136UK00001B/11/P